MISFIRE

What to Do When Things Aren't Running on All Cylinders

MITCH SCHNEIDER

Schneider, Mitch.
Misfire : what to do when things aren't running on all cylinders.
ISBN 9 781733 718400

Printed in the United States of America
Set in Minion Pro and Trenda
Designed by Fredrick Haugen
Misfire Icon by Brann Haugen

To Lesley
Ryan & Dana

Introduction

Section B: You Know What You Don't Know

Section C: You Don't Know What You Know

Section D: You Know What You Know

Foreword

Let me begin by warning you of the power you're now holding in your hands. *Misfire* undoubtedly will change how you feel about your business, your world, and your role in it. It will pick you up and put you back down on a different path—well equipped with a useful set of navigational tools to lead you to your best life.

For far too long we've come to believe that books which make you better at running your business, and your life, must be self-help books telling you what to do and not to do. *Misfire* proves that a more effective way to transform a person's life is through a story. And, believe me, this is a great tale disguised as a business book. Or perhaps a business book hidden within a compelling story.

A very long time ago, I was a speaker on a panel addressing an auditorium of small business owners. I gave my presentation: a collection of impressive facts and charts with some decent humor, and even a life lesson or two. I sat down satisfied with myself.

Then Mitch Schneider spoke. I had heard of him, but had never met him or heard what he had to say. I was somewhat startled at his presentation. There were no 'fact inventories' or charts and graphs. Most speakers who address business audiences speak only to the brain. Not Mitch. Sure, he spoke powerfully to every mind in the room, but he got there via the heart. And that, my friends, made all the difference.

I realized then that Mitch had learned a better way to help small business people. Not only with business process advice but with a fresh approach that offered a better journey and outcome.

Mitch's presentation did two things for me. First, it changed forever the way I think about teaching and presenting to impact people's view of their personal values, hidden strengths, and resilience to succeed. Second, it started a friendship with a man I admire and have learned from with every encounter—to this day.

Part of Mitch's magic is rooted in the fact that he has long been a small business person himself—struggling, succeeding, sliding backward, and getting ahead again. Like you, he's sweated the payrolls, woke up screaming in the night, worked way too long and hard, and felt the weight of responsibility for his team. Mitch has done all this and more.

However, unlike some, he resisted the temptation to linger on the dark side of small business. Instead, he uncovered a different way to find one's best life, and then he taught thousands of others.

Misfire is Mitch's ninth book, but it's his first work of fiction. It's a novel about two small business owners who, after a chance encounter, change each other's lives. It's the story of how this unlikely pair, one from the automotive world and the other from construction, meet. It chronicles how one becomes a mentor to the other at a time when the latter desperately needed fresh thinking and renewal. For this exploration, martial arts provide a robust framework and guidance to an elevated life of personal discipline, commitment, and a clear mind—at work and at home.

However, that is far from all the book is about. Mitch seamlessly weaves into the story authentic and powerful business lessons—real fundamentals that every small businessperson can apply right away.

Today in my life, as I flirt with retirement, I am the founder and chairman of a successful training and coaching company for small businesses. I say successful, not only because we are consistently profitable, but because we have transformed the lives of so many through our work.

So much of what makes my company successful can be traced back to things I've learned from Mitch about how to run a business, how to find the strength in the tough times, and how to savor the good. Even the fundamental techniques, tools, and strategies we use in my business to reliably make others more prosperous can be found in this book.

If you're a small businessperson fighting the battles to get on top of (or stay on top of) your world, then you and Mitch are good friends who just haven't met yet. Get acquainted through *Misfire*. You'll have a mentor and a friend for the rest of your life.

Ken Brookings
Founder and Chairman
The Aspire Institute

Introduction

This is a book I never thought I'd finish. Frankly, it's a book I never thought I'd even start. But, after more than thirty-seven years spent writing, speaking, and trying to help other small business owners achieve the success they so richly deserve, it's a book I knew I would eventually have to finish.

If you are familiar with my work, you will find this a bit different from anything I've done in the past.

Unlike the eight-volume Automotive Management Series I wrote, or the countless columns on shop management and life in the repair community, or pieces written for warehouse distributors, counter professionals, and manufacturers, this is unique.

It's a fable of sorts: an allegory incorporating much of what I've learned and written about in the past but in an unconventional way.

It is the story of a small business owner who woke up one day to find that his cherished Corvette, his family life, and his business had all failed him. And, it's a story about how he managed to get them all running the way they were meant to run.

To a large degree, it's my personal journey. The story of our family business: where it needed to be, and what we had to do to get it there.

If you aren't a member of the automotive aftermarket, but you are a small business owner—notably, an independent contractor—I think you will find many of the business management principles discussed within the pages of this book just as useful as if you owned an automotive repair shop or have been 'turning wrenches' your entire life. Because, in the end, this book is about people and business, service, and success, and almost everything in between.

It's about what I know and what I've learned. And, the profound and positive difference those lessons have made in my life.

Hopefully, it will make a profound difference in your life or the life of anyone searching for a better way.

So, here's your invitation. The door to the Corvette is open, and the passenger seat is empty.

Get in. Get comfortable. Get ready.

We're about to go for a ride.

A ride that's guaranteed to help you create a better tomorrow!

MISFIRE

1

Chaos Reigns Supreme

"Son of a bitch!" Kurt winced, desperately trying to stifle his scream before it became a bellow.

Just another Monday, he thought to himself.

He had managed to quietly slide out of bed and head to the bathroom when it became apparent he wasn't going back to sleep. It was a short journey, but it was fraught with its own special danger at 3:57 a.m.

Laurie was sound asleep. The room was perfectly dark, and that meant stepping off the throw rug that bordered his side of the bed was like entering a mine field—a mine field littered with Max's Hot Wheels, a princess doll of AJ's, and even his own slippers.

He tried to exercise extreme care, sensing where each obstacle might be before committing his full weight to a tentative step. But that proved futile when the soft instep of his right foot found the business end of a tiny fire truck, surprisingly sturdy for its size.

He made it to the bathroom, closed the door, and checked to see if he was bleeding. He wasn't.

Kurt turned on the humidity fan which cast a faint green glow across the room, and started the water running in the shower.

Now it was just a matter of waiting for the water to reach a reasonable temperature. *The water heater*, he thought. *Another to-do for the list.*

He decided to shave at the office. That way he wouldn't have to turn the lights on in the master bathroom. He wrapped himself in a towel, grabbed a pair of slacks and a shirt from his closet, fumbled for socks and underwear from his dresser, then closed the bedroom behind him. He softly walked past the kids' rooms, and then padded down the stairs.

He was still wrapped in a towel when he reached the kitchen and shoveled eight tablespoons of the strongest espresso roast he had into the filtered paper. It was going to be a strong coffee morning and Kurt knew it.

He toggled the coffee machine on; the aroma of freshly brewed coffee filled the kitchen like a welcome visit from an old friend.

After Kurt got dressed, he brought out the stack of invoices and work orders he perpetually dragged back and forth from the office. He opened his laptop on the kitchen table and picked up where he left off on the work he failed to finish the night before.

For the next few hours, his entire universe was confined to his notebook and the papers that surrounded it. At least it was until he looked up to find Max standing at the entrance to the kitchen, one hand holding a Batman toy by the feet and the other wiping the sleep out of his eyes.

Kurt looked over at the digital clock on the oven. It was 6:47.

He took a deep breathe and tried to relax. He knew he wasn't going to finish the work he started, work that *had* to get done. Not now. Not with Max at the doorway. Not with Laurie and AJ headed down the stairs at any moment.

He was about twenty seconds away from the normal level of chaos that was breakfast at the Kerrigan household. He wasn't sure exactly when breakfast had become an interruption. But, it had.

"Hey, slick," Kurt smiled at his son. "What are you doing up so early? Shouldn't you be in bed dreaming about the great day you're about to have today?"

Max yawned. His arms went back as he tried to stretch the sleep out of his little body.

"It was the spiders, Daddy. They—," Max sputtered, his little eyes searching the shadows of his memory. "They were in my room again, all over my bed. And they were coming to get me. They wouldn't go away and I was scared!"

Max ran to where his father was sitting and climbed up on his lap. He stood on Kurt's thighs, looking him square in the eye.

"I was scared, Daddy!" Max insisted, "I was scared, and I called out, but no one came." He threw his arms around his father's neck.

"Are you sure you called out, buddy?" Kurt asked. "Maybe you just did in the dream and that's why no one came. You know your mother and I would never ever let anything bad happen to you!"

Kurt wasn't sure when Laurie had come down or how long she'd been standing at the entrance to the kitchen, but there she was with AJ clinging to her side.

The kids were two years apart, almost to the day and a handful. Max was five-and-a-half and Andrea Jean—aka AJ—was three-and-a-half. Two bright, curious, energetic squatters who had completely taken over their house and their lives.

"Let *what* happen?" Laurie asked.

Before Kurt could answer, Max spun around to see where his mother's voice came from. The Caped Crusader he'd been holding struck Kurt's coffee cup as he turned, sending a wave of lukewarm coffee cascading across the table and on to the office papers.

Kurt's jaw locked and his body tightened. His growl would have made a lion proud.

He couldn't stop the "Goddammit, Max" that slipped through his gritted teeth as he started wiping up the mess with a couple of napkins.

Laurie grabbed a handful of paper towels from the counter and passed them to her husband. Kurt dabbed at the coffee-stained financials in defeat, thankful that, at least, the computer was spared.

Max, oblivious to the lake of coffee on the table, continued with gusto. "The spiders, Mommy! They came back to my room to get me and I was scared. I called for you and daddy, but no one came!"

Laurie moved alongside Kurt and deposited AJ into his arms. She reached over and pulled Max close to her, cradling the back of his head with her hand.

"Well, my little man, you're safe now. Nothing bad is going to happen to you. Not while Mommy and Daddy are here."

Kurt marveled at how easily Laurie made parenting look, how good she was with the kids. He loved Max and AJ more than he could ever express in words, but felt awkward saying it out loud. In fact, there were times he felt uncomfortable just being around them. Certainly much more than he would have liked.

Like it or not, he was becoming his father and that made him feel worse. He loved his dad, but the old man was tough. Hard as nails. Closed off and distant.

Sure, he loved Kurt. But he was from a different generation. He never showed his love. At least not the way the fathers of Kurt's friends did. His Dad just wasn't that kind of touchy-feely parent.

Kurt promised himself he would make up for the affection he had missed when he was a child by doubling up on it when it came time to raise kids of his own. But, now, he was finding that a lot harder than he ever dreamt it would be.

2

Hi, Ho! Hi, Ho!

Kurt scooped up the computer and the remaining papers that covered his quarter of the table. He alternated the stained, and still damp, documents with sheets of paper towels hoping they would dry while Laurie got breakfast going.

This morning it was going to be oatmeal for everyone.

Kurt took his with peanut butter, a tablespoon of maple syrup, and a second cup of coffee. AJ loved hers with a drop of peanut butter, a little raw honey, and a sprinkle of brown sugar. Max had to have his with half a banana and brown sugar.

Laurie didn't sit down to eat with them. Later, after everyone else had finished and Kurt was on his way, she'd make herself a protein shake.

Kurt was half-done with his oatmeal before the kids had even started on theirs. Laurie looked up at him from the dishwasher.

"You know you shouldn't eat like that."

"Like what?"

"That fast. It isn't healthy." Laurie shook her head. "Besides it would be nice if you slowed down a little and had breakfast with your family before rushing out the door."

Kurt frowned back at her, "I'll slow down. But, for the record, I'm not going anywhere until everyone is finished. I eat fast. It's a bad habit. But you already knew that.

Laurie returned to emptying the dishwasher.

Twenty minutes later, Kurt placed the laptop and paperwork in his backpack as the kids and Laurie lined up at the door.

Kurt picked AJ up, "How about a kiss and a monkey hug before I head off to work? A big one that'll last me all day."

AJ wrapped her legs around Kurt's torso and her arms around his neck. She squeezed her father, happily trying to duplicate the snorts and grunts of a little monkey.

Kurt smiled, "Good one, monkey bones. Love you."

He set her down gently, then eyed Max. "What about you, Mr. Kerrigan? How about a hug and a kiss for your old man?"

Laurie shot her husband a look, "Kurt! You're not his 'old man.' You're his father. And that's how he should address you."

Kurt nodded in agreement, then looked at his son. "Okay, then, Mr. Kerrigan. How about a big hug and a kiss for your *father*?"

Max took a boot-camp step forward, saluted his father, and then jumped into his arms. "I love you, Daddy!"

"I love you too, buddy." Kurt winked at his daughter. "And you, my little princess."

He threw the backpack over his right shoulder and took two steps toward the door, then stopped short. He backed up, turned around, and took Laurie in his arms. "I love you too, Mrs. Kerrigan. Always have. Always will."

Both kids echoed their disapproval at their parent's show of affection with a chorus of "Ewwww! Gross!"

Kurt pulled himself away and opened the utility room door. Inside the garage, his tricked-out, 2008 C6 Corvette convertible awaited his arrival. Kurt headed toward the security of his shiny black beast.

It was time. Time for a mental health moment.

Even in late spring, work was normally just thirty to thirty-five minutes from the house. The freeway was the fastest and most direct route. But there were two other ways that would just as surely get Kurt to his destination albeit a bit later.

He could take surface streets to the office—adding another ten minutes to the commute—or he could get on the freeway, get off at the first offramp, and head up Drexel to the Canyon, then ride Mountain Crest, and the top of the mountain, all the way to work.

It would take a few minutes longer, he thought. *But it's a hell of a lot more fun!*

Well, not exactly fun. Lose concentration and I'll be hundreds of feet down the mountain—the Corvette wheels up like a cockroach on its back.

Nevertheless, that's where Kurt was headed. He brought the ebony Vette to life, cranked the stereo up, and put the top down.

He closed his eyes and listened to the deep throaty sound of the tuned exhaust and slipped his sunglasses on.

Kurt had spent a lot of money, money he really didn't have, to take the Corvette to the next level of performance. With the convertible dialing in at 563 horsepower on the dynamometer, he figured it was cash well-spent. In fact, it charted between the ratings of a Z06 and a ZR1—the top off-the-showroom-floor performers in Corvette's performance car line-up.

All of that power was hidden in a stock convertible shell. He had the ultimate 'sleeper.' The vehicle Kurt always wanted, but could never have when he was growing up.

He backed the Vette down the driveway, closed the garage door, and headed straight for Drexel Canyon Road.

That's Why They Call It Work

The ride to work was everything Kurt hoped it would be. It was challenging, exhilarating, and downright terrifying at times.

Kurt loved this road because it demanded a driver's complete and undivided attention. You couldn't drive Drexel Canyon, at least not like it was meant to be driven, without totally committing yourself to its challenges.

There was no room for distraction. No space for work-related problems. No thinking about the mess at home. No wondering about Laurie, the kids, or what the future held in store for them.

Sure, he was being a little selfish. If anything happened to him, the impact on his family would be catastrophic, even though he was well-insured. But, every once in a while when his anxieties got away from him, Kurt felt entitled.

He had the Corvette in Competitive Driving Mode. He was driving aggressively. Kurt knew that any distraction could easily result in sliding off the road and a sheer, 500-foot drop to the bottom of the canyon. Yet he treated the loops and hairpins like they were the road to redemption and tested himself at every turn.

Kurt was nearing work when he slid into the last tight turn at far beyond what anyone would consider a reasonable speed. The black sports car glided off the road on to the loose gravel of the shoulder. The loss of traction was a ballet of unbridled horsepower and high school physics.

That's when Kurt realized how perilously close to the guardrail he'd come. He immediately backed off the accelerator pedal and tried to pull himself together. The slide left him shaking.

He needed time to allow his heart rate and breathing to drop to normal. *Too fast and too close to the edge*, he thought.

Then he smiled, *But, damn, it felt good!*

He cruised the rest of the way in to work. Kurt glanced at his watch: forty-five minutes since he left home. A couple of minutes late. But, certainly, well worth the extra time.

He walked through the front door and received the normal greeting of raised hands and grunts. Everyone seemed to be where they were supposed to be, doing what they were being paid to do.

He walked over to his Administrative Assistant's desk and smiled. "What'cha got waiting for me this morning, Rocky? Which fires need to get put out first?"

Rochelle looked up and smiled, "Come on, boss. Things aren't that bad. At least not yet." With that, she handed him a half-inch thick stack of pink 'While You Were Out' notes.

Kurt took a quick look at the stack.

8:17 AM. thought Kurt, *She must have just finished this up.*

Rochelle had started working for Kurt so long ago no one could remember a time when she was not a part of the company. She had been sixteen—still in high school enrolled in a work/study program —when she responded to the part-time job listing Kurt had placed with the school's employment office. She'd been there ever since.

Kurt had been looking for an extra pair of hands to help with the never-ending ocean of paperwork he was drowning in, and Rochelle was looking for independence from an abusive home.

She was young, ambitious, tireless, and incredibly curious. There was nothing she wouldn't try. Nothing she couldn't do—as long as you could deal with the constant barrage of questions about how, why, or when anything needed to be done.

By the time she graduated from high school, Rocky (as she was known by everyone) was a linchpin at Kerrigan Construction, an indispensable asset. Kurt could not imagine life without her.

Maybe because she was the only one in the company who knew where everything was. Or maybe it was because she was always laughing, and that joyful sound was irresistible.

As Kurt headed toward his General Manager's office, Rochelle turned and called after him. "Don't pay attention to the time stamps. The really critical stuff is on top."

Rick, Kerrigan's GM, was on the phone taking notes when Kurt stopped by his desk. He dropped the pen he was holding and held up his index finger up, indicating the call was important. It would be a minute before they could catch up on the morning's events. Rick was the only one at the company there longer than Rochelle.

Kurt crossed the hallway to his own office, slipped the backpack off his shoulder, and placed it on his desk. He walked over to the coffee machine to get it started. He could already sense this was going to be a three-cup morning.

As the coffee brewed, he grabbed his favorite mug. The message reflected precisely how Kurt believed the day would unfold: *Things could be worse. But I'm not sure how!*

He slid behind his desk, placed the backpack on the floor, pulled the computer out, opened it up, and pressed the power icon. He could feel his neck and shoulders tighten as he rifled through the cascade of pink messages.

He wondered why he was still doing any of this.

Why was he so committed to a business that seemed, at the very least, ambivalent to his wants and needs?

The first message was from a client with a pretty comprehensive remodel. It had started out as a 'good job,' but quickly descended to the Seventh Level of Construction Hell.

It's hard to please someone who doesn't know what they want, Kurt thought to himself. *Hard to do a good job when the client and all the Fates conspire against you.*

They were six-and-a-half months into a job that had been scheduled for six. The estimate allowed for decent margins and everything looked good until it was determined that a number of things had never made it into the original bid—critical things that would now have to be included, line items that would destroy the contract price and his company's credibility if Kurt tried to recover them. Things Kerrigan Construction would now have to eat.

On the same job, there were a series of delays that fell one after the other like a line of clacking dominoes. Sub-contractor after sub-contractor was unable to meet the schedule, until it became obvious the job wouldn't be completed for another two to three weeks.

The client was breathing fire when Kurt finally got her on the line. Ten minutes later she was still venting. In the end, he got her calmed down, but not until he was forced to make some pretty substantial concessions on the final project cost in order to compensate for her inconvenience and disappointment.

The next call mirrored the first. More problems, only different. This time it was the city and delays in getting the right inspector out to a jobsite at the appropriate time. When the inspector finally did arrive, there were more problems. None of them quick. None of them simple or easy to resolve.

Kurt continued to work his way down the stack, one little pink 'While You Were Out' at a time until they were all gone—more than three hours of crisis management and damage control.

It was almost eleven-thirty when Kurt tossed the last note in the trash. He sat back and stretched, totally exhausted. He was spent, both physically and emotionally.

But, finally, it was over.

Then a horrible thought formed in the back of his head: *Rocky has been at her desk this whole time building another stack of disasters for me to deal with!*

Kurt shook his head, *No lunch today. Not for you, mister.* He reached into the backpack and pulled out a protein bar.

"Hello, my little friend," he quipped in his best Al Pacino 'Scarface' impersonation.

Rick was at the door, his eyebrows cocked in amusement and empathy. "Tough morning, huh, boss?"

Taking a seat, he continued, "I haven't gotten anything done yet either. Been putting out fires and playing catch up since I got here. I don't know what's going on. But I'm pretty sure it isn't supposed to be this hard. Not all the time anyway."

Kurt laughed. Not the kind of laugh that results from someone telling a great joke, but the nervous kind that happens when things are falling apart and there isn't much anyone can do about it. It was the kind of laugh when you know you're in trouble, but don't quite know how to handle it. Kurt shook his head.

"No, Rick! It isn't supposed to be this hard. I don't know what it is. All I know is that I'm trying like hell to figure it out, because I know it can't go on like this for very much longer. Hell, *I* can't go on like this for very much longer!

"I just can't find the answers I'm looking for and that bothers me more than anything else. But, don't worry. I'll find a way. I always have, haven't I?"

Rick thought about this long and hard. He tried his best to be upbeat. "You brought us through the Great Recession and we're still here. We've just got to make it easier. Less painful."

Kurt smiled in return, "Let's take a break and see where we are. Maybe an idea will bubble to the surface."

For the next couple of hours, Kurt and Rick went over all the leads, referrals, and bids that had come in. They processed the ones that still had to go back out to clients. All the while, the clock on the wall kept ticking.

Kurt shrugged his shoulders. He was angry, frustrated, and overtired—a bad combination.

"That's it, buddy. I know it's only been a few hours, but I just gotta get outta here. I got nothin' left."

Kurt pushed his chair back from the desk. "I think I'm going to head out early and surprise Laurie and the kids. After this morning, I need it."

Rick nodded in understanding. "Don't worry, boss. I got this!"

Kurt gathered his stuff and walked out. Rick followed and closed the office door behind them. He waved as Kurt headed off.

Kurt didn't notice.

In fact, he didn't even look up as he plodded through the office. He made a beeline for the security and comfort of the Corvette— squeezing behind the wheel, and tossing his backpack on the floor in front of the passenger seat.

The morning had been brutal and he knew he was nowhere near sharp enough for the canyon. So, this time, it was going to be the freeway home. He sped out of the office parking lot.

Kurt slipped under the overpass, made a right turn on to the onramp, and pressed the accelerator pedal to the floor. The Vette's rear tires started to smoke and squeal as they lost contact with the asphalt.

The ebony vehicle entered the freeway at just over 90 miles per hour before Kurt brought his right foot off the accelerator pedal.

He looked to his left and entered the number three lane only to find another Corvette tracking him. It was a bright red ZR1, more race car than commuter vehicle. The driver was grinning and trying to goad him into a race by goosing the pedal, forcing the ZR1 to leap in front of Kurt's black convertible, then slowing down to come back alongside.

Really? One-forty-five. And this clown wants to race?

Kurt was too tired to play that game. At least, not right then. He ignored the other driver who finally got the message. The red ZR1 accelerated, leaving Kurt behind to deal with what little traffic there was at that time.

4

The Black Corvette

The black Corvette roared down the Interstate. Kurt was lost deep in his own thoughts.

The road, the other vehicles, the drivers, and their stories were irrelevant. There was just too much to think about—too much to worry about—to consider anyone or anything else.

Business was down. Sales were off. Profit non-existent. Today had been one more horrible day in a string of bad days that had been going on for far too long.

At the moment, the only thing on Kurt's mind was, *What am I going to do? How do I get things back on track?* Lost in thought, the only reminder that he was driving far beyond the 65 MPH speed limit was the glow of the heads-up display.

With his palm pressed hard against the surface of the steering wheel, he opened and closed the fingers of his left hand. They were stiff. His hand hurt as he released his grip on the wheel and scratched his chin.

What happened and how do I fix it?

He backed off the throttle, tapped the paddle shift one gear lower, stabbed the accelerator pedal again, and leaned to his right as he took the sleek black machine deep into a turn.

This car was his refuge. *The only thing I can depend on,* Kurt thought as he came around the bend. Looking ahead he could see the traffic start to congeal along the emerging stretch of highway.

Kurt's father had taught him to drive at least a quarter mile ahead, a half-mile when possible. That meant constantly scanning the sides of the road and the horizon for potential hazards—as well as for any vehicles that were being driven erratically, like the red ZR1 who had toyed with him earlier.

The same red ZR1 that was, just now, slamming into the back of a moving van.

Even before traffic came to a screeching halt, well before an iridescent wall of crimson brake lights lit up in front of him, Kurt's instincts kicked in. He slammed the brake pedal hard while simultaneously pulling the Vette toward the shoulder, his eyes darting from the car ahead to the rear view mirror—checking to see how aware the drivers behind him were of the pending emergency. He didn't want to avoid a front end collision just to get rear-ended. Luckily, there was room to maneuver.

He felt the brakes chatter as the anti-lock brake system engaged. His black Corvette came to a stop safely behind and to the right of the vehicle ahead. The car rested at a slight angle to the highway, its passenger side tires on the shoulder.

Kurt checked his rear view mirror again. He punched the red triangle on the dash engaging the Corvette's emergency warning lamps. They blinked in rhythmic response.

He surveyed the situation ahead: he was less than a hundred yards from the accident. At this angle, Kurt saw the red Corvette wedged under the moving van's liftgate. It was jammed tightly, almost to the windshield.

There but for the grace of God go I, he thought. His heart pounded faster in realization of the consequences.

That could have been my Corvette. My crash! Laurie could have been sitting next to me. Or one of the kids!

Cars and trucks were scattered in every direction. It reminded him of Max's room on a Saturday morning with all the Hot Wheels and Matchbox vehicles carelessly strewn across the floor. But this wasn't play time. It was real.

That's when he saw smoke start to billow out from under the red Corvette's cracked and crumpled hood. Kurt looked around, but no one else moved. The cars and their drivers seemed frozen in time.

Without thinking, he released his seat belt and emerged from his vehicle already at a sprint. Evading debris near the accident, he arrived at the driver's side of the mangled ZR1 and tried to pull the door open. It was jammed. He grabbed the handle with his hand, firmly planted his foot against the chassis just behind the door, and pulled with everything he had.

Suddenly, the door came loose. The abrupt absence of resistance left Kurt stumbling backwards. He gathered himself, then raced back to the driver. The windshield was shattered and the airbag deployed; the man was slumped over the steering wheel, bleeding from facial cuts on his cheek and forehead.

"You okay? Can you move? Is anything broken?"

The driver shifted his head in the direction of Kurt's voice, but there was no response.

Kurt smelled the unmistakable odor of raw fuel. He looked down to see a river of liquid flowing under the vehicle.

No more time…

He shoved the deployed airbag out of the way, trying to release the driver's seat belt. It was wedged in at an angle.

Without hesitating, Kurt reached for his pocket knife, the one always clipped to his back pocket, and cut the belt at both the shoulder and the driver's waist. Then, he reached in and yanked the man out and away from the Corvette.

He stumbled back under the driver's weight. As Kurt collapsed, they both fell to the road twenty feet or so from the stricken car.

I'll bet no one teases me about carrying a knife again.

His butt on the pavement, he looked around. Cautiously, other individuals had emerged from their vehicles: some to get a better view, a few to help. Two men quickly dragged the injured driver away from wreck, while a guy in a blue jacket assisted Kurt to his feet just as the red ZR1 burst into flame.

Kurt stared at the fire, dazed for a moment, not noticing how hard he was breathing.

The guy in the blue jacket looked in him in the eye, "You okay?"

Kurt cleared his head a bit first, "Yeah. I'm good. I think." The reality of his situation hadn't really penetrated yet.

The stranger smiled, "You're a hero! You know that, right?"

He slapped his hand proudly on Kurt's shoulder, "I'm not sure I would have gotten out of my car if I hadn't seen you running over there. You saved that guy's ass!"

Kurt frowned slightly, not sure what to think.

Within minutes, he heard the sirens of the Highway Patrol and then an ambulance arriving. Soon the Fire Department was on the scene racing down the shoulder, followed by a TV news van. Everything was a blur.

A patrolman was asking Kurt a number of questions. Nearby the injured driver was attended to; the ambulance screaming away. A helicopter, its side emblazoned with the logo of a local TV news affiliate, hovered overhead.

Kurt answered each query to the best of his ability. When the officer needed contact information, Kurt handed over his business card.

Then the highway patrolman asked what he was driving. Kurt slowly pointed to black Corvette straddling the shoulder with its driver's door wide open.

Yes, that's mine, he nodded.

Traffic was moving slowly around the wreck as Kurt returned to his car. A flatbed tow truck was snaking its way through the traffic, trying to make it to the crash site. The highway patrolman motioned for him to move his vehicle.

Kurt was still a little out of it as he slumped back into the seat, the reality of the moment finally registering. He had no idea how much time had transpired.

Jesus! he thought. *What the hell is going on today?*

How could that guy not see the van? It was right in front of him.

Maybe he was spacing out, like me. Worrying about his company instead of the road.

Kurt shook his head and fired up the engine. Traffic was backed up for miles behind him. The officer he had spoken to earlier halted the other vehicles and waved him onto the freeway. Kurt slowly passed the perimeter of orange cones.

The road opened up ahead as he cleared the accident site.

I called and told Laurie I was leaving early and now I'm gonna be late. She's going to have a fit.

He reached for his sunglasses, preparing mentally to make up for lost time. He stabbed the accelerator pedal.

The black Corvette shuddered violently.

What the hell?

5

Mushin Automotive

The black Corvette recovered, at least for the moment. Its driver did not. What might have been a simple misfire to someone else was a sign of complete and utter betrayal to Kurt. He was furious.

The Vette had misbehaved like that a couple of times in the past and he'd taken it in to be looked at. But, of course, it never acted up while in the shop.

Now it seemed like every time he stepped on the accelerator the vehicle shuddered—not as violently as when he left the accident, but not exactly normal either.

What the hell is going on?

Kurt was focusing on the 'how' and 'when' of the misfire when the amber Service Engine Soon lamp caught his attention.

The light, the shaking… What next?

Kurt shook his head in frustration. He realized that he couldn't drive the vehicle very hard or very far the way it was running. The only question was what to do instead.

He was in a no man's land on the highway—halfway between home and work, too far away from either to make it there without the Corvette shaking itself apart.

He waited for the next highway sign to get a sense of exactly where he was: "Blue Ridge exit, 3 miles."

Blue Ridge exit?

Where had he heard that before? Kurt trolled his memory.

Oh, yeah! Frank from the Corvette Club. He told me about a shop right at the Blue Ridge off-ramp.

Frank had said, "If you ever have a problem with your car—and you're anywhere close to the Blue Ridge exit—you gotta go there. Hell, even if you don't have a problem, go there."

It was at a weekend gathering for the car club, a bunch of guys getting together for breakfast. Kurt remembered standing in the parking lot with a to-go cup of coffee in his hand.

"What's so special about it?" he asked.

"Kurt, you've never been to any shop like this in your life. Sure, the guy who runs it is a little different, but he knows his cars. You'll love the place. I'll bet money on it."

"Different? How?"

"I don't want to spoil the surprise. I tell you what… If you don't agree, I'll buy you lunch."

At the time, Kurt thought it was a strange recommendation. But what was even stranger was finding himself in the middle of a crisis at the foot of the Blue Ridge off-ramp right now.

He didn't believe in coincidence or fate. But he did believe in getting his Corvette fixed. Besides, what else was he going to do? He didn't know anyone close by, and he was terrified he could seriously damage the only thing he cared about.

Kurt suddenly felt the shock of momentary, yet crippling, guilt.

Well, the only thing I care about next to Laurie and the kids!

His chest tightened. He knew how tenuous his relationship with Laurie was becoming. It felt like the house they'd constructed together out of love and hope had become a battleground strewn with broken promises and unresolved commitments. They'd gone from agreeing on almost everything to fighting about, well, just about anything.

It seemed like there were times they couldn't be together in the same room for more than a few seconds before the tension would begin to build. Laurie's voice echoed in his head.

"Why are you always late? Why can't you make it home in time to have dinner with your children? To have dinner with *me*? When did we get relegated to last place?

"And there's never enough money! Not enough for the kid's school. Not enough to take a decent vacation. Whatever there is gets pumped back into that black hole of a company. It's always about Kerrigan Construction.

"You told me to quit my job, to abandon my career. You said I should stay home with the kids. I've been out of the workforce for six years, Kurt. What am I gonna find now? I'm trapped here in a house that's starting to fall apart."

Kurt sighed. Laurie was the only woman he'd ever cared about. The only woman he ever loved… still loved.

And the kids were his life.

But the business he started, the one they started *together*, was on life support and that pressure was taking its toll on both of them.

Kurt shook his head violently and pounded the steering wheel with his fist. He'd almost missed the ramp, which would have meant working his way back to the Blue Ridge area on surface streets, if he could find it at all.

He pulled off the highway, trying desperately to think of the shop's name: *Mooseen? Moo shu? Moo-something, dammit.*

Suddenly, it was right in front of him. The large illuminated sign glaring at him in Asian-style letters: Mushin Automotive.

Odd name, Kurt thought to himself, as he pulled down the driveway to the building. *Well, Frank said they worked on his Vette and did a great job. It'll be fine.*

Navigating toward a bright blue awning with the word 'Office' emblazoned on it, he slowed the vehicle to a crawl. A clean-cut young kid emerged from inside and waved him to park where he was. The kid was at the Corvette's side with a tablet PC in one hand and a bar code scanner in the other almost before Kurt could get the door open. He stepped out.

The facility sparkled in the sunlight. It was immaculate.

The young man hung the scanner over his left shoulder, reached out and took Kurt's hand in his. It was a firm, confident handshake.

"Welcome to Mushin Automotive, sir! How can I help you?"

The enthusiasm and genuine warmth of the greeting caught Kurt off guard.

"Well, er… I'm having a problem. A misfire or something. Actually, the whole car shakes whenever I accelerate. And the warning lamp came on about five miles back."

Kurt walked toward the front of the vehicle. "It's scary as hell and I was hoping someone could take a quick look at it, so I know what I'm up against—what I have to do next in order to get home."

"No problem, sir. You've definitely come to the right place." The kid was absolutely beaming. "Let me get some information on the vehicle and then some personal information from you, so they have it in the office when you get there. It will only take a minute."

Suddenly, the kid was everywhere: under the hood, inside the passenger compartment, all around the vehicle.

Kurt marvelled as the young man scanned the vehicle ID code, plugged some type of connector into a receiver inside the passenger compartment, turned the key on, turned the key off, walked around the vehicle, checked under the hood, and then started taking digital pictures with his tablet.

"Sure is a pretty car," said the kid, as he snapped away.

"May I have your name, address, and a phone number, along with a current email, so I can get them into the system?"

Kurt reached for a business card. He said, "Everything you need is on here."

"Great! The main entrance to the office is just under the awning. They'll be ready for you in a moment. And thanks so much for allowing us the opportunity to serve you."

Kurt couldn't help but return the kid's smile. He headed toward the office door.

The Office

The accident seemed like a distant memory: a dream sequence of something he'd witnessed, but had not been directly involved in.

He'd had a client dinner at an expensive four-star restaurant the week before, and the service there wasn't anywhere nearly as pleasant or enthusiastic as what he'd just experienced in the parking lot.

Now, as he opened the office door to Mushin Automotive and stepped inside, he found himself smiling.

Kurt removed his sunglasses and looked around. The lighting was more subdued than he expected and he was sure he could hear the sound of moving water. He turned toward the cascading sound.

What's that? A fountain in an auto repair shop waiting room?

As his eyes adjusted to the lighting he saw a tri-level waterfall and miniature Zen rock garden discreetly placed in the far corner of the room.

He scanned the office: brush paintings, calligraphy, and sculpture. All of it Asian, all of it chosen with great care. Then he noticed the scent of incense.

Incense? Wha...

Cumulatively, it was an assault on the senses: unexpected and out of place—albeit, not altogether unpleasant.

Who decorated this place anyway? Am I in a repair shop or a Zen day spa?

Kurt could feel the tension leaving his body as the atmosphere washed over him. He liked it: the peacefulness and relaxation.

Boy oh boy, was Frank right. This is one unusual place.

Kurt was experiencing a degree of sensory overload. Perhaps that's why it took a moment for him to realize there was no service counter. No artificial barrier between client and service provider.

There were, however, two desks—modern, open, and elegantly simple in design. They each had a bare minimum of the things you would normally find on a desk: a telephone, a calculator, two flat-screen monitors, one single fresh cut flower, and not much else. There were two chairs on the client's side of each desk with a single chair on the management side.

Both desks were placed at odd angles, not at all where Kurt would have expected them to be in order to maximize the available space. But it was obvious there was nothing conventional about this office or the people who had put it together.

That's when he noticed the large glass partition between the office and the shop. If the office was a shock, the shop itself was downright astounding.

Instead of the bold white, red, and blue stripes that seemed to be synonymous with every service area Kurt had ever encountered, this shop was rich in earth tones and bright accents. The lighting was as close to daylight as you were going to find inside a building, and the entire area was 'operating theater' clean.

Instead of banners, racing posters or product signage, there were brush paintings and calligraphy—except that these were murals painted directly on the walls.

The technicians wore loose-fitting smocks more consistent with what you would find in a martial arts studio than the stock work shirts and pants seen everywhere else.

But, more importantly, there was something decidedly different about the way each person went about their tasks.

Everyone that Kurt could see through the glass moved with a purposeful and athletic grace. There was no wasted effort, no unnecessary motion, no sense of the anxiety that one normally experiences in most automotive repair shops.

The workers weren't smiling, but they weren't frowning. They were totally absorbed in what they were doing. Kurt was taken by the contrast between this calm shop floor and his own place, Kerrigan Construction, where it appeared that everyone was perpetually in crisis mode—including himself.

"Welcome. I'm Allie," said a soft voice.

Kurt jumped. He didn't mean to, but he couldn't help it. The fact that he never saw or felt a person nearby until she spoke had him rattled. Yet here was Allie standing by his side.

"How may I help you today?"

Wearing slacks and a Mushin polo shirt, she was tall and slender, just as warm and kind as the young man outside. Kurt guessed she was in her late twenties or early thirties.

An athlete? he wondered. *Or maybe a dancer?*

He finally fumbled a response, "Hi, I didn't mean to jump like that. It's just that I've had a hell of a day and I'm kind of out of it."

Allie seemed genuinely interested, "Would you like to tell me a little about it?"

Surprised by the question, Kurt walked over to one of the chairs and sat down. "Well, there was this accident on the freeway, just before my car started acting up. A guy in another Corvette plowed into the back of a moving van. He was wedged under the liftgate."

"How bad was it?" Allie asked with concern in her voice.

"Bad enough. I managed to pull the guy out just before his Vette caught fire. I've never done anything like that before."

"That was brave."

"No. I'm no hero. I just imagined myself in that car. Any kind of distraction and it could've as easily been me. I had to help."

Allie took one of the client seats next to him as Kurt continued.

"But it wasn't me, luckily. So I got back in my car to head home and that's when it started shuddering and shaking. And, now, here we are."

Allie reached out and gently touched Kurt's forearm. "Well, my first question is: Are you okay?"

Kurt shook his head, "Yeah, I guess I am."

Allie noticed that, despite his insistence everything was okay, his left foot was beating a steady rhythm on the office floor.

"Can I offer you something? Maybe an herbal tea? Some cold water?" she asked.

"An herbal tea sounds good if it isn't too much trouble."

"Not at all," responded Allie. "Let me get that for you."

Allie returned with a steaming cup of freshly brewed herbal tea. Her voice was reassuring as she continued, "Listen, Mr. Kerrigan, you don't need to worry about your Corvette. You're in the right place. Whatever it is, we can take care of it."

Kurt relaxed into the chair and smiled. He was actually feeling a little better. Allie leaned forward, she was holding a computer tablet very much like the one the young man had used outside in the parking lot.

"Now, tell me about your Corvette. What's it doing that you no longer want it to do?"

Introductions...

"It's misfiring, I think. Jerking and shaking. I don't want to drive it the way it's running," Kurt replied.

"No worries." Allie replied. "But I do have a question. How did you hear about us?"

"Frank, one of the guys from my Corvette club told me this was the place I had to go to if I had a problem. The misfiring got really bad just before I hit Blue Ridge."

Allie beamed, "Frank McMasters? He's great! Please thank him for us the next time you see him. In the meantime, let me write this up for you and assign it to one of my Master Technicians. Just keep in mind it may take a bit."

As Allie spoke, Kurt glanced out onto the busy shop floor. She sensed his apprehension, reached out, lightly touched his forearm.

"We work almost exclusively by appointment. But I promise we'll still find a way to squeeze your Corvette in somehow."

Kurt's look of concern intensified as Allie smiled and went on.

"Kurt, we're very good at what we do. And I promise you will have an answer as quickly as is humanly possible. I promise we'll stay within our initial estimate as well. Unless, of course, something unforeseen pops up, in which case you get to decide what comes next."

Kurt was visibly frustrated.

"Can't you tell me what's wrong just by what the car's doing?" he asked. "I mean, it sounds pretty straight-forward, doesn't it? I'd kind of like to know what you think is wrong and what it might cost before we go any further."

Allie smiled again. This wasn't the first time she'd been forced to deal with a potential client's anxieties.

"Unfortunately, cars aren't that simple anymore. Today's vehicles are dynamic organisms complete with their own primitive kind of artificial intelligence.

"Because each driver is unique, and each vehicle is operated in its own environment with different demands, every vehicle brings with it its own distinct set of challenges.

"To find out what's wrong we need to know everything there is to know about you and the vehicle: where it's driven, when it's driven, and how it's driven."

Allie's response was logical and Kurt reluctantly found himself nodding in agreement.

"Someone will need to drive it in order to experience the symptoms that brought you to us. We'll need to inspect it and probably have to run some tests. We'll evaluate the results, then formulate a diagnosis.

"After that we can create an estimate, at which time you get to decide whether or not to proceed. If you want to go ahead, we'll order any parts that are necessary, install them, and then retest the vehicle to confirm it's really fixed.

"All of that takes time, tools, technology and an experienced technician."

"Come on, Allie!" Kurt responded. "That's a lot of steps. I can't believe you don't have one of those computers you just plug into the car. The kind that just tells you what's wrong."

"We do!" Allie replied enthusiastically. "And, in the case of your car, we call that computer Robert."

"You call your computer Robert?" Kurt looked confused.

Allie was still smiling as she looked out at the shop floor, "Robert's not a computer. But, in the process of diagnosing what's wrong, he'll use a scan tool—the kind of computer you mentioned —to create a window into the car's central nervous system."

Allie stood up. "Please come with me," she said. "I'd like to tell you a little bit about our shop, show you what we do, how we do it, and why we feel that our way makes us different from everyone else. When we're done, and if you're comfortable with what you've seen, we can get the paperwork together and get started."

With that, Kurt set down his tea and joined Allie as she walked out into the shop. Just a few steps inside, Kurt stopped. There was the sound of rushing water again, not the blare of rock music or country and western common to just about every other shop he'd ever been in. This was quiet, soothing, and relaxing.

As they entered the work area, Allie pointed out various pieces of equipment and introduced him to several technicians working in the ten stalls that made up the shop. Each seemed to have their own work space and though it was clear from the patches on their tunics they were all Certified Master Technicians, each seemed to have their own area of specialization.

Each one was courteous and respectful, but stopped only long enough to appear courteous and respectful. They had work to do, and it was clear they were all about getting that work done.

Robert's area was at the very end of the shop: the last two of the ten bays hidden from the street. Kurt suddenly realized that—although Allie had never raised her voice above a low, almost conversational tone—he had been able to hear her every word.

There was virtually no noise in the shop except for what sounded like what he'd heard while watching a Discovery Channel special on Tai Chi, kung fu and the Shaolin Temple in Northern China. It was an eerie kind of quiet considering there were four technicians working on at least nine vehicles.

As they approached a late model sedan with the driver's door open, Allie called out, "Robert, you have company."

It was obvious Allie was talking to the torso and pair of legs hanging out of the front door of the vehicle. The rest of the body was wedged into the area under the dash in a jumble of angles that would have made a Chinese acrobat proud.

Slowly, and with great care, Robert extricated himself from under the dash until he was standing by the open door. Then, just as slowly, he began to stretch. Allie smiled broadly as Robert folded himself in half, placing his palms on the epoxy-covered concrete. Her eyes moved between the two men as Robert pulled himself upright and she continued with her introduction.

"Kurt, this is Robert, our lead drivability technician and Mushin's owner.

"Robert, this is Kurt. He's brought his C6 here for you to look at when you have a moment. I'm going to leave him with you while I head back to the office. I'm sure Kurt has got some questions for you and I know you will have a few for him."

8

Purpose

The man who had just pulled himself out of the vehicle looked to be in his early fifties. He was muscular, yet moved like everyone else in the shop: gracefully and with purpose. The one thing Kurt noticed almost instantly were his eyes. They were ocean water blue and laser piercing.

"I apologize for not being available when you pulled in, but I was trying to convince my patient here to cooperate and I finally succeeded."

Kurt tilted his head as he looked at the car.

"What exactly were you doing under there?" he asked. "That was quite a position you managed to get yourself into. How can you work like that? How can you see what you're doing? There can't be enough light."

Robert smiled, "There isn't *any* light. And, as far as squeezing myself up in there is concerned, it's what I do. What I have to do. So I don't think about it much. I just do it."

Kurt frowned. "If there isn't any light, how can you see what you're doing?"

"I can't. At least, not with my eyes," Robert said as he reached for a red shop towel.

"Listen, it's too dark to see and the working area is too close for a light. Certainly too close for anybody's eyes to focus clearly, least of all these old eyes. I just close them and see with my fingertips.

"It's not the kind of thing you think about because the more you think about it, the more impossible it becomes. I've taken enough of these apart over the years to know what it looks like from behind and to know what it feels like by touch."

Kurt gazed at the sedan: a high-end German import. Robert finished wiping his hands and set the towel down. He shrugged.

"I want to fix the vehicle. The vehicle wants to be fixed. It wants to be whole again. We are both part of the same reality, so I become a facilitator more than a technician or a mechanic."

Robert smiled wryly, measuring Kurt's reaction.

"Have I frightened you yet?"

Kurt shook his head and returned a nervous smile of his own.

"Well, maybe just a little," he admitted.

"Well then, let's talk about your Corvette," Robert said. "What's it doing that's causing you pain?"

Kurt was confused. He'd never been in a 'car place' where people were this relaxed. He'd never been in a repair shop where they explained things as clearly.

"It isn't running right," Kurt said. "It won't accelerate like it used to. It kind of chugs and jerks along. It doesn't have the power it used to either. What's worse is that the problem is intermittent. I never know when it's going to run right or run like crap. It's become like everything else in my life: a real pain in the ass."

"Do you have time to go for a quick road test to see if the vehicle is still symptomizing right now?" Robert asked.

Kurt nodded his yes.

"Did you finish up the paperwork in the office? In our business, the job can't even get begin until the paperwork is completed."

Kurt shook his head.

Robert gestured for the two of them to head back to the office.

"Well then, we'll have to make a stop up front, and get the appropriate documents signed. I'll start with a visual inspection: obvious things that could cause the symptoms you described. From there, we'll road test the vehicle to verify those symptoms. Then, if we need to, we'll start a regimen of formal tests and inspections.

Robert made eye with Kurt as they walked through the shop.

"Does that make sense?" he asked.

Kurt nodded.

"I'm not driving it running the way it was when I brought it in," he said, his voice straining. "Something really bad is going on under there. As far as I'm concerned, you've got all the time you need. I'll just have to call home and let my wife know I haven't run away or been kidnapped. I'll rent a damn car if I have to, but I want it fixed."

Kurt realized he was rambling; talking too fast. He felt himself tightening up all over again.

The Beginning of Process

Robert walked completely around the vehicle twice. He knelt and looked under the Corvette, checked the tire tread, and swiped his finger around the inside of each tailpipe. It seemed as if there was always at least one part of his body contacting the vehicle.

He opened the door, reached inside and pulled on the hood release. Under the hood, he scanned the coolant reservoir, checked the oil, and rubbed a drop between his thumb and forefinger. Then he removed the oil fill cap, held it up to his nose, lightly moved his hands along the large air inlet duct, and then across electrical connections that seemed to be everywhere under the hood.

Kurt found himself fascinated with a process that could only become that fluid, that natural, with hundreds or even thousands of repetitions. It was obvious Robert had done all of this before.

"Let's take her for a quick ride so we can see how it's running. If she misbehaves I may have a better idea of where to start and how to proceed. That will save me time, and you money."

Robert sensed the tension creeping its way back into Kurt's body. He spoke calmly as he placed a hand on the Vette's fender.

"I realize you're a little nervous about having your lady handled by a stranger, but I can assure you that all my people love and respect the cars and trucks that find their way here at least as much, if not more, than their owners."

Robert smiled broadly as he pointed Kurt toward the passenger seat. He reached for the driver's door, and looked over at Kurt.

"And the vehicles that come here wind up loving us back."

Kurt was surprised at how easily Robert slid behind the wheel. His Corvette wasn't all that easy to get in or out of. It was low and close, and a lot of people seemed reluctant to ride with him because of the initial struggle getting in. Robert adjusted himself to the driving position as Kurt got into the passenger seat.

Immediately Kurt felt uncomfortable. He'd never sat in his own passenger seat before, not even when he first went to test drive the car. Not being in control just felt wrong somehow. It was the same feeling he'd come to know and loathe at work.

Robert confidently pushed the button marked 'start' and the Corvette sprang to life—its speakers throbbing to the bassline of some hard rock song. He reached for the entertainment center controls, then stopped and looked at Kurt.

"Would you mind if I turned the sound system off? It's bit of a distraction."

Kurt hadn't realized how loud the stereo was while he was driving. He nodded.

"Sure. Do whatever you have to do to get her back on the road and well again."

Robert took a deep breathe and sat there for a moment with his eyes closed, both hands on the steering wheel. Kurt watched as whatever residual tension the technician may have had completely left his body.

"Do you think she's going to cooperate and misfire when we take her out?" Kurt asked.

"We don't have to worry about that. She's misfiring right now," Robert replied.

Robert shut the Corvette down, reached in his pocket, and pulled out a small clear plastic rectangle. He inserted it in the same receiver the young kid had used when Kurt first arrived at the shop; then he restarted the vehicle.

Kurt could see a bright blue light intermittently radiating out from the rectangular object.

"What's that?" he wondered.

"It's a kind of flight recorder," Robert said. "A device we use to capture real-time data as we drive. It allows us to know what's going on in the vehicle's engine and fuel management systems. I can see almost every sensor and actuator, without having to hook up a dozen pieces of equipment. It allows me to focus on driving the car —how it feels and what it's doing—rather than the equipment."

‡

Robert turned the Corvette around and stopped in front of the office. Both men exited the car. Robert held the office door open for Kurt. Allie was sitting behind her desk deeply involved with her computer. When she realized they were standing at the foot of the desk, she slid a tablet toward Kurt—explaining the initial charges again and indicating where he needed to sign.

Kurt hesitated. He thought about what he'd seen so far along with the possibility of unknown expenses.

What the hell, he thought. *I don't have much of a choice.*

Kurt signed the authorization and slid the tablet back to Allie.

The two men got back into the Vette and took it out to the street and onto the freeway.

Robert handled the car with the same grace he showed earlier exiting the late model sedan. Effortless and poised: in control.

The Corvette responded appropriately.

Robert had it in Competitive Driving Mode and was tapping the shift paddles up and down—driving the car as if it had a manual transmission. The transitions were flawless, smooth as glass.

This massive composite of steel, plastic, carbon fiber, fiberglass and rubber embraced its new driver in a way Kurt had never experienced.

They'd only been driving for a few minutes when the Corvette suddenly shuddered on acceleration. The Service Engine Soon lamp came on almost instantly.

"Dammit!" Kurt shouted as he pounded the dash with both fists hard enough for the glove box to open. Robert remained unruffled.

"Everything okay?" he asked with his eyes on the road.

"No!" Kurt bellowed, pushing the glove box up until it locked. He shook his head and chuckled sarcastically.

"Everything is not okay! But, up until now, it was everything but the Corvette. This car was the one thing, the only thing, I could depend on.

"And don't get me started on my business! We were doing great for a long time—for years—and now we're struggling just to get by.

"Nothing seems to go the way it's supposed to anymore. You know that old expression: 'When it rains, it pours'? Well, it's true. And, right now, it's raining like hell."

Robert listened quietly as Kurt continued his tirade.

"You own a business. You know. Things are tough at work and you find yourself doing everything you can to make it better. Then it all bleeds over into your personal life.

"You're spending too much time at work trying fix something, not really knowing how it was supposed to work in the first pla—."

Suddenly, Kurt caught himself in mid-rant. He took a breath.

"I'm sorry, I have no idea why I'm even talking about this. I mean, with you. You don't know me. You don't know my situation. Why would you care?

Kurt's pain was visceral; it filled the passenger compartment. As Robert glanced over at him, he remembered the feeling. This pain was one that Robert knew too well. It was a pain reminiscent of a time and place he had worked hard to leave behind.

"I get it," said Robert. "It falls into the 'been there/done that' category of experiences you'd rather not revisit. Don't apologize. Anyone who's ever been in business understands."

Robert had started a business knowing nothing about the mechanics of running one, and that lack of knowledge had all but destroyed him. To survive had taken a strength of will he didn't know he possessed, but also the humility to look for and accept assistance from anyone willing to help him.

Kurt's pain was something Robert could empathize with as someone who had walked the same rocky path. He removed his right hand from the steering wheel and reached out, barely touching Kurt's left forearm.

"I understand. I know where you're coming from. It's a place I only revisit when heading there results in something constructive.

"I almost lost Mushin once. More than once, really. But, I was fortunate and pulled through it. I had to.

"I love what I do. I love the people I do it with, just as much as I love the people I do it *for*. So, for me, there was no alternative. I had to make it work."

Robert chuckled. "My passion and pride wouldn't let me fail."

Kurt had been averting his eyes as Robert spoke. After a few seconds, he looked over at the stranger he'd just entrusted one of his most valuable and important possessions.

"You know," Kurt said, "I started pounding nails when I was in high school. I did it part-time after school. It was perfect for me. I was big, strong and looked older than I was. I lied my way on to a construction sit, loved the work and never looked back.

"Didn't matter what they had me do. I didn't care. Every crappy clean-up job. Every truck that had to be loaded or unloaded. As long as I could get caught up in my work and someone was willing to teach me something new, it was worth it.

"I got into the Carpenter's Union Apprenticeship Program and worked my way up. I became a Journeyman and did just about every job you could do on a construction site. Everything. Didn't matter what."

"I don't know when I realized it wasn't about framing. It wasn't about building stuff or any of the physical things we did that made the job so satisfying."

Kurt smiled. He was proud of what he'd accomplished. But, now, he was terrified of losing it. He took a deep breath and sighed.

"We change lives. Not sure when I realized that, but we do. What we do is lasting. Maybe transformational. And, when it's done right, damn! When it's done right, it's beautiful."

"I can relate," Robert nodded. "When you think about it, we don't just fix cars at Mushin. We're in the freedom and mobility business. Delivering freedom feels a whole lot better than just doing oil changes, changing spark plugs, and fixing broken stuff."

Kurt looked over at Robert, more than a little surprised. He couldn't remember talking about something so deep, so personal, and having whoever he was talking with actually understand.

"Yeah, it was great." Kurt responded, "And then the Recession hit and it just about killed us! It took the joy out of all of it.

"I'm not going to lie, Robert. I hate it now. I hate going into the office. I hate waking up in the middle of the night panicking over payroll, thinking about where the next job is going to come from, or how I'm going to get the jobs I'm working on finished without any major problems."

"And, through it all, the only thing that gave me any peace, the only thing that could make me smile—other than my wife and kids —was this damned car. Now even that's gone to hell."

Robert was quiet, driving the vehicle harder, listening to the engine. For a moment or two, Kurt wasn't sure if the mechanic had even heard what he'd said.

He sat uncomfortably in the silence.

"There's an answer to every question," Robert said, eyeing the road. "Ask the right question and the right answer will reveal itself."

Kurt frowned. He was in no mood for proverbs.

Robert turned the Corvette around. It was time to head back.

"I think we've got what we need," he nodded to himself. "Now it's all process as we inspect, test, analyze, and evaluate. Don't worry about the Corvette."

Robert deftly shifted the transmission and raced down the road.

Kurt wasn't sure when his focus had changed from his current reality to Robert's driving, but it did. Suddenly, he no longer cared about any of it. He was in awe of Robert's driving skills.

"Where did you learn to handle a vehicle like that?"

10

An Absence of Mind

"Like what?" Robert cocked his head inquisitively and brought the vehicle to a stop in front of the open door to the last service bay. They both exited the vehicle and moved inside the shop.

"Like you were driving just now," Kurt said. "I've never seen anyone handle a car like that and I've been to three different driving schools: two NASCAR and one SCCA. You were in *control*!

"What you did was impressive. I've felt like that occasionally, playing football or once or twice when I was long distance bike racing. But that's the first time I've ever witnessed it: the way you and the car came together."

"It's hard to explain," Robert said, obviously uncomfortable. "I wasn't anything more or less than I always am. The car is alive. I'm alive. The car has energy. I have energy. The car wants to perform the way it was designed to perform. And that's why I exist, my purpose.

"The car wants to be well as much as I want it to be well. Enough to allow me to become an integral part of it. But, to do that, I have to leave my conscious self behind so that I can give myself to the vehicle without reservation. Then I can actually experience it."

Robert leaned against his tool cabinet and looked at Kurt.

"No matter what you may think. I wasn't controlling anything, because there wasn't any *I*."

Kurt was trying desperately to wrap his mind around Robert's perspective, but couldn't do it. It was like trying to grab a handful of water from the ocean—more was lost than retained.

Robert asked, "Do you know what *mushin*, the name of this shop, means? Do you know what it is or where it comes from?"

"No." Kurt said. "It sounds Asian; Japanese or Chinese maybe. But I don't know what it means. And I don't have any idea what that has to do with me, my car or that damned Check Engine light."

Robert took a deep breath and smiled.

"It may have everything to do with the light if you leave the car with us. Do you know anything about Eastern philosophy or what folks in the West refer to as the martial arts?"

Kurt shrugged, "Not really. Just the stuff I've seen on TV or at the movies. You know, *Crouching Tiger Hidden Dragon*, Bruce Lee, and Jackie Chan. Stuff that's all stunt doubles, props, and special effects. But none of that is real."

Robert responded softly, "Well, that isn't exactly where I was headed, but it's a start.

"*Mushin* is a state of mind. More accurately, a state of *no mind*, a state of being without the interference of conscious thought or thinking. Individuals who embrace the martial arts, or the wisdom associated with Zen, or even the mindfulness movement, refer to that state, a state of *mushin*, as having a mind like still water.

"If you visualize a reflection pond, like the one on the National Mall in D.C., you can begin to understand. When the air is still and the conditions just right, the water in that shallow pond reflects everything that surrounds it. It reflects everything, but retains nothing."

Kurt nodded, doing his best to follow along. Robert continued.

"If you can imagine your mind doing that, that's the kind of mind I'm talking about. *Mushin* takes a fair amount of dedication and endless practice. It comes from doing something so often you ultimately do it well without thinking about it. You do something so well, you are more *being* it than doing it."

"World class athletes know this state. They refer to it as being in the zone, a place where time appears to be suspended and they feel detached from the outside world."

"Like when I was on the bike, right?" Kurt interjected.

"Yes," Robert nodded. "But I'm not sure if that's the same as practicing a martial art. *Mushin* allows a heightened state of awareness. It removes the id and the ego. It eliminates conscious thought: the time it takes for the mind to process, analyze, and respond.

"As we are all made out of the same stuff, the same material as the rest of the universe, it's a kind of plug into the great cosmic connection that joins us all."

Robert paused and cocked his head. "Too much?"

Kurt was captivated. "No, keep going," he said.

"Okay, then. People who have experienced this state of being often described it in terms of an instant application of what they have practiced accompanied by a sensation of time standing still or slowing down. Often it is followed by a kind of echo, the ability to experience whatever it was that took place a second time, outside the actual event—almost as if there was a ripple in time itself."

As Robert became more animated, Kurt was drawn deeper into his explanation. If nothing else, he felt he needed to know how this was going to impact the car problems he was experiencing.

Aside from that, he was stuck there.

What else can I do other than be polite and listen? he thought.

Robert wiped off one of the tools he had removed from the vehicle he was working on when he was first introduced to Kurt, then moved toward his tool cabinet to return it.

"This state is action independent of conscious thought: instant action. It's the direct result of heightened situational awareness, constant practice, and a willingness to trust the suspension of self. The samurai called it *haragei*. Practitioners of Zen call it *zanshin*."

Robert opened the middle drawer of his top cabinet. Suddenly, there was an incredibly loud pop followed by the variegated hiss of compressed air escaping at high velocity.

One of the quick connect air fittings had blown off the end of a compressed air hose. It rocketed across the shop propelled by the air compressor's 125 pound-per-inch pressure.

The hose was thrashing around like a cobra on crack, with the fitting headed toward the other end of the shop—straight for the back of one of Robert's technicians, a large man who was hunched over the fender of a silver Jeep Grand Cherokee.

The technician must have heard the noise, but there was no way he could know the fitting was headed straight at him. No way to move fast enough to dodge the missile.

Time slowed to a crawl.

The projectile moved so fast it was virtually invisible.

Kurt was mesmerized.

This is going to be bad, he thought.

But—before he could shout a warning—the technician moved with a purpose and speed Kurt had never witnessed before.

He swung his left leg out in a 180-degree arc to his right, pivoting on his right heel. Then, he dropped his body to the right as he turned. Crouching slightly, his left hand dropped to his left thigh with his palm open and his right hand came across his body in what appeared to be an attempt to block the projectile.

There wasn't a sound.

No noise of the blocked fitting being deflected and hitting anything. Not the ceiling or the floor. Not a wall. Not another car or technician. It had disappeared. Or so it appeared.

Only, it hadn't.

The technician who—just seconds ago—seemed to be headed to an emergency room, opened his right hand and there it was. He had somehow managed to snatch it out of the air!

Kurt exhaled.

While this was going on, another technician had wrestled the air hose into submission and clamped it shut with a pair of Vise Grips.

Kurt stared. It was the most amazing thing he had ever seen.

There was no time for thought, no way for the technician to know he was in trouble other than the 'pop' and the sound of air escaping from the end of the hose. No time to respond if, or when, he finally did realize it.

"Jason!" Robert called out. "That was impressive! Strong work!"

Jason chuckled as walked across the shop toward his boss.

"Damn, Robert!" he said. "If ah didn't know any betta' I'd think someone was tryin' a kill me!"

As he approached, Kurt could see that the man was immense—tall and broad. Jason shook his head and dropped the coupling into Robert's hand.

"It's a damned good thing we train as hard as we do, boss. Otherwise, we'd a been headed to an ER somewhere."

He gave Robert a high five.

"Gotta say, thank you for that one!"

"You did well, Jason," Robert said proudly. "Good to know that your perfect practice worked out perfectly today."

Kurt shook his head. He looked at Jason.

"I've never seen anything like that! You couldn't have seen that fitting coming at you. It was moving so fast nobody could have seen it! How the hell did you do that?"

Jason shrugged his big shoulders innocently.

"Hell, I don't know. It's kinda like when you're foolin' around with a bunch of friends an' somebody tells ya to close your eyes while someone else brings an open hand to yer' face an' you can feel it, even if ya can't see it. Kind of a proximity sense, I guess.

"Only here you train your awareness to be sensitive to speed and distance as well as intent. It's like when we train blind-folded. After a while, ya just know where everyone is and what they're gonna do almost before they do."

He looked at Robert. "Did I explain that right, boss?"

"As well as anyone can, Jason," Robert confirmed.

"Train?" Kurt asked, "Where, and in what? How does it work? If what I just saw really happened, how come no one knows about it and everyone isn't trying to learn it?"

Robert held up a finger. "One moment," he said.

He sat down at a workstation built into the corner of the bay, opened a small cabinet, and pulled out a sliding tray with a laptop. Alongside the laptop was the faded picture of a young woman.

I wonder if that's Robert's wife, Kurt thought.

Robert removed the flight recorder from his pocket, plugged it into a USB cable, and began typing. The results were apparent.

"Well, you *did* see what you just saw," he said. "And, some people do try to learn it. Some actually succeed. But, unfortunately, few are willing to make the sacrifice necessary to do the work. At least, not outside some very small, specialized circles.

"Finally, some people do know about it, mostly those of us who have dedicated our lives to achieving a different level of awareness. The big problem is Western culture. Here we are too fixated with what's going on around us to focus on what's inside. We're too busy with superficial distractions to recognize what is real.

"Our minds are cluttered, doing one thing while thinking about the other things we could be doing. We're not in the moment, not being present at times."

Kurt nodded in agreement, encouraging Robert to continue.

"There was a scene in the movie *The Last Samurai* where Tom Cruise's character, Captain Ahlgren, was trying to learn *iaidō*, the art of Japanese sword fighting. He was having a hell of a time and in the process taking one beating after another. One of the samurai watching acknowledged his effort and, ultimately, tried to help him. Did you see the movie?"

"Sure. Three times," Kurt said, smiling. "It was amazing."

"Do you remember the scene?" Robert asked. "Do you recall what the samurai told Cruise?"

"Not really."

"He said, 'too much mind.' Most Westerners walk around putting too much mind into everything they do, because they are unwilling to do the work that, almost certainly, guarantees success.

"It's a universal principle. Sweep away the clutter and you make room for greater awareness. Eliminate the mess and every aspect of performance improves. No matter what type of competition you're in, that is what consistent excellence is really all about."

11

The Sound of One Hand Wrenching

"That sounds great," Kurt said, flatly and unconvinced. "Maybe it works in kung fu or karate. Maybe even for fixing cars. But what about all of us stuck out here in the real world? Folks just struggling to get by? We can't all become black belts.

"I'll bet you couldn't make this stuff work in my business, although I'd certainly like to know how you made it work in yours.

"And what about my car? How is this higher consciousness stuff supposed to get my Corvette running the way it's supposed to?"

Robert listened intently, then changed his tone.

"You're right," he said. "I can't possibly make this work in your business. But you can.

"You don't have to become a black belt. Although, to be honest, it wouldn't hurt. You just have to embrace the principles and try to master the discipline. It's a process."

Kurt felt the need to defend his challenge.

"For me maybe," he countered. "But what about my employees? I can't haul them off to live in some kind of Zen temple on the side of a mountain somewhere."

Robert nodded as he scanned his people on the shop floor.

"Making it work for your employees is different," he said. "Inside the company, start with communication. Share what you're trying to accomplish—the why and how of what you want to do. Tell them how this new approach will benefit each of them. It'll take stamina on everyone's part. It'll take the strength to follow through when you hit an emotional dip. But change will come."

"That's it?" Kurt scoffed. "If I'd only known it was that easy I would have jumped all over it a long time ago."

Robert brushed off the sarcasm. "Well, you know about it now," he said. "So the question is: What are you willing to do about it?"

Kurt was silent.

Robert continued, "You know, the man who guided me when I first started as a mechanic had a favorite saying we still use to this day. He'd say: 'You gotta wanna fix the car.' If you do, everything else will fall into place. If you don't, nothing else matters.

"All the training in the world won't help. Neither will having the best tools and equipment. Nothing will help.

"In the end, you gotta wanna fix the car."

Robert breathed a heavy sigh, as if he'd experienced a moment some place in the past he wished he could return to. The quiet was thick, isolating the two men. In the shop, everyone was fully engaged in their work, each intimately involved with the vehicles in their service bays in an intricate ballet of their own choreography.

Robert shook off the memory and continued.

"As far as how we fixed this business is concerned, I'll be happy to share that with you." He hesitated for a moment. "But not without a cost."

Kurt looked over at Robert and thought to himself.

Great. Now, I've hired myself a consultant.

Robert couldn't help but notice that Kurt was shaking his head back and forth ever so slightly.

"I don't mean money, Kurt. The 'cost' is entirely existential. If you really want to change your company, there'll be conditions. Conditions and certain expectations.

"You'll learn the same way I learned. I'll teach you the same way I was taught, the same way everyone here has learned."

"Everyone here?" Kurt asked.

Robert nodded, "Yes, everyone here." He gestured across the entire service area with his arm.

"It won't always be fun. It won't *ever* be easy. But it'll be worth your time. I can guarantee that. What do you think? Are you up for the challenge? How badly do you want to fix what's broken?"

Kurt looked down and mumbled, "This is the strangest damned place I've ever been. I come here to get my car fixed and wind up with a Baccalaureate in Asian Studies."

He locked eyes with Robert. "How do I know it will work? Why should I take the chance?"

Robert shrugged, "You'll have to answer that for yourself. But, based on our conversation, that black Corvette isn't the only thing in your life that's misfiring right now.

"You have to determine what you do, whether you take action now, sometime in the future, or not at all. You're the one who has to make it work. It's your hands that are on the wheel.

"But let me say this as gently as I can… What have you got to lose that you aren't already in the process of losing?"

Kurt was quiet for a long time. He tapped his left foot nervously.

"What about my car?" Kurt asked. "I can't even get home with things the way they are right now. How am I supposed to change my whole damn life without any wheels?"

"Your Corvette?" Robert smiled. "I've captured all the data I need to bring her back to showroom-level performance. In fact, I can make her run even better.

"Are you up for that as well?"

Process and Art

Kurt was sitting at a table in the company lounge as Robert placed a beautifully-crafted cup in front of him filled with green tea.

"You know something, Kurt? Most people think things like process, science, craftsmanship, and art are all mutually exclusive. But they aren't. I think they can co-exist. In fact I know they can, because that's how we fixed this place."

Kurt reached for his cup and made a face.

"Don't you mean this is how *you* fixed this place?" he asked. "After all, you're 'the guy' around here, aren't you? The boss."

"No, I mean *we*." Robert said calmly. "Process must include everyone. The Japanese call it *kaizen*: 'change for better'. But in business it's translated as continuous improvement that includes everyone in the organization. That's the hard part: getting everyone to buy in. We did it through education and training."

"What kind?" Kurt frowned. "Six Sigma, QS9000 stuff?"

"No," Robert laughed, "Martial arts training. As beautiful as they are to watch and as deadly as they can be in application, the martial arts are based on science.

"Regardless of the style, properly executed, they represent a deep understanding of physics and body mechanics. The delivery of maximum power with an absolute economy of effort. It's all about activities and outcomes—knowing what your desired outcome is and finding the most efficient way to get there."

"But you said your teacher didn't study martial arts," Kurt said.

"That's right, he didn't." Robert responded, "But he studied life. He learned that, for lessons to be effective, they have to be relevant. They need to be meaningful to everyone involved. If a lesson is meaningful, it can be internalized and then executed.

"I started working here around the same time I began training in the martial arts. It was something to do after working all day.

"By watching Jerry work, I learned that all things are integrated, connected in some profound basic way. When I struggled, he urged me to apply what I was learning in the *dojo*—qualities like patience, dedication, discipline, situational awareness, and good judgment—to what I was doing in the shop.

"At the same time my *sensei*, my martial arts instructor, was encouraging me to apply everything I knew, everything I had learned outside the studio, to my practice on the mat.

"In the West we break things down in order to see them as individual acts or discreet events. In the East the approach is more integrated, with everything being part of a greater 'whole.'

"I didn't get that at first. Then one day I realized that fixing cars and practicing martial arts were based on the same principles. Whether I was working on perfecting a kick or installing a bolt without stripping it, it was the same.

"And fixing a business, especially ones like ours where we serve the public, isn't any different. The same principles work with equal effectiveness. I'm confident of that."

Kurt was hooked, enthralled by the spell Robert was casting over him. His mind raced with the expectation, the possibility that perhaps he'd found a way out of the wilderness.

"Your marriage, however," Robert smiled, "that's a different story. You may have to figure out how to fix that on your own."

"*My marriage?* Kurt thought.

Suddenly, he realized that he hadn't called home to let Laurie know where he was, that he might be late, or even why.

God, she's probably getting dinner ready. The kids must be hungry, fidgeting in the playroom. And here I am off the grid.

Kurt winced. To him, the Corvette's problem was still a mystery. And how the hell he was going to get home? And, when he finally did, his car trouble would be responsible for another ruined dinner, another late night catching up on the never-ending stream of paperwork he had stuffed into his backpack.

Kurt felt the tension rising up inside him. He took a long deep inhale and exhale until the stress faded.

Something about Robert's confidence was intriguing.

Maybe I can get back on track. Stop freaking out on every little problem. This guy knows something I don't know, that's for sure.

He was being drawn into Robert's universe, his philosophy. And it was actually starting to make sense.

Kurt wondered if it was possible to apply the principles that Robert believed in to his own world, to Kerrigan Construction. He wasn't sure.

It would be interesting to try though.

He stood up, looked at Robert, and reached for his cell phone.

"I have to call home, but I want to pick this up again when I get back."

Scrambled Eggs and Cold Toast

Kurt left the shop and walked to the corner. He squinted at the glare on the screen of his phone and swiped to the appropriate icon to call home. He glanced at his wrist: it was almost 5:00.

The phone rang for a while before Laurie finally picked up with a cheerful, "HiIIii!"

Her voice, Kurt thought, *when she's happy, it's almost musical.*

"Hey, it's me," he said, doing his best to match her positivity.

Suddenly, the energy drained away. He could almost hear Laurie readjust herself, imagined her shoulder tensing against the phone as she cradled it closer to her ear.

"Hey," she said flatly. "What's up? Is everything okay?"

"No, not really. The Corvette started to act up on the way home and I had to stop at a shop off the Blue Ridge exit. That's where I'm calling from."

"Blue Ridge? It's almost dinner time, Kurt! You were supposed to be home early. Remember?"

"Laurie, please! This isn't my fault. The car started shaking itself apart; the engine light came on. I was almost in an acci—"

"Of course it started shaking itself apart," Laurie interrupted. "You drive like a maniac whenever you're alone in that thing!"

"Give me a break, honey. Please. You don't know what kind of a day I've had."

Kurt didn't want a fight, but it was too late.

When did I become the enemy?

He searched his mind, looking for happier moment
floated past like he was shuffling through a stack of old
smile, a dinner together, a weekend getaway, Max walking across
the room on his own, the first time he held AJ.

Was that it? Kurt wondered. *The tension of a second child?*

It doubled the work. More than doubled the cost. That's for sure.

*No. It isn't the kids. It can't be! It was the damned economy. It was
trying to get things back to where they were. I spend way more time at
the office trying to make things work than I ever have.*

*That was my mistake. Thinking of the business as the 'well', the
origin of our security. Thinking that if I just take care of the business,
it'll take care of us.*

Kurt sighed. The equation didn't work; it was all lop-sided. The
business was getting almost everything from him while Laurie and
the kids got almost nothing.

Life was all about taking care of Kerrigan Construction, taking
care of his clients, taking care of his employees so they, in turn,
could take care of *their* families. He closed his eyes in resignation
and tried his best to remain calm.

"Listen, here's the bottom line: I'm stuck at a new shop I've never
been to before. I have no idea if they can fix the car immediately, or
if they have a loaner for me or what. My whole day's gone to hell
because of this."

Kurt felt his chest tighten as his internal dialogue ran wild, filled
with all the words he wanted to say but couldn't.

"You know I'd rather be with you and the kids. It's just that this
is a bad time at work. Try to understand... Please."

The silence was long and uncomfortable. Finally Laurie spoke.

"I want to, honey. I try to. But it's always a 'bad time' at work."

As she lowered her voice Kurt heard his wife walk to a quieter
room, farther away from the children.

"It isn't fair," she continued. "Not to me. Not to the kids. It's not
fair to you either. You spend sixty hours a week there, I'm guessing.
More, if you count all the time you're here working at the kitchen
table or your office upstairs.

"That business demands more than our kids did were when they were babies. You're constantly wiping its nose and cleaning its bottom. At this rate, it'll never grow up. Sometimes I'm not even sure you want it to."

Kurt nodded his head in silence.

"It's a bad habit now, Kurt, a chronic condition you've grown accustomed to. You'll keep doing what you've been doing, devoting more and more time, making more excuses. But it's a bottomless pit. Whatever you're doing isn't working. I wish you'd see that."

Laurie was working hard to keep it together. She didn't want to lose control and go over the top again. In the quiet, Kurt softened a bit, realizing that she was right. Too right. This was on him.

"I promise you I will fix this," he said. "We'll get our lives back. Just give me a little time to figure it out and make some changes. Believe me, nothing is more important than you and the kids."

Laurie's tone brightened slightly.

"Okay," she sighed, "just give me a call when you're on your way. I need some idea of when you'll be here. I can hold dinner, but not forever. The kids are starting to get antsy. If you can't make within an hour, I'll warm something up when you get here."

"You don't have to do tha—"

"Shut up, Kurt. It's a peace offering. Take it."

For maybe the first time that day, Kurt smiled slightly.

"Thanks," he said.

"And stay safe, honey," Laurie said. "No speeding, okay? I want you home in one piece."

Kurt realized that this would have been the perfect time to tell her about the wreck he witnessed earlier, but he let it go.

"Thanks. I will. Love you."

Laurie spoke softly, "Love you, too."

14

Laurie's Lament

Laurie tapped the red icon at the bottom of her phone and stared at the image of her family huddled together in the snow on its face.

'Love you, too.' That last remark echoed in her mind.

Am I being completely honest? she wondered.

Her mind drifted back to the snow-covered mountains that day. It was their last vacation together—playing outside in the cold, pushing Kurt into the snow, the children laughing in response, the warmth of the cabin at the end of the day, snuggling under Kurt's arm in front of the fireplace while the kids fell asleep nearby.

Of course she loved Kurt. It was hard not to. She loved him almost from the second she laid eyes on him.

Laurie had been out with a group of friends when one of them pointed Kurt out from across the room. He was young and tan. Not hard to look at. What was not to like?

She worked up the guts to move across the room to say 'hi' and found that he was kind and considerate as well, even ambitious. Not like so many of the other guys she had dated.

And he made her laugh, all the time. His sense of humor was irrepressible; his laughter was contagious.

She couldn't remember enjoying anything as much as their courtship. Kurt made her feel like she was royalty wherever they went, regardless of what they were doing.

For the first time, she could see herself raising kids and spending the rest of her life with someone, with this incredible new guy in her life.

That's exactly what they did. And, for a long time, things were pretty much 'happily ever after'.

Now it seemed like she rarely had anything to smile about.

She looked at the kitchen table, there were four places set, each awaiting the meatloaf and vegetables she was almost ready to serve.

Why even bother making a decent dinner every night?

It seemed like Kurt was coming home later all the time.

Max and AJ would probably be fine with peanut butter and jelly sandwiches, or a bowl of cold cereal.

It wasn't that long ago that she felt like the two of them were the envy of all their friends. Laurie was living a dream come true, a dream she bought into because of Kurt's abundant confidence.

Kurt started out working for a large contracting company, doing well. But quite often he would come home miserable, angry that things at work had become unbearable. His boss was a decent enough person, but Kurt complained the guy didn't know a damn thing about running a successful contracting business.

The flow of work in and out of the company was completely unpredictable. They were either crazy busy, or way too slow, which left Kurt and everyone else unable to budget for anything. And, as erratic as the projects may have been, the cash flow was even more unpredictable.

"Besides," Kurt told her, "after all my years working inside the trade and the resume I've built up, this is the logical next step. I need to leave and go out on my own."

Kurt was convinced he knew everything he needed to know about running a construction company, because he knew everything there was to know about running a job site.

"We can do this, babe. I know we can. We'll just need to sacrifice a little in the beginning: the first year or two maybe."

"But we've just started putting something aside," Laurie insisted. "You have security there. I'm doing well at my firm, but not enough to carry us both for more than a few months."

"It'll be tight," Kurt agreed. "But we can make it work. A few late nights and a few extra bucks for Contractor's School to get my license—then we can have it all. I won't have to deal with anybody's incompetence. And I can do the kind of work I've always wanted to.

"I promise I'll build a company that supports the two of us—that supports our family when we have one. Then you won't have to work anymore unless you want to."

He was so passionate and his dream so vividly clear, she couldn't help but get caught up in the vortex of his enthusiasm.

They had their share of scrimping and cutting corners just to get by, their share of late dinners while he was getting his license. When he graduated, they opened the company out of one room in their tiny apartment. It was tight, but they felt they were working together toward a common goal.

They were happy, despite the struggle.

Then, after a couple of years, the company finally did exactly what Kurt had predicted it would: it was a 'success'. They found themselves with more work than they could handle—backlogged so far ahead that they had to turn jobs away. There was money in the bank. More than they ever imagined, more than they could spend.

Kerrigan Construction grew from just Kurt (and one of the guys who left the old company with him) to a crew of five. He turned in his beat-up pickup truck for a shiny new F-250. They moved from their small apartment to a home in an upscale neighborhood. It was a house to raise children in. It was 'heaven'.

When little Max arrived, even though Laurie managed to move up from one challenging position to another at every company she ever worked with, she was happy to quit her corporate job and dedicate herself full-time to her new baby.

She was content with the choice she made. Then there were two kids, and she knew she needed to be at home at least until they were both in school.

But, when the economy tanked, the rug was pulled out from under their world. New construction went down. People stopped renovating. And accounts receivable dried up.

Laurie saw a growing threat.

What if he can't pull the company back from the edge? What if I have to go back to work? How do I explain the hole in my résumé?

She felt resentment, insecurity, and anger—more anger than she wanted to feel.

She was angry enough to think about what life would be like with only her and the kids. Without all the excuses. Without all the late nights. Without Kurt in the picture.

Of Mice and Menus

"How'd it go?"

Robert did his best to seem cheerful, but it was getting close to five and he'd seen enough clients make late evening phone calls to know that Kurt probably caught a little hell on the other end.

Kurt shrugged as he walked back into the lounge. From the orchestrated chaos at the office to the disappointment he had just caused at home, he wasn't in the best mood. He collapsed into the chair directly across from Robert and eyed his tea cup. Robert had refilled it. The tea was piping hot with tiny wisps of condensation spiraling into the air above it.

Kurt didn't know how to thank him. He put his hands around the cup to enjoy the warmth. It was somehow reassuring. Then he returned to the subject at hand.

"Before we start talking about all this principle stuff again, I really need to know what's going on with my car."

"Well," Robert said, "I've got some good news and some bad news. Which do you want first?"

Kurt sighed, "Give me the 'good news' first.

"The good news is we've identified the problem. We know what we need to do to return your car to like-new performance."

"Okay, what's the 'bad news'?"

"We can't finish this evening. It's too late to get parts. In fact, we won't be able to complete the repair until Wednesday at the earliest. And, to complicate things, all our loaners are out. I'm afraid you'll need to rent a car or have someone pick you up."

"Terrific," said Kurt dryly.

He thought about calling Laurie back, then imagined her trying to get the children ready and into the SUV.

Forget it. That's way too hard with the kids.

Kurt sipped his tea as he thought about his options.

"I think I'm going to rent a car if that's possible."

"Absolutely," Robert said. "I'll have Allie make the call for you. They're close, but honestly, it could be a half-hour until they can get out here. In the meantime, let me tell you what we fou—"

Robert stopped for a moment, cocking his head to one side. He had an odd almost playful expression. He continued.

"I've got a strange question for you, so bear with me for a moment. Do you keep the Corvette inside? Enclosed, in a garage?"

"Of course!" Kurt said. "Take one look at her; you know she's never spent a night in the rain or outside in the cold."

Robert nodded his head.

"Do you have a dog or a cat?" he asked.

"What? I have a dog. What has that got to do with anything?"

"What kind of food do you buy? Is it hard like kibbles? Does it come in a bag? Do you keep it in the garage?"

"You're kidding, right? Are you some kind of Doggie Detective? It's hard food. It comes in a forty-pound bag; we keep it in a plastic bin near the door in the garage. Why do you ask? You think Ranger is responsible for the misfire?"

"No," Robert responded. "But I think you and Ranger might share some uninvited 'guests' who like the food you buy as much as he does. There's evidence that critters have been picking up a little 'take out', dragging it to the top of your intake manifold, and then camping out on top of your engine. I'm guessing they like the warmth it offers after you shut the vehicle down.

"They pulled down some under-hood insulation to make things a bit more comfortable while they chowed down on the dog's food. Then, they snacked on some of your under-hood wiring and insulation for desert."

Kurt was speechless.

"As a result," Robert continued, "some of those bare wires—wires that went to the coil packs that fire each spark plug—went to ground instead, causing the coils to fail, and a spark plug or two to misfire.

"I've already had someone remove the nest and clean up the mess. But we had to order the coils and connectors. They'll take until tomorrow to come in. After we repair the wiring, we'll give her a road test. When we're done, I'm sure everything will be fine.

"Better than fine actually. We checked the software level on your vehicle's computer, determined there was a performance upgrade available, and have already re-flashed the computer.

"All you have to do is manage your rodent problem. Put your dog food in a closed metal container, if it has to be kept in the garage at all. Sweep the floor regularly. And enjoy your Corvette."

"Just like that?" Kurt asked.

"Just like that."

Opportunity Cost

"Okay, since the Corvette's squared away, let's dig in. What's all this principle stuff about?"

Kurt took a swig of tea and set the cup down.

"I mean, I think I get it. But I'm not quite sure what it has to do with me, or running a construction company."

Robert looked across the table at Kurt. His gaze was intense.

"Let's start with this," Robert said, "I'm not here to sell you anything. Or convince you to *do* anything.

"I can help, but it won't be without cost. I'm talking about you having a little skin in the game. You need to show me that this will be worth *my* time—that you'll listen. That you're committed to the change that needs to take place."

Kurt shifted uncomfortably in his seat.

"I'm here, aren't I?"

"Right," Robert scoffed. "You're here because your Corvette failed. You have no choice. I need to see what happens when you have a choice, whether or not you actively *choose* to engage with these principles.

"So, here's how it's going to work. I'll share a number of our guiding principles with you before you leave the shop tonight, the ones I feel are most important. In addition, I'll give you copies of our Employee Handbook and our Policies and Procedures Manual."

"Thank you," Kurt said. "That sounds like it has to help."

"Maybe," Robert countered, "But I won't explain how to actually implement them, unless you agree to train with us for a year.

"Train'?" Kurt sat back in his chair. "What do you mean?"

Kurt felt stomach knotting up. Unperturbed, Robert continued.

"Same thing goes for Strategic Planning. No, forget it. We won't talk about how to do that for quite some time, actually."

Kurt wrinkled his brow. Suddenly, he was unsure.

"Have you done this before? Helped another business owner turn their company around?"

Robert wrapped his right hand around his chin, thought for a moment, then smiled.

"You know something? I haven't," he said confidently. "Not a business anyway. But I have helped more people than you can count straighten out their personal lives."

Robert looked Kurt square in the eye.

"You want to try this or not? Ultimately, the choice is yours."

Without hesitation, Kurt nodded affirmatively.

Robert smiled and handed him a sheet of paper.

"Okay, here's a list. When you get home later, go online. There's a few YouTube links that I believe will help you understand the *why* of what we do here. Also, there's the URL's of a couple of bloggers I think you should be reading. It's all pretty foundational. Afterward, I'd like you take a critical look at your business based upon some of those teachings."

"You're giving me homework?" Kurt said, raising an eyebrow.

"This is essential stuff," Robert said. "Stuff you probably should have started doing long ago. We need to create a model of your business as it exists today—baseline measurements to determine a starting point—then track how you're doing as we move forward. Numbers that we can take a look at every few months or so.

"A big part of what I can offer depends upon an assessment of what I see. In the martial arts, we call it situational awareness: an honest appraisal of where you are. Like being aware of your environment, knowing your capabilities, thinking ahead. It's hard to catch someone by surprise if they are fully aware of their situation."

"Like when Jason snatched that fitting out of the air?"

Robert smiled and nodded, "Something like that."

"But what about goals and objectives? The usual stuff."

"I was just getting to that," Robert said. "After we've established a baseline, we'll sit down to create a set of realistic goals. I believe that goals need be SMART: Specific, Measurable, Achievable, Realistic, and Time-Based. Believe me, there's no point in planning a trip to a destination you can't reach."

Kurt smiled, "Goals have to be attainable. I get that."

"That's why your Strategic Plan needs to wait. A good plan is designed to solve a problem. This process is how we decide which problems need to be addressed before we start building that plan.

"In fact, every choice from here out will be decided on the basis of how it relates to your objectives. You'll pursue activities that embrace your values, and abandon those that don't. We'll get to the Strategic Plan as soon as we can, but—if what you're telling me is true—we have to stop the bleeding before we do anything else."

Robert tilted his head toward the door.

"Let's walk up to the office and get you those manuals."

‡

Robert handed him two relatively-thin manuals.

"Here. I'm not going to say a lot about them now. Hopefully, they'll make sense when you're ready. If you have a question, the answer will be more valuable if we talk about your company as it functions in the real world rather than discussing things abstractly."

Kurt nodded his head. It was Robert's turn to appear tentative.

"You still want to do this?"

"Yeah, of course," Kurt responded.

"That's interesting, especially since you haven't asked what the training entails. Or how often you're expected to be here."

"Doesn't matter," Kurt shrugged. "I've tried everything: business books, seminars, consultants who didn't do a damned thing. It's obvious something good is going on here. It's worth a shot."

There was a mischievous glint in Robert's eye.

"Okay then. I'll be reminding you of this conversation every time you want to quit. And, I promise, you will want to quit."

"Is this about the martial arts stuff?" Kurt asked, frowning. "Do I have to break concrete with my forehead or something?"

Robert laughed, "Not right away."

The look of abject terror on Kurt's face said it all. Robert smiled.

"Actually, breaking is related to the second principle: energy. And we'll definitely be spending some time on that.

"But, for now, let's start here. Scientists say that energy cannot be created or destroyed. I agree. There's energy in everything, whether organic or inorganic. It's everywhere, all around us.

"Since it takes energy to achieve anything we desire in life, we have to learn how to harness and conserve it. How to focus it.

"In the Chinese tradition, that energy is referred to as *chi*. In business, that energy can be defined as resources. Not just money and materials, it's everyone in your organization—and includes the combined energy they bring to work with them every day.

"No matter how hard you train in the gym, or how big your business is, resources are finite. You only have so much.

"When those resources are gone you're in real trouble. In the training you'll receive here, we want to achieve the maximum impact with the least amount of energy expended. You can't do that if you squander your resources.

"You must continually question how they're being allocated. Will they better serve my purpose if they are deployed elsewhere? Hopefully, the answer will be 'no'. Because, if they can, that's where they should be invested.

"The third principle is power. In martial arts, power comes from the core. The Chinese say that core is *xià dāntián*, the 'golden stove', the area below your belly button, inside the abdomen. Let's just call it the 'center'.

"In business, your center comes from your people, or more appropriately from your leadership of them—how well you're able to unleash their talents and abilities. How well you help them learn to lead others, so the burden of ensuring the company's success doesn't always fall on your shoulders.

"The fourth principle is the concept of force versus impact. The fifth is flow. The sixth is the principle of hard and soft. I realize I'm just rattling these off now. Not explaining much."

"That's okay," Kurt smiled. "I kind of assumed we'd circle back to each one when the time was right."

"Exactly. So, the seventh principle isn't actually from martial arts at all, although it might as well be. I call it: Do the work."

"I thought I was already," Kurt said, sighing.

"Well, there's working hard. And there's working *smart*. You'll learn the difference. The eighth principle is something we call blending. The ninth is balance. I think the tenth is as much an observation as it is a principle: pain cancels technique."

Kurt nodded even though he wasn't sure he fully understood.

"If that has anything at all to do with the stupid mistakes I make when I have a headache, I understand."

Robert chuckled, "That's maybe one small aspect. But there's a lot more to it than that. Hang in there with me, I'm almost done.

"The eleventh is leverage. The twelfth is continuous learning. It addresses the idea that achieving a black belt is only a gateway to further knowledge, not the culmination of your training.

"Throw in flexibility, and you have a baker's dozen—a little over one per month to master by a year from now."

"Sounds like a lot."

"Definitely," Robert agreed. He looked away then back at Kurt.

"Two more things I almost forgot… We're going to talk about muscle memory and something everyone here lives by: meticulous attention to detail, or MAD for short."

Coming Attractions

They left the office and walked through the shop. Things were winding down; the process of cleaning up had already begun. The entire team was fully involved in preparing the shop for the next business day. It was a sight to behold; everyone doing something that contributed to the ultimate goal.

Kurt was mesmerized by the meticulous attention to detail they all demonstrated—regardless of what their assigned, or chosen, task may have been. Their pride was manifest in everything they did.

Kurt and Robert crossed the alley that separated the businesses on Blue Ridge Drive from the residential neighborhood behind it. Across the alley, directly behind the shop, was a high white wall with a row of bamboo growing along the inside perimeter.

Where the other houses along the alley had two-car garages, this one had only a heavy wooden gate with a large orange *torii*—the type of gateway found at the entrance of a Shinto shrine. The formerly detached garage was connected seamlessly into the house.

Robert opened the gate and Kurt entered a world he did not expect to find behind a repair shop. They walked a stone path through a zen rock garden alongside a koi pond. It was magnificent.

The pair climbed the three steps that led to the back porch. Robert kicked off his work boots and placed them in one of the many rectangular compartments bracketing the door. Kurt was trying to determine just how many spaces for shoes there were.

Thirty? Forty? Geez, how big is this class going to be?

He counted six pairs already there in addition to the two compartments they used.

Robert beckoned, "Come with me and we'll get you set up for your first workout Wednesday morning."

The two men walked deeper into the facility.

"Class starts at 5:30 a.m.," Robert said over his shoulder. "It runs for about an hour and forty-five minutes. You're expected to be here on time. Every day, Monday through Friday."

Kurt laughed, "You're my 'car guy' now. So getting me here is kind of your responsibility."

"Don't worry. The Corvette won't be the problem."

Robert pointed out a row of tall vertical lockers.

"We've got lockers for your stuff." Then he gestured to his left, "Down the hall's a shower, if you want to clean up afterward."

Kurt admired the surroundings: spartan but functional.

"All the comforts of home," he said.

"Pretty much. Oh, one more thing. When I say we start at 5:30, I mean 5:30 sharp. So get here early and be ready to 'do the work' when class starts. If you need to warm up or stretch, do that before whoever is leading the morning's workout takes the floor."

"Aye aye, sir." Kurt responded as if he'd been given an order.

"Now, let's see what size you are."

Robert disappeared.

‡

"Take these and try them on," Robert said, handing Kurt an outfit composed of off-white pants and a robe-like top.

"The uniform is designed for judo. It's heavier than the standard *gi*, in that it's made to withstand serious practice that includes grabs, holds, and throws.

"It should be loose enough to allow movement and flexibility without getting you tangled up. Not a bad model for work either.

"The shin guards are to protect you as you learn how to block and strike with your legs. The gloves are a lot like boxing gloves, only they have a bit less padding. And the fingers are removed at the first knuckle, so you can execute hand maneuvers more easily.

"Goggles for your eyes; helmet for your head. You *will* be getting hit and kicked, in the head at times."

Kurt noticed that Robert finished his sentence with an almost imperceptible smile.

"About the kicking, you'll need a protective cup. Get a good one and wear it. Trust me, not having one is a mistake you will only make once. Unless, of course, your goal is to sing in a boys' choir."

Robert stopped. He ran through a laundry list in his mind.

"What did I forget? Ah, yeah, two towels. And bring something to drink—something with plenty of electrolytes. You're going to be working hard. Once you've demonstrated your commitment here on the floor, we will move on to your business."

Robert smiled, "We good?"

Kurt nodded and returned the smile.

"I'll see you Wednesday morning at zero-dark-thirty."

Home Again! Home Again! Jiggety Jig!

Allie had made arrangements with the nearest car rental office for a mid-sized sedan. When Kurt returned to the Mushin office, a guy was there to pick him up. Kurt checked to see that he had his new manuals, then said his good-byes to Allie and Robert.

Soon he was waiting in line to sign the rental paperwork and receive the keys to an under-powered, underwhelming import.

He walked outside into a sea of bland cars until he reached the vehicle whose plate number matched the one on his key fob.

Kurt stared at the unremarkable vehicle for a while. He stared until he realized that standing there staring at it wasn't magically going to get him home.

Finally he unlocked the doors, threw his stuff across the back seat, adjusted his seat and mirrors, dragged the seatbelt across his waist and shoulder, and took off.

Kurt wasn't sure how long he'd been driving before he realized he was having second thoughts.

What the hell did I just do? A year commitment? Getting up before the sun? Well, I guess I do that already. But I do it to work on the business, not to get my ass kicked! Am I crazy?

All he could think of was the old, black-and-white Laurel and Hardy comedies he used to watch with his grandpa when he was a kid. Oliver Hardy's admonition to his friend, "Well, this is another fine mess you've gotten me into, Stanley!"

Well, Kurt, this is another fine mess you've gotten yourself into!

Why couldn't he have just said no? It would have been so much easier. Now he had to deal with this whole new world of... what?

Martial arts? Zen? Give me a break!

He accelerated up the on ramp. How could any of this change his world even a little? It was already coming apart at the seams.

Kurt's jaw tightened as the car in front of him puttered along.

What is this clown doing?

The vehicle ahead was slowing down and then speeding up again—like a hesitant turtle trying to cross a busy intersection.

Brake lights on. Brakes lights off. On, then off again. Geez...

He checked his mirrors, saw a break in traffic in the lane to his left, stabbed the accelerator pedal, and jerked the wheel.

The modest sedan performed like the Little Train That Couldn't.

It wanted to respond, but there weren't enough ponies hiding under the hood to make that happen. It was a painful reminder that Kurt wasn't behind the wheel of his Corvette.

Note to self: Do not do that again.

‡

Kurt grabbed his cell phone and quickly swiped to Favorites. He tapped 'home' and put the call on speaker.

Laurie picked up, "HiiIIii!"

"Hey, it's me. I just left the repair place, and I'm on my way home. With traffic like it is right now, I should be there in less than a half-hour."

Kurt knew it wouldn't take that long, but it was better to under-promise and over-deliver.

He could feel Laurie relax a little on the other end.

"Great," she said. "I'll do my best to keep the kids from tearing the place apart, but it's been a long day. And, well, they're starting to get a little hyper."

"I understand. That's okay."

"What about the office? Do you have to stop there first?"

"No," replied Kurt. "Didn't even call. I can fix whatever's broken tomorrow. Oh, and about tomorrow… Well, Wednesday anyway. We have something to talk about after the kids are down."

"Can't we do it now?" Laurie asked.

"No, honey, it's too complicated, even for me. Still, I think you might like it. At least, I hope so."

"Kurt Kerrigan, you are a man of mystery."

"I'm not trying to be. Listen, let me concentrate on the road, so I can get home soon."

They exchanged friendly good-byes and Kurt returned his full attention to the highway.

‡

A short while later Kurt parked the embarrassing rental on the street. He came through the front door, took two steps, and stopped. Both kids were in their pajamas playing quietly on the family room floor: the regular pre-bedtime ritual.

Collectively, the little duo heard the front door open and shut. They looked up, realized who it was, and bedlam ensued.

They jumped up in unison and ran toward Kurt at full speed. As they neared him, each child hurled themselves into the air. Kurt barely had enough time to drop all the papers he was holding so he could catch them both without a trip to the emergency room.

"Daddy, Daddy, Daddy! You're home!"

"We were almost ready for bed!" Max said. "But I told Mommy we can't go to bed unless you give us a kiss first."

"And read us a story," said AJ brightly. Kurt laughed.

"Kisses. A story. The whole works," he said. "Let's head upstairs."

Laurie stood in the hallway, smiling.

"Not quite yet, Mr. Kerrigan. Your dinner is ready."

A Reluctant Hero

Max and AJ were in the family room, flipping channels on the TV as Kurt polished off his meat loaf in the kitchen. Laurie sat beside him, nursing an herbal tea.

Warm meatloaf is better than cold meatloaf, he thought, *or no meatloaf at all, right?*

Even though he missed dinner time, it felt special to be home 'this early.' Laurie looked tired, but somehow as beautiful as ever.

Suddenly, in unison, Max and AJ exploded with excitement.

"Mommy! Mommy! That's Daddy's car! It's on TV! Look it!"

Kurt turned his head toward the family room. Laurie leaned back in her chair so she could see the television better.

The local news was reporting on an accident and resultant fire that had crippled traffic along the freeway for nearly two hours earlier that afternoon.

In a two-shot with aerial footage of the scene, the program's female anchor looked into the camera with practiced sincerity as she brightly read from the tele-prompter.

"This is the story of 'Vette Valor' and a mysterious Good Samaritan; an unknown Corvette owner who risked his own safety earlier today to save another Corvette driver, a complete stranger."

The aerial shot was replaced with a male reporter at the scene standing near the moving van that was rear-ended in the accident. The reporter's image cut to full-screen.

"Thanks, Sandra. As you can see, traffic has not yet returned to normal. The Highway Patrol still has the far left lane coned off as they investigate the crash site. Though it seems fairly obvious the driver of the red Corvette failed to stop in time."

The reporter shook his head.

"About the injured man… We've been told that he was taken to Westside Memorial Hospital and is currently resting in 'serious condition.' As you can see, things could have been a lot worse."

The reporter went on to describe a 'nameless hero' who raced out of his own vehicle, a black Corvette, to pull the injured driver away from the mangled car just before it burst into flames.

"The rescuer left before we arrived onsite, but luckily News Chopper 6 is our 'eye in the sky'. Don and the team shot footage of what we assume to be the reluctant hero' and his Corvette leaving the scene."

Sure enough, there was a black Corvette convertible, about a hundred yards behind the burning wreckage, re-entering traffic from spot near the shoulder.

There was no denying this was Kurt's Corvette either. He always covered his front driver's seat with a bright red sweatshirt emblazoned with unmistakable yellow graphics. It was his alright.

"Who was this bashful hero?" the reporter wondered. "And why didn't he remain at the scene? I'm sure the family of the injured driver would like to thank him personally."

Kurt sat silently, thinking of a thousand other places he'd rather be. Laurie had her hands on her hips, her head tilted to one side.

"Just another day at work? Really?" she asked, sarcastically. "Is there anything you'd like to tell me? Something that you may have forgotten to share?"

AJ had moved across the room to her mother's side—hands on her hips, her head tilted at the same angle.

"Yeah, Daddy? What did you 'forgotten' to share?"

Kurt shook his head in surrender. *Busted*, he thought.

He knew the best thing to do was to come clean, tell the whole truth. He recounted every detail he could remember. The kids' eyes lit up in admiration.

"Daddy's a hero!"

Laurie, however, was strangely quiet. She sat near Kurt as he told the story of the crash and his subsequent adventure at Mushin.

I have no idea why I rescued that guy. Maybe it was just because he had a Corvette. Maybe I saw myself trapped in there.

In the end, he spent more time describing his encounter with Robert and the man's offer to help Kurt fix the business than he did on any heroics.

Laurie stood up. For some reason, in this moment, it seemed like she towered above him. It could have been the events of the day finally catching up with him, but he felt small and tired. He hoped to hell she didn't start a scene in front of the kids.

Unexpectedly, she grabbed the corner of Kurt's shirt and pulled him to his feet. This was the man she had fallen in love with. Tough and strong. Selfless and brave. Too brave. Stupid brave.

She embraced him and kissed him on the cheek.

"I'm proud of you, honey! What you did was so courageous."

Kurt relaxed into her embrace and returned it. Then, just as quickly, she pulled away.

"Brave and dangerous," her eyes were loving but firm.

"You saved that man's life. But you could have been severely injured yourself. You could be lying in a hospital bed alongside him right now. Promise me you'll never do anything like that again."

Kurt had no words.

"We need you here, honey," she continued.

"Me and the kids. They need a daddy. And I need a husband."

The kids squeezed in for a hug. Tears started to form in AJ's eyes, probably more from her mother's tone than her actual words.

Kurt put one arm around his wife and the other around the kids. He kissed them all. He knew he loved them more than anything, but he also knew his own soul.

He doubted he'd do anything different in future; anytime there was any type of trouble where he could make a difference. That was just hard-wired into him. It was who he was.

20

Hope is a 4-Letter Word

Kurt helped Laurie get the kids into bed. It felt like something he hadn't done in a long time. There were so many missed meals and broken promises rooted in when he'd get home from work every day that he didn't bother keeping score anymore.

He was so happy to read a story to Max and AJ they were able to negotiate for three each. He helped them under the covers, kissed each one on the forehead, and told them how much he loved them. Laurie gave a kiss to each child as well. Lights were dimmed. Doors closed. Dreams were on their way.

Later, downstairs, Laurie was at the sink doing the dishes. Kurt dutifully took a plate from her and dried it with a towel.

"Sorry they pounced on you like that," she said. "I'm trying to teach them, but it's been a while and they were pretty excited. That news story didn't help much either."

"No, it was great," Kurt said. "I'd trade that kind of chaos for what goes on at work any day."

He lifted a stack of dry plates to a space in the upper cupboard.

"Today was nuts," he continued, "The wreck just punctuated a really bad day. I had a terrible morning. Problems on a host of jobs. Rick and I spent more than an hour just trying to plot our way out of the mess. But we can't seem to get beyond just reacting."

Laurie nodded quietly. She'd heard all this before.

"I was trying to get home early when the accident happened. Right after that the Corvette started misfiring. I thought it was going to shake itself apart. I was afraid to drive any further."

Laurie stopped scrubbing long enough to brush a wisp of hair away from her left eye, "Why did you pick this particular shop?"

Kurt turned to answer and started laughing instead.

"What's so funny?" Laurie frowned.

"You."

Kurt took the corner of his dishtowel and brushed away the soap suds that formed a huge second eyebrow over Laurie's left eye.

"One of the guys in the Corvette Club had suggested a shop he liked near where the misfire started. A shop by the Blue Ridge exit.

"The place was crazy. Some kind of zen/martial arts auto repair shop complete with a rock garden and meditation music. And the owner was straight out of a Hollywood movie. Like Mr. Miyagi with technicians snatching projectiles out of the air or something."

"What?" Laurie asked.

"Long story," Kurt said. "But, for some reason, I felt safe there; I trusted him. I told this Robert guy all about how the company was in trouble. How it was sucking me dry, causing problems everywhere. I don't know why. I just started talking and I couldn't stop. He said he understood and told me it could be fixed. No. Actually, he said *I* could fix it. And, honest to God, I really think he can help—"

Kurt stopped. Laurie was staring at him, arms crossed. He knew that look, the 'Are you crazy?' one. The rest of the dishes would have to wait.

"Who is this guy, Kurt?" she asked. "What makes you think he can help with our business? He's just a mechanic, right? What could he possibly know about the construction industry?"

"See, that's the thing," Kurt said. "He doesn't have to. What he's got to share is… ah, um… universal. He says the principles he has to teach me can be applied to anything."

"Anything?" Laurie said. "Really? That's quite a promise. Did he, by chance, happen to mention how much this was going to cost?"

"No," Kurt responded. "Well, yeah. In a way. But, listen, I know I've tried things befo—"

"Yeah, expensive things," Laurie interrupted. "Especially the consultants. All of them full of B.S. That place is like the Titanic! Nothing and no one has been able to turn the monster around."

"Let me finish, please," Kurt insisted. "That's the amazing part. Essentially, it isn't going to cost anything."

"Essentially?"

"Well, my time. It's going to cost me time and effort. And I have to buy a few things like workout stuff."

"Excuse me?" Laurie wrinkled her nose. "The mystic mechanic is a personal trainer, too?"

"Workouts are a part of the process. A bunch of people will be there. I'm not really sure about the connection yet. Maybe he wants to see if I have the will power to even show up."

"What's this guy's name again?"

"Robert."

"Okay… So why would Robert help a stranger for free? He's got his own problems, I'm sure. What does he get out of it?"

"I don't know. I guess the satisfaction of 'paying it forward', helping somebody else like he was helped in the past. He struggled with his business, too. But he came out of that dark tunnel wiser. It's going to be a school of hard knocks education, I think."

Laurie nodded. Her eyes were softer. She was listening.

"Robert will guide me, but I have to do the work, the heavy lifting. I think the training is about showing up, showing him that I'm serious enough to put some emotional skin in the game."

"Hold on, Kurt," Laurie said, holding up a hand. "You've always been athletic. But that was quite a while ago."

She playfully glanced down at his belly. Kurt was carrying around an extra fifteen pounds or so he knew he didn't need.

"I'm not going to become a black belt or anything," Kurt said, shaking his head. "I'm just going to let him know I'm tough enough to take whatever he has planned for me. Tough enough to do whatever it takes to turn the business around."

Laurie looked concerned again.

"How much time is this going to take? You're never home now as it is. How many more hours can you be away?"

"The workout sessions are early in the morning, before you guys even wake up. The place is on the way to work. I think the rest is more about me reading things he assigns. I can do that at home."

Kurt smiled.

"I've got a good feeling about this. I'm going to make it work. I promise."

Laurie touched the back of his arm, and looked into his eyes.

"Listen, honey. I love you and know you can do just about anything you put your mind to. Whatever you do, *we* do it together. Like you always say: In for a penny, in for a pound."

Kurt moved closer, put his arms around his wife, and held her. This was one of those times he didn't have to think about why or how much he loved her.

21

Restless Nights

Laurie was sleeping when Kurt finally got the house squared away: doors locked and alarm set. He entered the bedroom, walked to her side of the bed, and moved her pillow gently—just enough to give her a kiss on the cheek.

Then came the normal ritual of washing up and getting ready for bed himself. It wasn't until he crawled under the covers that he realized the TV was still on. Laurie insisted it was her brand of 'white noise'—the best way for her to get to sleep.

There was some *Cops*-style show on. 'Real crime, real victims.' Not a genre Kurt was fond of. But the chase scene on a freeway caught his attention. The camera alternated between the dash cam on the police car in pursuit to a helicopter high above.

A quarter mile ahead a red car was weaving erratically between three lanes of slower-moving traffic. A red car out of control. The red Corvette, its driver inattentive and unfocused, smashing into the backend of a moving van—wedged under the liftgate.

The driver, cut and bleeding, barely breathing. Gasoline running beneath the car aimlessly seeking a spark. A mysterious stranger, the Good Samaritan, dragging the battered driver of the red car to safety. The red Corvette engulfed in red, orange, and yellow flames.

A film reel unspooled in Kurt's head, flashing light on the walls of his memory then dropping to a pile of twisted celluloid on the floor. It looped in perverse variations.

Now Kurt was stuck inside the burning vehicle, blood dripping down his face. He looked weakly around at the cars stopped on the highway. No one got out. No one helped him. It was a frozen tableau. He felt the flames. He wanted to scream, but no sound escaped his open mouth.

He squeezed his eyes shut, but the images kept coming. He ran to the Corvette, its hood cracked and crumpled under the van's liftgate. Rick and Rochelle were trapped inside, pounding on the windows. Kurt glanced under the hood. There was no engine in the compartment, just stacks and stacks of pink While You Were Out slips. They caught fire. He ran to open the door. He was too late.

Kurt snapped up and out from beneath the covers like one of AJ's jack-in-the-box toys!

He looked around the room to get his bearings. He tried to breathe normally but couldn't.

It was only a dream.

He dropped back down to the damp pillow. He realized that things were really a lot worse than Laurie realized. He was hiding the truth about how deep a hole the company was in. The shame and guilt of it was gnawing at him.

Kurt always kept a lot of credit cards, more than he needed. They were all Kerrigan Construction cards with the statements mailed to the office. But, like most cards issued to a small business, each was personally guaranteed.

Until recently, he had only used one or two. But, as things got worse, he started leaning on the cards more heavily. He was at a point where the business would have to get better just to service the debt. If things didn't get better, he could lose everything.

Everything.

Laurie didn't know. He hadn't told her.

He knew it was his own arrogance, his own pride, that allowed things to get this bad.

Maybe that's why Robert's offer is so appealing, he thought. *It's a last ditch, heroic effort to save the business—my only option.*

He sighed, then looked over at Laurie. She was sleeping soundly, oblivious to that fact that she was a helpless passenger taking a fateful cruise on the Atlantic.

She's right, Kurt thought. *Kerrigan is the Titanic. I'm the captain and I'm steering her, the kids, and my employees straight into an iceberg.*

Kurt clenched both fists tightly. Suddenly, he burst out.

"Okay. That's it! I'm in. All in!"

Laurie stirred a little. He hadn't meant to say that out loud. But it felt right. It felt like this bold declaration needed the forcefulness of his voice, needed to be manifest in the world.

I'm going to show up on Wednesday and prove to this guy that I'm serious. Do whatever he tells me I have to do. Go big or go home!

Kurt rolled over, pulled the covers up to his neck, and closed his eyes. For the first time in weeks, he fell into a deep, restful sleep.

22

0:DARK:30 – Wednesday Morning

Kurt wiped the sleep out of the corners of his eyes. It felt as if he had just gone to bed, and that was pretty much reality. He had risen at four, hit the shower, and an hour later was in the parking lot at Mushin Automotive. He walked behind the building, and crossed the alley to the house where he had received his uniform.

He felt silly wearing it now. He had to roll the pants up around his waist to keep the bottoms from dragging on the ground. And he had no idea how to tie the tunic so it didn't look ridiculous.

Kurt had filled a gym bag with his work clothes and a toiletry kit crammed with a razor, shaving cream, and assorted items. The bag seemed heavier than it should have been.

Got enough stuff in there, Kurt? he thought. *It must look like you're leavin' home.*

He was tired, and he hadn't done anything but try to stay awake. Worst of all, he'd resisted the urge to stop and get some coffee. He was afraid of having anything in his stomach if the workout was even mildly intense.

He kicked off his sandals and placed them in one of the small cubbies. That's when he noticed a brass plate over the door. The sun wasn't up yet; Kurt had to strain to make out the engraving:

> THE STUDENT DOES NOT PAY THE TEACHER TO TEACH:
> THE STUDENT PAYS FOR THE OPPORTUNITY TO LEARN.

Interesting, he thought.

Like everything else at Mushin Automotive, it was certainly a very different spin on things.

As he walked down the hallway to the main room, Kurt became aware of the intense quiet. He smiled.

Good, I'm early!

He had something to prove and hoped Robert would recognize the effort he'd made.

Then he noticed the open door. He entered the room to find eighteen people there before him, spread across the floor in three rows of six individuals each. There were men and women—of just about every age, shape, and size—sitting on the polished wood floor stretching. A young man was silently leading them through a series of exercises. Not a word was spoken. He led the group by example and each student followed to the best of their ability.

"Howdy, Mr. Kerrigan. Welcome!"

The voice came from behind. It was Jason, the young guy who had miraculously snatched the fitting out of the air what seemed just a few hours earlier. He cocked his head.

"How's the world treatin' ya?"

"I'm fine, Jason," Kurt answered. "Thanks."

Kurt didn't hear, nor did he feel, Robert come up behind him until the intimidating rumble of the man's voice startled him.

"In the studio," Robert said, "everyone is addressed by their last name and appropriate prefix. Jason would be Mr. Widham. Allie, Ms. Knox. And I'm Mr. Taylor. It's a sign of respect for those who have preceded you on this journey."

"Sorry," Kurt stammered, "I didn't know. It won't happen again."

He looked at Robert and then down at his gym bag.

"Is there any place I can put this where it'll be out of the way?"

Robert looked at Jason and the next thing Kurt knew the bag was over Jason's shoulder and on its way out of the room. As Kurt watched this, he noticed the entire area for the first time.

The studio's interior space was significant, filling what must have been the living room and dining room of the original structure. Yet it was spartan—simply an open, rectangular work space.

The two side walls were punctuated with images tracing the genealogy of each of the martial arts taught, along with racks of traditional weapons used in each. Here and there were class pictures that went back years.

The wall up front—the focal point of the studio—had at its center an altar with images of the founders of each of the disciplines taught, the flags of each of the nations from which the arts came, fresh flowers, and incense.

In the back was essentially one large ceiling-to-floor mirror that went wall-to-wall across the room. It was punctuated by two barre bars, one significantly higher than the other, that sliced the mirror into three sections.

Looking down, you could see there were two polished wooden floors that made up the studio. The larger of the two took up most of the area, extending from the altar in front, two-thirds of the way across the room, leaving just under ten feet between the edge of the main surface and the mirrors. It was a gleaming maple, polished to the point it almost looked wet.

Along the back, and five feet on either side, was a border of hickory, also highly polished.

The back and sides were used for moving around the actual practice floor and to stretch out, to practice before and after class and to watch when you weren't formally called to the floor.

Robert brought his hands together in a single loud clap. The stretching stopped immediately; every head turned his way.

"This is Mr. Kerrigan. He'll be joining us. He's never worked out in the arts before, and has no idea what he's in for.

"This is an experiment. I promised to help Mr. Kerrigan with his business, but only if he allowed us to help him from within the context of our world. In other words, his participation here isn't exactly voluntary. It is a condition.

"He did not stumble upon us out of a burning desire to find his true center. He's here because I insisted he be here. Treat him with respect and help him as you would anyone else searching for 'The

Way,' but don't allow him to give less than his best. If you do, you will insult him and demean yourselves."

Robert turned his attention from his students back to Kurt.

"Mr. Kerrigan, you have about fifteen minutes to warm up and stretch before we begin. I urge you to use the time wisely."

And, with that, the master mechanic exited the room.

23

On the Floor

Kurt used the remaining fifteen minutes to warm up and stretch everything he could think of stretching in just about every way he could think of stretching it.

He used all the yoga poses he could remember, all the stretches he had learned playing sports in high school, and even some of the Williams moves he mastered while in physical therapy for his back.

He wasn't convinced it would all be necessary, but decided he'd rather be safe than sorry.

C'mon, how hard could this be? he thought.

There were people on the floor older than him. Even a couple that were, for lack of a kinder word, just plain big. He was certain he could hold his own with any of them.

As he was sizing up the other students, Robert, Allie, and Jason moved to the front of the room. Everyone snapped into formation with almost military precision—three rows of six students evenly placed on the floor to take advantage of the available space. And there was Kurt, all alone in the back, in a row of his own.

That's when he noticed the belts that everyone had tied around their *gis*. They were all white, though some were not as bright as others. Even Robert's belt was white, though tattered, badly frayed, and almost black in places from what was, evidently, a lifetime of use. And everyone had tied their belt in, what appeared to be, a perfect square knot. Everyone, of course, save Kurt.

Robert surveyed the room.

"Ready," he said. It was not a question.

"Mr. Widham," he continued, "please take the class through the beginning exercises while I help demonstrate what we are doing for Mr. Kerrigan's benefit."

Jason waited attentively for his *sensei* to give the final word.

"Begin," Robert said quietly.

The two men bowed deeply from the waist. As their torsos moved down, their heads tilted up to maintain eye contact with each other. Then they turned and bowed to the class.

In unison, each of the eighteen students placed an open left hand over their closed right fist and returned the bow.

What followed was elegant, almost like a ballet. Both Jason and Robert dropped their weight slightly, brought their arms together in front of them—open left hand alongside a closed right fist—and then brought both hands to their right hip. They stepped forward with their left foot, planted it, and then followed through with the right, while moving both hands forward. Finally, they retreated to their original position, saluting the class with an open hand and a closed fist.

Wow, thought Kurt, *that was something to see.*

Everyone on the floor bowed in the same manner and followed through with the same salute. Everyone, that is, with the exception of Kurt who felt awkward and ignorant.

The Four Stages of Knowledge

Kurt shifted uncomfortably as the class followed Jason's direction with practiced precision. In a moment, Robert was alongside him providing encouragement.

"Don't let this bother you," he said in a lowered voice. "No one knows what they don't know until someone points it out, until someone shows them or guides them. This is no different. That's why you're here, isn't it? To learn and grow."

Kurt nodded silently. He still felt awkward.

"Not knowing what you don't know," Robert continued, "is the first stage of what we refer to it as the Four Stages of Knowledge. In fact, this First Stage: You don't know what you don't know, is especially worth noting for your business. After all, how could you? It's what most people call ignorance."

Robert smiled, trying to ease Kurt's anxiety.

"The Second Stage is: You know what you don't know. We like to think of that as the beginning of wisdom.

"The Third Stage is: You don't know what you know. It's that state in which you're able to perform beyond your own realistic expectations."

"How's that even possible?" Kurt interjected.

"It's based on things you were exposed to, but weren't aware you actually knew. Knowledge and wisdom are all around us. They have a way of seeping in even when we remain unaware.

"And, finally, there's the Fourth Stage of Knowledge: You know what you know. Some people see this as confidence. Some may see it as arrogance. We see it as performance and, most importantly, results. Keep all that in mind as we progress; it will come up a lot."

Kurt tried to stifle a nervous laugh.

"Well, I'm certainly in Stage One with that salute," he said.

"The salute?" Robert smiled. "It's a kind of formal greeting, like a hand shake—a sign of mutual respect from one martial artist to another. In many cases, the greeting is unique to a school or style, much like a fingerprint.

"Sadly, for some, it's a meaningless ritual. We don't focus on it, but the origins of our salute are relatively clear. The open hand means peace, the absence of malice. The closed fist indicates a weapon, the martial artist's ability to defend him or herself.

"In some disciplines, the left hand covers the weapon. In others, it remains open and alongside. In ours, the way we position our hands—the left hand open and alongside a closed right fist—shows that we come in peace, but are prepared for the alternative if it comes to that."

"Got it," Kurt smiled, loosening up a little.

"Regardless," Robert continued, "the quality of your salute won't be judged until you've been with us for a while. For the first few weeks, let's focus on the basics: balance, body dynamics, and movement through time and space. The beginning of your practice is all about control, self-control really. It's about you, your mind, and your body."

The class was moving through a tightly choreographed series of punches, kicks, blocks, and parries. Kurt counted the repetitions in the back of his mind.

Sets of twenties, maybe, he thought.

"You control nothing," Robert continued, "until you learn to master yourself. You'll learn nothing until you open your mind. And that won't happen until you determine there's sufficient reason and reward for all the effort.

"What you will learn here is a blended martial art. It's many styles, mastered over the years, refined until there's little wasted effort. We use elements of kung fu from China; *kenpō* from Hawai'i;

gōjū-ryū, shōrin-ryū, isshin-ryū, and *shōtōkan* which all originated in Okinawa; *jujutsu* from mainland Japan; *taekwondo* and *hwa rang do* from Korea, a bit of capoeira from Brazil, krav maga from Israel, *eskrima* from the Philippines, wrestling from the Greeks, and boxing from England and America."

"The school's philosophy is borrowed from my experience with *isshin-ryū*: There is no first strike; there is no second strike."

Kurt shrugged his shoulders. He looked lost.

"What does 'no first strike, no second strike' mean?"

Robert answered, "No first strike means that we never use our art, our skills and abilities, as the aggressor. We never strike first. However, if attacked, we respond hard and fast with whatever it will take to end the incident as quickly as possible. So there should be no need for a second strike in our response. Understand?"

Kurt nodded, "I think I do."

"No first strike/no second strike is everything you need to know if you want to stay out of trouble," said Robert, "or just enough to get into more trouble than you'll ever be able to get yourself out of."

Kurt processed the philosophy carefully.

"Everything you learn here," Robert continued, "is relevant not only to your life but to the problems you're having with your business. There is some overlap with things discussed in quality campaigns, zero defects, and becoming a Six Sigma 'black belt.'

"But, honestly, I can't speak to the effectiveness of those means. I just know that *our* way works. And it can lead to a *real* black belt, if that's what you want. But the thing about martial arts training most people fail to realize is that earning a black belt signifies the very beginning of your education, not its culmination.

"If that's the case," Kurt laughed, "we'd better get started."

For the next seventy minutes that's exactly what they did. While Jason drilled the rest of the class, the two men worked off to the side, one-on-one, with Robert firmly correcting Kurt's every errant movement.

They started with the basics: a proper stance; inward and outward blocks; upward and downward blocks; front kicks, side-kicks, and rear kicks. Robert coached Kurt on each new move, showing him how each block was potentially a strike, quietly reminding him to breathe.

"Oxygen is energy," Robert said. "Learn how to breathe; it's a critical skill. Learn how to absorb oxygen; store it; manage it wisely and efficiently. It could save your life one day. Ignore it; take it for granted; squander it… And you cannot, and will not, prevail."

Kurt did his best to imitate his teacher.

"Breathe in through your nose," Robert coached. "A deep breathe. Relax your upper body. Westerners work too hard drawing their energy into their chest. They pull their stomachs in and push their chests out. It changes your center of gravity.

"With Eastern philosophy, the center of your energy is a couple of inches below your navel. Keep it there and you're centered. Keep it there and it's much more difficult to knock you off balance.

"Let each deep breath fill your diaphragm. Don't worry about what you look like. Let your belly expand and keep your energy where it belongs.

"Once your lungs are fully expanded, hold that particular breath for a second or two, and then fully exhale through your mouth. This works better if you curl your tongue slightly and hold it against the roof of your mouth. Breathe like that and you'll see a profound difference in your energy level and your attitude."

The workout was an exercise in what Robert referred to as 'controlled contact'—just enough contact and just enough control to get your attention.

Each of Robert's strikes was deliberate, forcing Kurt to block just as thoughtfully. Robert was throwing straight punches, hooks, upper cuts, and jabs from every conceivable angle and position on the floor. He balanced the punches with kicks—side, straight, and roundhouse—in an endless choreography of constant motion. Each attack was measured, executed with precision. Yet, from Kurt's perspective, the entire sequence appeared to be without rhyme or reason, totally unpredictable.

After just fifteen minutes, Kurt was soaking wet and gasping for air. He wasn't sure if his shoulders and forearms hurt more from the constant movement or from Robert's contact. All he was certain of was that they were screaming for mercy.

I have nothing to worry about, Kurt thought. *Pain is irrelevant. If this keeps up for another hour, I'll be dead anyway. So who cares?*

Robert, on the other hand, was breathing normally. His heart rate, essentially, was at rest.

"I think that's good enough for your first day," he smiled.

Five minutes later, the entire class was on the floor doing leg lifts, push-ups, and crunches. They quickly followed this with wind sprints across the polished wooden floor which, by this time, was glistening with perspiration.

"Ready," Robert barked.

Everyone took their original places on the floor and snapped to attention. Robert bowed to Allie and Jason, and then to the class. The class responded and bowed in unison as if joined by a common spirit, then stood at attention once again.

Allie and Jason bowed to each other, and then to the class.

"Get something to drink," Robert said.

The class responded with a deep formal bow once more. Then, after a collective sigh of relief, each individual bowed and then backed off the floor.

Start the Sentence With "I"

When the last of the other students had exited the studio's main room, Robert turned to face Kurt.

"You know, a minute ago," he said, "I mentioned that you can't control anything until you learn to control yourself. That's nearly impossible if you don't understand what personal responsibility is all about.

"If you have a moment, I'd like to tell you a little story. One that changed my life. It was the favorite story of one of my favorite people, and I hope you'll find it as useful and meaningful as I have.

"My friend Randy was the president of a warehouse distribution company we sourced the majority of our parts from. He told this story anytime he wanted to stress the importance of accountability.

"It was the dead of winter outside Pittsburgh, where the dead of winter really *is* winter! Randy was working as a rep for one of the major parts manufacturers in the automotive aftermarket, and the greater Pittsburgh metro area was his territory.

"His son, Curtis, who was five at the time, was playing outside early one Sunday morning. All of a sudden, the kid is banging frantically at the utility room door.

"Randy gets up from the table where he was reading the Sunday paper, opens the door, and finds his son standing there crying his eyes out. Curtis was covered in mud and snow, tears running down his cheeks. He could barely catch his breath.

"Both Randy and his wife Sandra tried to get the boy to breathe, to stop crying and tell them what had happened. When the little guy finally composed himself, he looked up at his father, and shared his tale of woe.

"Billy Sullivan, puh... punched me in the nose," he said. *"He punched me in the nose and pushed me down the hill!"*

"Sandra was still sitting at the kitchen table when she suggested that Curtis frame the incident differently.

"Start the sentence with 'I,' Curtis," she said. Curtis started over.

"Billy Sullivan punched me in the nose," he said, more confident and angry this time, *"and he pushed me down the hill."*

"Sandy pushed her cup of tea forward as she eased her chair back from the table. She crossed the room to where the boy was standing and tenderly knelt down in front of him.

"Honey, I want you to start the sentence with 'I'."

"Curtis bit his lower lip in frustration; he knew there was no escaping his mother's demand. He repeated the story yet again.

"I... I kicked Billy Johnson in the stomach. Then he punched me in the nose and pushed me down the hill."

As the story ended, Robert smiled.

"Personal accountability defined in elegant simplicity," he said.

Robert waited for Kurt. The silence lingered for a few seconds. Kurt shifted uncomfortably as the meaning slowly dawned on him.

"Okay," Kurt said, "I think I get it."

"It's pretty clear, really," Robert responded. "Your business is in trouble? Start the sentence with 'I'. You're probably the one who broke it. You'll probably be the only one who can fix it.

"You can't get your people to understand what needs to be done, or to go along with any new policies you need for a turn-around...

"Start the sentence with 'I'.

"You're the one who has to set an example for your employees.

"You're the one who needs to live those policies. You're the one who needs to explain them and see that they're executed properly."

"Okay," Kurt said, nodding in agreement.

"Problems at home?" Robert asked. "Not getting along with the wife? Feeling distant from the kids? They don't understand you?

"Start the sentence with 'I'.

"Your wife doesn't understand how hard you're working to turn things around? Start the sentence with 'I'. Show her, don't tell her.

"Be the partner or the parent you are capable of becoming. The person everyone wants and needs you to become. The person they deserve.

"Become the leader your people will want to follow. Become the leader they need. Then watch 'em line up behind you!"

Basic Theory

Kurt stood there blown away. How could an idea that simple be so powerful? How could he have missed it? He was speechless and didn't know what to say even if he could speak.

Whatever happens in the future, he thought, *I'll be starting my sentences with 'I'. I am going to take ownership.*

He thanked Robert for the advice, bowed and backed away. He needed to shower and head to the office. Suddenly, an image of that bland rental car flashed before his eyes, sitting there in the parking lot like a beige bug waiting to be put out of its misery.

I can't believe I'm stuck driving that thing for another day.

He shook it out of his head. Robert was walking away as Kurt cleared his throat and called out.

"Mr. Taylor. About the Corvette," he asked, "Do you think there is anything else wrong with it?"

"Well," Robert said, "it has the multiple misfires we talked about the other day. Past that, we'll have to install the new parts when they come in and then see. In the meantime, we'll be inspecting the rest of the vehicle to ensure there isn't anything else there you need to know about. But the inspection isn't complete; we'll have to wait for the results."

"That's it?" Kurt wondered.

"That's it. We identify and eliminate. We find out what's causing the engine to misfire and remove the cause. Then move on."

"That sounds so simple," Kurt said, nodding his head. "Hey, I know this may be a stupid question, but what is a 'misfire' anyway?"

"Well," Robert quipped, "unless you already know the answer, there is no such thing as a 'stupid' question.

"Technically, a misfire refers to the failure of the fuel charge in one or more of the cylinders to ignite properly when it's supposed to. That almost always results in incomplete combustion. A misfire occurs when one of several conditions are either not met, or not met at the appropriate time: that is, too early or too late. This could be things like too much air and not enough fuel, or the reverse. It could be no spark or inadequate spark, as well. You get the idea."

"Not sure I do," Kurt replied, mystified but genuinely interested.

"Let's talk basic theory," Robert said. "There are four necessary components that must come together for an internal combustion engine to run. You need the right mixture of air and fuel—the ratio is 14.7:1—in order to achieve what the engineers refer to as Stoichiometric Efficiency."

"Stokey...?" Kurt frowned.

"Sorry," Robert chuckled, "sometimes I forget I'm talking to a *civilian*. It's a technical term. It doesn't really matter what it's called.

"The point is you must have adequate compression. And then sufficient spark to light the mixture off and start the burn. It all has to come together at precisely the right moment. Everything must happen perfectly, six hundred to six thousand or more times a minute under every conceivable driving condition and under all possible temperatures and loads.

"The wonder isn't that vehicles misfire every once in a while. The wonder is that they run at all."

"I'm amazed," Kurt said, "that you knew what was wrong with my car so quickly—why and how it was misfiring the way it was."

"I knew the Corvette had a misfire," Robert said, "the minute I got behind the wheel and started the engine. I could feel it: sense it, more than anything else.

"I needed to drive the vehicle to get a feel for what it was doing and under what circumstances. Then I needed the right equipment to determine exactly where and how the misfire was occurring.

"I guess it's a combination of intuition and experience, with a little intellect thrown in."

Kurt shook his head. He was impressed.

"I wish fixing stuff was as easy in the real world," he mumbled. "My business is misfiring all over the place and I'd give anything to plug a magic little rectangle under the dash, so to speak, to find out what's wrong. Then fix it."

"You can," Robert smiled. "We did it here. Not with a magic rectangle, but with information. You must keep data on the jobs you complete, right? If you do, the basic principles are the same.

"You can harvest the performance data from your business in the same way the flight recorder gathered it from the Corvette. Then you can compare that data to an ideal set of known, good specifications.

"Truth is, all businesses need a combination of critical elements to come together for them to perform properly. The first step is identifying what they are. The second is understanding how they work together. Then all you have to do is create the policies and processes necessary to facilitate their effective execution.

"In principle, there isn't a hell of a lot of difference between your business, martial arts, or auto repair."

Suck, Squeeze, Bang, Blow

"Hold up," Kurt said. "You're saying the workout we just did is like repairing a car? There's a parallel between fixing my car and fixing my company? I think that might be stretching the analogy a bit. Don't you?"

"Not really," Robert replied, "Think about your Corvette. You love it, right? But do you have any idea what's under the hood?"

"The engine?" Kurt furrowed his brow.

"Yes," Robert said. "Did you know that it's a 6.2-liter, 430 horsepower, LS3, V-8, four-stroke, internal combustion engine?"

"Actually, I did. I know it's an LS3 and I know it was rated at 430 horsepower from the factory. That's why I bought it. But as far as what that means is concerned, I haven't got a clue. I just put gas in it and check the oil every once in a while."

Robert nodded his head. He'd heard that all before, too many times. Fill it with gas; check the oil; bring it to the shop when the engine light goes on, or it makes a funny noise.

"Okay, then," he said, "Let me explain. Four-stroke refers to the number of times the piston moves up and down to complete a working cycle during the two rotations it takes to make it all happen. The strokes are intake, compression, power, and exhaust.

"You have to get a combustible mixture into the chamber as the piston moves down. That's the first stroke: intake.

"Once the mixture is present, you compress it to create pressure and heat. That's the second stroke: compression, with the piston moving up.

"With enough pressure and heat inside the chamber, the mixture will burn when ignited. You ignite it on the third stroke: the power stroke. The mixture expands and forces the piston down again.

"After the mixture burns, you need to push the by-products out so you can get some more combustible mixture back into empty cylinder. That's the fourth stroke: exhaust. Then you start the process all over again.

"Get an old technician involved in this conversation and, within a few minutes, you'll hear him talk about suck, squeeze, bang, blow. It's slang for the same four events."

"Suck, squeeze, bang, blow," Kurt repeated softly.

"If you think about it," Robert continued, "all businesses go through the same four cycles and the demands in each step are nearly identical. When the cycles don't mesh together seamlessly, efficiently, and effectively, you could call that a misfire."

"Okay," Kurt interjected, "I'm trying to follow you here. What's the mixture in my business, the stuff that goes into the engine?"

"Your customers, of course," Robert answered. "They're what your business needs to run, right? You need people to buy the stuff you have for sale, regardless of what your products or services are. Marketing and advertising deliver customers, your combustible mixture, to the business. That's your intake.

"Not enough of the right kind of customers, or too many of the wrong kind, and you're likely to experience a misfire. Your job is to learn how to discern between the two.

"Compression is about turning potential customers into clients —determining their wants, needs, and expectations. Then the heat is on you to create appropriate solutions for them: opportunities.

"Creative pressure is always present when you're looking for solutions and serving customers. But the failure to listen can cause unnecessary pressure, a different kind of squeeze.

"Do this right and you make a sale. Do it wrong… Pressure someone to accept a solution that benefits you first, or provide an answer, even the right answer, before they're able to hear it for themselves, and you can lose a valuable opportunity. Misfire.

"Getting the actual work done—the tools, training, technology, and staffing required—that's your power stroke, your 'bang'. Not enough work is an obvious problem, but imagine a workload that's too heavy with too many good jobs or, worse, too many bad ones. The chicken running around with its head cut off. Frantic activity without any thought. Without any results.

"Another way to misfire during the power stroke is to have inadequately-trained craftsman, a lack of efficiency, or policies and procedures that undercut your productivity. To my mind, you can't overstate the importance of getting this cycle right.

"Finally, exhaust is about completion, your quality control, and follow-through. The end of the process is not the time to blow it. Quite often, this part of the process feels like it's superfluous after the 'real' work is done. It's not. Follow-up is crucial. It probably does more than anything else to build lasting relationships with your customers.

"Actually, connection and generosity should be your guiding principles through all four stages of the customer cycle. When you fail to connect authentically; when you don't take the time to give that extra minute to listen and truly understand a concern; when you forget to say 'thank you'… These are the ways you leave your customer feeling unheard, unappreciated, and invisible. This is how and when *you* cause the misfire.

"If you can understand these four—what they are and how they work—you're on the way to understanding how your business really works. And that, my friend, is the first step to fixing it."

Kurt smiled. He was starting to understand what Robert meant when he said the Second Stage of Knowledge (knowing what you don't know) was the beginning of wisdom.

‡

"Will you be around after I shower and clean up?" Kurt asked tentatively.

"Probably," replied Robert, looking at his watch. "Why do you ask?"

"Well, I was hoping you'd have a few minutes to continue this discussion. There's so much I'm trying to wrap my head around."

"I'll make as much time as I can," Robert committed.

Kurt bowed, backed away, and headed for the shower.

28

D-Words

By the time Kurt made it to the men's locker room, the majority of the other students had already cleaned up and were on their way.

He had felt fine while he was talking to Robert. But now, in the silence, Kurt realized he was so tired he could barely keep his head up, so sore he could hardly move. He flopped down on a bench.

It was impossible to recall the last time he'd given that much of himself to anything, let alone a workout.

The few men who remained in locker room came over and introduced themselves. They seemed pleased he was there.

There's a genuine sense of community here, Kurt thought.

He stripped off his uniform and laid it on the bench in front of the locker Jason had chosen for him. He couldn't remember the last time he had perspired like that. He held up the *gi* in wonder.

This has to weigh three times more than it did when I put it on.

Steam filled the locker room and the shower felt good. Better than any other shower in a long time.

He was exhausted, but it was a different kind of exhaustion. Not the beaten-down, bone-tired weariness he felt leaving the office every night. This was a very satisfying kind of tired, tempered by the accomplishment of finishing a difficult and demanding task.

He looked at his body in the mirror as he dried off. His forearms were swollen. There were reddish welts, slowly turning purple, that identified every strike he had blocked.

His legs felt like Jell-O. The shin guards absorbed some of the impact from the blocks and kicks, but he was sure he could identify every spot where contact was made.

As Kurt finished putting on his work clothes, Robert walked into the locker room. He was dressed for work across the alley.

"How was your first workout?" he asked. "I'm sure it wasn't what you expected, but I have to say I am encouraged you made it through without quitting or throwing up. Not everyone does."

"I did," Kurt smiled. "But I don't know about the cost. Or how I'll feel tomorrow either. Nevertheless, I'm in."

Kurt reflected for a moment, rubbing a sore forearm. He looked down at his gear bag, then back up to Robert.

"I guess I should ask how often I'm expected to show up."

"Someone is here every morning," Robert said. "Generally at five or just a few minutes after. We went over the basics today because there was someone new on the floor. That's one of the reasons we finished early. But that isn't often the case.

"There are other classes offered at different times, many of them very specific in content. But this is where I want you to be for now.

"As far as when you come back, that's up to you. All I'll say is that I see your attendance as a measure of your interest. And *your* interest will determine the level of *my* interest when it comes to helping you. We can start talking more about your business after you've shown me that you have mastered a few of the D-words."

"D-words?" Kurt asked. "What are D-words?"

"Words critical to your success," Robert said. "Your personal success as well as that of your business. Words like discipline, desire, determination, and drive."

Kurt shifted uncomfortably. He frowned. He felt like he'd just been indicted.

"Are you saying that I don't have any of those traits?" he frowned. "I'm super driven."

"That may be," Robert countered. "But we just met. I haven't seen it demonstrated. To my mind, the D-words are foundational elements of character. And character is at the core of who you are.

"It's about the decisions you make and the actions you take when no one else is around to witness those choices. Let's see what kind of choices you make over the next thirty days.

"In the meantime, if something really critical with the business comes up, let me know. We can work our way through whatever it is before things get too far out of control."

"I appreciate that," Kurt said. Then he paused for a moment.

"I don't want to assume anything here. So could you tell me how you define your terms? What do these D-words mean to you."

Robert looked at his watch.

"I've only got a few minutes, but I'll give it a shot," he said.

"Let's start with desire. Simply stated, it's something you want, something you would like, right. We've all got desires of one kind or another, both personal and professional. Maybe to run a marathon. Or to increase sales to over a million dollars.

"The real question is: What do we do with those desires? Sadly, most of us do nothing more than fantasize. We're satisfied using our desires to fuel our daydreams and not much else. We're not willing to take that next step. We're not willing to 'do the work'.

"For desires to be more than the stuff daydreams are made of, someone, somehow, has to sprinkle them with a little action."

"That's where discipline comes in. It's the mental toughness to do what has to be done, even when you aren't motivated to do it."

Kurt leaned in, "I'm following you, but drive and determination, they seem like essentially the same thing."

Robert pondered the comment for a moment.

"Not really," he said. "Drive is all about motivation, the self-motivation needed to fuel discipline. Like when you say 'I am driven to fix my business.'

"Certainly there are external forces that could drive you to do something. Even something you don't really want to do. But, for the most part, when I talk about drive, I mean the fire in your belly that compels you to do whatever it takes to accomplish your goals."

"And determination is different, how?" Kurt responded.

"Like a lot of these words, determination has more than one meaning," Robert said. "But, when I talk about determination, you can be pretty sure that I'm talking about a firmness of purpose, about being resolute.

"You can have desire. But without determination, discipline, and drive, how do you get it done? If all you've got is determination, your efforts will probably remain unfocused. Discipline is only a means to end; never an end in itself. And if you're just driven, the chances are high your journey will take longer and cost more, physically and emotionally, than if the D-words were in harmony. That's the point: getting them working together."

"Thanks for the explanation," Kurt said. "Over the next few months, I'm going to show you just how dedicated I can be."

Robert smiled broadly.

"Dedication," he said. "I should have mentioned that as well. It's one of our favorite D-words here at Mushin."

"Is it really all that different?" Kurt asked.

"It is. And, for me, the difference is powerful. That difference is passion, your passion for the task at hand. Your commitment to see that task through to its best completion. No matter the difficulties. Regardless of the inconvenience, or the obstacles, or even the cost."

Robert looked Kurt hard in the eye.

"When you say you're 'dedicated' know what that means. Know what it means to *me*."

Kurt took it all in for a moment. He shook his head.

Every word with this guy is like falling down a rabbit hole.

Robert grabbed his gym bag at a nearby locker, ready to go. Kurt motioned for his attention one last time.

"Are there any other D-words you may have forgotten?"

Robert stopped in his tracks, smiling mischievously. Then he burst out laughing. The mechanic reached into his shirt pocket and pulled out a small blue, octagonal jar. He tossed it Kurt's way.

Kurt held the jar up trying to determine what was inside. It was opaque and the label was handwritten in Chinese characters.

"It's called *dit da jow*," Robert said. "It's a Chinese ointment that will help you with the welts, bruises, and soreness. Just be careful. Use it sparingly. Less is more when it comes to this D-word."

Robert picked up his bag again and headed for the door. Kurt twisted the jar open and checked it with a hesitant sniff. His head snapped back. His eyes filled with tears.

"Oh, my God! What the hell is this stuff?" he moaned.

Robert turned around, still smiling.

"One more thing, Kurt… It stinks. And, it burns like hell if you aren't careful about where you apply it. Don't rub your eyes or touch anything, um, sensitive, after you've handled it either. Not until you wash your hands thoroughly."

Kurt shook his head and eyed the blue jar suspiciously.

"This stuff is nasty," he said.

Robert sensed Kurt might be having second thoughts after the workout regardless of his insistence that everything was fine.

"You still up for this?" he asked. "It's not too late to back out."

Kurt thought about it for a second or two. He felt the soreness in his body and projected how much more it would hurt at four the next morning, when his alarm went off. He set the little jar of *dit da jow* down on the bench. Then he placed his right hand alongside his left, and bowed to his new teacher.

"I'm here," he replied. "But can I steal just a few more minutes of your time when I'm done, *sensei*."

Robert stopped, looked at his watch again, and then back at Kurt. He rubbed his chin and replied.

"Sure, Kurt. I'll wait for you in the studio."

Neither Good, Nor Bad...

Kurt found Robert sitting on one of the chairs at the back of the studio carefully going over a handful of papers. He looked up as Kurt entered the room. Robert smiled.

"Feeling any better?" he quipped.

"Physically or mentally?" Kurt answered. "Physically, I'm still standing; mentally, not so much."

"That's not good. What do you think is causing your distress?" Robert's concern was obvious; the question sincere.

"To be honest," Kurt responded, "the business has gotten so bad it's painful showing up in the morning. Nothing works the way it's supposed to, not the way it did before. It just plain sucks."

Robert's demeanor softened.

"My *sensei* would say that things are neither good nor bad," he offered. "They just are. You have to deal with them the way they are, not how you would like them to be.

"We assign values to things. We frame them. We place them in the context of our experience and then judge them. But things are rarely 'good' or 'bad' intrinsically. Once we get past that, the world becomes a much easier place in which to operate.

"For me, it started with my teacher. Although 'teacher' is not an appropriate description; he didn't really 'teach' me anything."

"How can you teach without teaching?" Kurt asked.

Robert laughed.

"I think you're starting to get it! That was a very zen question for someone who claims not to know anything about zen. Just like

Jerry… He was a zen 'master', although he never actually studied Zen or the martial arts.

"I worked with him for a lifetime. I sat at his feet, so to speak. But he never taught a formal lesson in his life. Never answered a question directly. In fact, if he answered at all, it was with another question. But I learned every day.

"He taught me everything about personal responsibility I'd ever need to know. This was right at the very beginning of my career. And all it took was a broken bolt."

Kurt furrowed his brow, and raised a hand in gentle protest.

"How did he do that? What did he say?"

"Looking back," Robert said, "it's actually kind of funny. But it didn't seem so at the time.

"I was a kid just starting out in the business. I didn't know my butt from a hole in the ground, and Jerry—he owned the place—hired me and made my education his personal responsibility. I guess I was a kind of a project for him.

"In any case, one of the first jobs I got assigned was an exhaust manifold R&R. That's Remove and Replace. As easy as the job may have sounded at first—R&R Right Side Exhaust Manifold—like everything else, it required a minimal level of skill and finesse.

"I went over to the vehicle, an old Chevy station wagon, figured out which tools I needed, and went to work. Honestly, I had no idea what else I might have to remove before I could even get to the manifold. The only instructions I'd been given was 'no power tools'.

"Everything I did in the shop, at that time, had to be accomplished with hand tools. No air or electrical tools allowed. That was a privilege to be earned. It didn't make any sense to me, air tools help speed a job up. But I wasn't signing the paychecks.

"Anyway, the first bolt came right out. The second bolt was another story. I leaned on the ratchet a bit, but it wouldn't budge. So I did what any nineteen-year-old kid who never worked on anything mechanical before would do, I leaned on it a little harder."

Kurt winced in advance. He knew where this was headed.

"I leaned on it hard enough to snap the head off the bolt and skin the knuckles of my right hand in the process.

"Well, as you can imagine, I felt embarrassed and more than a little lost. I walked over to where Jerry was working with the broken bolt head cupped in the palm of my hand.

"Jerry was a big guy; not tall, but imposing nonetheless. He was bent over a car and all you could see from behind was his massive back and shoulders. That, and the smoke curling around his head from the cigarette hanging out of the corner of his mouth.

"He had this raspy, coarse-sounding voice that seemed to rumble up from somewhere deep in his chest. A thick Brooklyn accent, too. Quite frankly, I was terrified of him. He seemed to sense I was there, although he never looked up. Finally, he acknowledged my presence with a grunt.

"Yeah...?" was all I got. And it caught me off guard.

"'I was taking the manifold off when this bolt broke,' I said.

"Before I could say another word, this is what I heard.

"While you were watchin' it?"

"The only response I could muster was, 'Huh?'

"Jerry had gone silent. He continued working on the car he was buried in. I stood there a moment confused, then tried again.

"'I was taking the manifold off the Chevy when this bolt brok—'

"He cut me off again.

"While you were watchin' it?"

"He was more insistent this time. More impatient with me. I remember thinking to myself: What the hell is this all about? What kind of a question is that? Suddenly, I realized that the bolt didn't break itself. It had help.

"I broke it. I snapped the head off the bolt.

"I went back over to where Jerry was working and tried talking to him again, only this time I started the sentence with 'I':

"'I was working on the Chevy wagon and, while I was trying to remove the manifold, *I* broke one of the bolts.'

"Jerry stopped what he was doing and turned toward me.

"What did it feel like?"

"I was lost again. What did it *feel* like? Well, I felt like crap at the moment. But I suspected that's not what he meant. And I knew being a smart ass would get me kicked out the door. I really wanted to work there. I sensed he could make a profound difference in my life. So I stared at the bolt and admitted sheepishly that I had no idea how to answer the question.

"While you were leaning on whatever it was you used to loosen the bolt you broke... What did it feel like just before the bolt snapped?"

"'It felt like it kind of gave a little, almost like it was stretching.'

"Then why did you keep leaning on it?"

"There it was: personal responsibility defined yet again. All in a couple of short sentences.

"The bolt didn't break by itself. I broke it. It was a pretty powerful life lesson.

"If you are doing something that feels wrong—if you encounter an unnatural amount of resistance—trust your instinct, follow your intuition, and stop. At least for a moment or two. Sheer force might not be the answer. Listen to what the universe is trying to tell you and stop before something bad happens.

"Along with accountability, Jerry proceeded to teach me about commitment as well, repeating his mantra over and over again:

"You gotta wanna fix the car! If you do, you'll find a way.

"If you don't, all the training, time, tools, and technology in the world won't help you."

Robert got up from the chair.

"He taught me about process, science, craftsmanship, and art. How they all come together if you let them. And he did all that without ever lecturing or looking in a book.

"How much do you wanna fix your business, Kurt?"

Life – Imitating Art – Imitating Life

Kurt walked into the parking lot in front of Mushin Automotive. For a brief second, he was looking for the the smooth curves of his Corvette, then he remembered the awful truth.

He trudged over to the blah beige rental car and sized it up.

If there is a God, he thought, *may this be the last day this rental car and I spend together.*

He opened the door, slid behind the wheel, and prepared himself mentally for the short commute to work.

The freeway drive passed without incident. Kurt was so lost in his own thoughts that he arrived at Kerrigan Construction without noticing there were only a few other cars parked in the lot.

Without thinking, he unlocked the front door, disabled the alarm, and headed back toward his office.

He stared at the pile of papers on his desk, each one precisely where he'd left it the afternoon before. He took a deep breath, just as Robert had taught him.

He felt the tension exit his body, closed his eyes and did it again. The muscles of his neck loosened; his shoulders dropped. There was a pleasant sensation in the middle of his forehead.

That's better, he thought.

Kurt walked to his office door and looked back toward the front door: the room was empty. He went back to his desk.

This was the first time, in a long time, he was the first one to arrive at work. It was an odd feeling. The stillness was palpable.

He found his mind racing, bouncing back and forth across a dozen areas of the company's operations. Each one important. Each one urgent, worthy of action. But, together, it was overwhelming.

He reflected on his first conversation with Robert: the concept of *mushin*, no mind.

Too much mind, he thought. *Focus on the goal. No mind.*

He took another deep breath. He focused solely on his breath.

In through your nose. Pause… Out through your mouth.

Three-count in. Pause… Four-count. Exhale. No mind.

He wasn't sure how much time had elapsed when he realized that his manager was staring at him from the other side of his desk.

"Everything okay, boss?" Rick asked. "What are you doing here? It's just after eight. Is something wrong?"

"What do you mean, Rick? Does there have to be something wrong for me to be here at eight?"

Rick shrugged as if to imply 'Yeah, we both know the answer to that question'. Kurt knew how unconvincing he must have sounded. He leaned back against the spring in his desk chair.

"I worked out early this morning," he said. "Then I decided to come straight to the office. You know, get some quiet time to think about where we are, what we have to do to reach our goals."

"Sounds great. Come up with anything?" Rick asked.

"No, not really. Not yet anyway."

"Well, if you do, let me know. Seems like we're at the point where we sure as hell need to do something."

Kurt looked across the office at the clock hanging on the wall off to his right. It was ten minutes after eight.

Apparently, he and Rick were the only ones in the office. Kurt remembered a time when he came in an hour or two before anyone else got there. And how, back then, he was still there for at least an hour after everyone else was long gone.

It was easy in the beginning. He was virtually on his own. There was no one else around. He did it all. That meant coming in early and leaving late every day, weekends included. Even when things started to get better—and sales picked up and they hired more people—he still managed to maintain the same intense schedule.

Just to be sure everything was moving in the right direction.

Kurt couldn't remember the last time he'd been there this early.

Hey, it's ten past eight, he thought. *Ten past, and only two people are here. Where is everybody? What am I paying them for?*

Kurt closed his eyes, and took another long thoughtful breath.

You gotta wanna fix the car.

He opened his eyes, got up from the desk, and looked at Rick.

"Is anyone else here besides you and me?"

"No," Rick said. "But a couple of crews went out at seven."

As one employee after another dribbled in, Kurt stood there in his doorway gauging their reactions when they realized the boss was there before they were. It wasn't until 8:20 that everyone who was supposed to be in by 8:00 had arrived.

Kurt felt his face flush; his blood pressure began to climb.

How long has this been going on? he wondered.

He felt an irrational surge of anger bubbling up inside him. He decided to cut it off before it could take control.

Breathe…

After a few breaths, he felt the intensity of his anger subside.

Kurt went back to his desk. He needed a fresh perspective. Then he remembered the list of resources that Robert had given him.

Maybe there's something here that can help.

He searched the list, running his finger down the page.

I'm sure they're all good. Just see what jumps out at me…

His finger stopped at 'The Golden Circle by Simon Sinek'. Beneath the heading was a URL. As Kurt's computer booted up he realized there was an email alert from Mushin Automotive.

Better check that first.

It was marked 'urgent'; the time-stamp was an hour earlier.

I wasn't expecting anything when I left the shop last night.

The email contained an attachment with a short explanation about its contents—a digital report. A general vehicle inspection had been performed on the Corvette.

Kurt opened the attachment and was blown away. He counted more than forty specific items that had been inspected, almost all of which had been marked 'satisfactory' in green.

The few items that weren't marked in green were maintenance related. They were 'preventive maintenance' items, things suggested for service now or in the near future. Except that on the Mushin form, the items were called 'productive maintenance'. It was a subtle difference to be sure, but one that Kurt noted.

Each item was accompanied by a link to an animated video that explained the system it pertained to and the benefits of the service being suggested. It was interesting, educational, and very different from anything Kurt had experienced anywhere else, including his regular shop or even the dealer. The reports from other shops were always printed and attached to the invoice, lost in the stack of papers. This digital inspection was much more comprehensive.

He opened the top drawer of his desk, pulled out a notebook, and wrote a note to call Allie at Mushin with questions about the process behind creating the form. There was something here he felt was important enough to follow up on.

I bet we could use a report like this here.

Just then Rochelle buzzed in on the intercom.

"You've got a call from the car place," she said.

"Thanks, Rocky."

He picked up the phone. It was someone from Mushin calling to ensure his initial impression of the shop was positive and that he was 'delighted' with his experience so far. Kurt assured the caller he was more than impressed. He hung up the phone with a smile.

Kurt added 'customer satisfaction call-back' to his note, then placed the notebook in the upper left-hand corner of his desk with a red Post-it note on top. Red to remind him that it was crucial.

He clicked over to an open browser window on his laptop, and found the video he had chosen from Robert's 'homework' list. It was a TED Talk called 'How Great Leaders Inspire Action'.

Impressive, he thought. *More than four million views.*

Kurt clicked 'play' and sat mesmerized for eighteen minutes as Sinek talked about leadership, the similarities between Apple, the Wright brothers, and Martin Luther King. He watched a second time only this time he took detailed notes.

This guy's whole analysis is elegantly simple, yet brilliant.

Sinek talked about his concept of a 'golden circle'. The What, How, and Why of every company's struggle to exist. His contention was that most organizations on the planet fail to understand the very nature of *who* they are and *what* they are all about.

Instead, most start out by telling you *what* they do. Then they follow what they do with *how* they do it: 'We make such-and-such and it's different from our competitors because of this special thing'.

But rarely, if ever, does a company attempt to explain their *why*. Why they do what they do.

In Sinek's opinion, great and compelling companies, inspiring and innovative companies start out with Why. It's at the very core of who they are and what they do. It was something they did before they answer their What or How.

Kurt got up and left his office. He stopped at Rochelle's desk.

"Hold my calls," he said. "Don't forward anything to my cell. I'll be back in a little while. I've got something important to work on, and I don't want to be interrupted."

Rochelle nodded politely. She saw that spark in his eyes again. A spark that had been gone for far too long. Whatever had gotten under his skin, whatever brought him to the office early today, it had to be good.

Kurt walked out into the bright sunlight. It felt good on his face. He reflected on the Sinek video. The sudden clarity it brought him was blinding.

I've lost my Why. Without it, the What and How are meaningless. Meaningless to me, to my people, probably even to our clients.

I need to find my Why before I take another step.

Insanity: The Definition

There was a park near the office, just outside the business district, that had long been one of Kurt's favorite hiding places. He used to go there all the time until they started construction on the new Senior Center. He felt he'd lost his refuge when construction began. It was too noisy and hectic. He hadn't gone back since.

When he left the office, he had no intention of driving to a park. Certainly, not to this one. And, yet, when he put the little import in park and shut the engine down, there he was.

Kurt took a breath, closed his eyes, and exhaled. He had stopped in the cool of the shade. It was quiet, except for the faint chirping of birds. There had to be a reason this is where he ended up.

If nothing else, it seemed like a good time to call Mushin and ask about the email and digital inspection he'd received. He dug through his wallet until he found Allie's business card. In a few seconds, he heard her bright voice on the line.

"Good morning! This is Allie at Mushin Automotive. I can help you."

It was the second time he was greeted with the same salutation.

Wow, he thought. *'I can help you.' That's one hell of a positive way to answer the phone.*

"Hi, Allie. It's Kurt Kerrigan. The black Corvette late Monday afternoon. And this morning's workout too, I guess. Have you got a minute? I have a question or two I'd like to ask."

"Sure, Mr. Kerrigan. Or is it okay if I call you Kurt?"

"Sure," he smiled, "Kurt works as long as we're not in class. How's that?"

"Great, Kurt. Is there a problem?"

"No. My experience on Monday was perfect. And the follow-up this morning was great. Unexpected, but appreciated. That's not why I'm calling, though. I want to talk about the inspection."

"Do you have a question about any of the items that were identified?" Allie asked.

"No, the inspection was awesome. Easy to read and understand. I've already made a note to have the service items performed.

"My question is about where it all came from. I was really impressed. How did you develop it? I'm trying to figure out how I can use something like it in my business."

It was quiet for a moment or two before Allie responded.

"Okay, got it," she said. "I may have to put you on hold for a moment or two if I get a call, but I think I can help you with what you're trying to figure out."

"That would be great! I would appreciate it."

"No problem," Allie said. "We started with inspections a long time ago. Back then, they were only for internal use—to move from quantity control to quality control, if you know what I mean.

"Bear with me for a minute while I channel Robert…"

Kurt could hear the smile in Allie's voice.

"Do you know the definition of insanity, Kurt? It's doing the same thing the same way every time you attempt it, while still expecting the results to vary somehow."

"I've heard that," Kurt said. "It's nuts, right? If you do the same thing the same way every time, the result will always be the same. There's no reason for anything to change."

"Exactly," Allie said. "And we figured that out. You see, in our profession, the problem is that every mechanic and technician has created their own knowledge base. The only thing we've got to ensure any kind of consistency is voluntary certification.

"There aren't any industry standards, no generally accepted procedures, like in accounting. So everyone learns either from someone else, from their own master, or they have to build a set of skills and abilities on their own. Which means that just about everyone has their own way of doing everything."

"No consistency," Kurt interjected. "I can see that."

"Right," Allie continued. "Robert convinced all of us, both here and in the studio, that consistency is critical. If you can't explain or describe what you're doing in terms of a process, then you don't really know what you're doing.

"Consistency is one of the key ingredients in our secret sauce. The inspections are a means to adhere to a standard in the service bay. It's critical to our success."

"But you mentioned everyone took a different path," Kurt said, "a different journey before they worked for you. How do you build consistency in that environment?"

"Good question," Allie said. "Our answer was to create sets of pin-point inspections designed to ensure that the key elements of any service, maintenance, or repair operation were covered. You know, considered and then addressed.

"Then we realized how rare this was. How rare it was for any of our competitors to be doing anything like it."

"That's for sure," Kurt said. "At every other shop I've ever gone to you're lucky if they staple a sheet on the back of your invoice with a couple of checkmarks ticked. You head out the door without any discussion, no explanation."

"That's been my experience as well," Allie said. "So once we realized just how unique our process was, we realized it could be a 'differentiator'. It was something that set us apart, something that suggested how special our approach was. And it worked.

"We started off with seventeen physical inspection sheets. They covered almost everything we do; we used them for years. When new technology appeared, the switch to digital inspections wasn't much of a leap internally. But digital gave us a completely different level of flexibility, visibility, and credibility.

"It gave us the opportunity to use the inspections both 'in house' for quality control purposes, and externally to educate our clients.

It created awareness, interest, desire, and action. Especially, when the reports were combined with images and streaming video."

"I know," Kurt said. "The videos are what jumped out at me."

"Cool," Allie said. "Is that what you were looking for? If it was, I can email you copies of some of the original inspection sheets that Robert and the techs built in the beginning."

"This is great, Allie. More than I was looking for."

Kurt thanked her and hung up the phone. He looked out at the park and the tranquil beauty it presented. He closed his eyes and took another deep cleansing breath.

He could sense that he was already thinking more clearly.

Now all I have to do is figure out how to integrate this whole notion of checklists and inspections into my construction business. How they can augment the punch cards we're currently using?

Situational Awareness

After Kurt finished the call, he carefully extricated himself from the rental. It seemed like every muscle in his body was screaming at him from the trauma of the morning's workout. He was convinced that even his hair hurt.

As he headed toward a bench underneath a magnificent old oak tree, he caught a glimpse of figures moving out the corner of his eye. He turned and walked over to get a closer look.

Standing in the grassy field, just over a small rise, were about twenty seniors. Barely audible to Kurt were the relaxing tones of Asian music, much like what he'd heard at Mushin. The group of seniors followed the lead of a slender, very frail-looking old man. He moved with a fluid grace that Kurt had never seen before.

His curiosity piqued, Kurt walked closer looking for a place to sit. There was no bench, so he sat down to watch with his back against a sturdy oak. He slid down the tree's trunk and arranged himself on the ground.

If getting down is this hard, I can't wait to try and get back up.

The old man leading the class saw Kurt and motioned to him.

"Come! Join us," he said with a smile. "Please!"

Kurt hadn't wanted to make a scene. And he certainly didn't want to struggle to his feet again. He waved sheepishly.

"Thank you," he said. "But go ahead. I don't know what you guys are doing. I wouldn't want to distract you."

"You won't distract us," the man beamed gently. "We're doing tai chi, the long Yang form. There are more than one hundred poses. Where we are doesn't matter. Join us and try to follow."

"I'd love to," Kurt replied, "but I had a killer workout this morning and my body is crying out for mercy. Not sure it can handle any more strain."

"There's no strain," the man shook his head. "Join us. You'll see."

The old man was insistent. A few of the other students were looking his way. Kurt realized this was an argument he was not likely to win. He didn't want to insult the elderly gentleman, so he slowly eased his back along the side of the tree, wincing as his thighs cried 'help'.

Kurt walked to the end of the last row. He watched carefully, and tried to follow the movements being demonstrated.

"Breathe in through your nose," the man told the class. "Gather your energy. Breathe out through your mouth. Focus that energy outward."

Kurt realized he was hearing virtually the same instruction he'd heard hours earlier all over again.

"In through your nose," the man continued. "Out through your mouth. Relax. Without effort."

The old man's voice was reassuring; the music was soothing.

Kurt disappeared into the practice. The gentleness of it, the flow, worked deep inside him. His stiff muscles stopped grumbling.

Before he realized it, the music had ended, and the group was disbanding. The old man walked over to Kurt, and bowed softly.

"Was this your first time doing tai chi?"

"Yes," Kurt nodded.

He looked down at his work clothes and realized he'd been sweating. But he was in much less pain than before he started.

"You did well," the man smiled. "Have you studied before?"

Kurt laughed.

"Sure! For about two hours, just this morning. I wouldn't exactly call that studying, but it was something."

"Well, whoever showed you, has taught you how to breathe correctly. That's the foundation for success in the martial arts."

"I appreciate you opening a space for me," Kurt said. "I'm sorry. I didn't mean to be rude. My name's Kurt. Kurt Kerrigan."

He reached out his right hand. The old man took Kurt's hand into his own, and placed his left hand on top, embracing it warmly.

"I'm Chou Li. Very pleased to meet you, my friend."

Chou Li's eyes smiled as he gently shook Kurt's hand.

"Can you tell me more about the movements we were doing?" Kurt asked. "You said something about the Yang long form?"

"Yes," Chou Li nodded, "the long form was developed by a man named Yang nearly two hundred years ago. It's a series of one hundred and eight movements, designed to help you remain healthy, to help your body remain resilient.

"But, also, if applied correctly it can provide an impenetrable defense. Remember it's still a martial art, though not necessarily an aggressive one. Beyond the health benefits, tai chi is primarily about protecting yourself.

"Like so many other things in life, you must first open yourself to the universe. You must expand your awareness. Extend your senses."

"I pretty much know where I am," Kurt chuckled. "I'm in a park on a hot day in a damp shirt."

Kurt checked his watch. He'd been there an hour.

"I really have to be getting back to the office. I've been gone too long already. God only knows what's gone to hell in the few minutes I've been here with you."

Chou Li shook his head slowly. His eyes were stern.

"Look at you," he said. "In an instant, all your calm, all your peace is gone. Dispersed to the wind."

The old man reached out and touched Kurt's shoulder.

"You are too tight," Chou Li said. "Too rigid and vertical. All straight up and down. No room to breathe."

Kurt tried self-consciously to soften his posture.

"You're using too much energy standing," Chou Li continued. "There's no energy left for your senses, none left for your body."

Kurt huffed and slumped his shoulders. Chou Li was right.

"Mr. Kurt, please allow me to show you something. If you have the time, that is."

"I'm no good at the office," Kurt said, "all locked up like this."

"Ah, this is true," Chou Li smiled.

The old man raised his hands, gracefully moving them through the air.

"This is a type of training. There's contact, but no strikes. It's called 'pushing hands' or *tuishou* in China, where I am from. It is an energy exercise. An exercise in awareness, in sensitivity."

Kurt watched him move, uncertain how to engage.

"It should be easy for you," Chou Li said. "All you have to do is cause me to lose my balance. Pull or push me off center.

"But there's a catch. To make things interesting, we only have two points of contact. The back of my right wrist against the back of your right wrist, with the fingers of my left hand touching your right elbow, and the same for you. You can pivot around the wrist, but you must never lose contact."

Chou Li extended his right arm bent at close to a ninety-degree angle with his hand open and fingers extended. He beckoned.

"Shall we? It will only take a moment to demonstrate my point."

"Sure," Kurt said. "Why not?"

Kurt mirrored the old man's stance, extended his right arm and made contact. Immediately, Chou Li started moving his arm in a circular pattern. Kurt felt the old man's power radiating through his own arm to the back of his wrist. He felt the subtlety of that energy with the fingertips of his left hand as they barely touched the old man's elbow.

This guy's rail thin, Kurt thought, *but he's as strong as a superhero.*

Chou Li led him through a series of movements—the 'original movements of tai chi', he called them. Kurt followed the patterns intensely, then found himself attempting to lead. With almost no change in speed or direction, the old man lightly directed him to one side and then to the other in larger, more dramatic movements. Without warning, Kurt fell forward.

Chou Li caught him with an arm. Kurt regained his composure, ever more determined to knock the old man off balance. After all, he had to outweigh him by a hundred pounds.

Kurt met Chou Li's arm with his own. He thought of patterns and circles, breathing deep, contact without striking. Within twenty seconds, he was falling again.

The old man barely moved. His feet were rooted in the ground. His arm was as supple as a willow branch, yet as hard as steel. As much as Chou Li allowed Kurt to move him he was always able to turn that energy against the larger, younger man.

"Why can't I move you?" Kurt asked, frustrated.

"How do you do that? Are you a mind reader? Because you seem to know where I'm going to move before I do."

"I do," Chou Li nodded. "I can sense it in your muscles, in your bones. I can feel your intent before you even think about it. Your body decides before your mind does."

"How?"

"Your body is filled with energy. It moves through meridians, pathways. Like an electrical force runs along the outside of a wire carrying current.

"You generate that energy. It's a force that extends beyond the shell of your body. With training and practice, you can feel it. You can learn to read that energy and control it. 'Pushing hands' is just one of many tools that will enable you to do that."

"I wish I could do that with my business," Kurt mumbled.

"You can," Chou Li smiled. "You can do something like this with every aspect of your life. A business has energy. The only difference is that it's cumulative. It's a combination of the energy of everyone working there. Everyone, whether they contribute or detract."

Kurt listened attentively. That was the second time in two days someone insisted Kurt could fix his business if he really wanted to.

33

Energy

"You sound just like Robert," Kurt said, "the guy I started working out with this morning."

Chou Li smiled and tapped Kurt's shoulder playfully.

"Ah, your *sifu*," he said. "If I sound like him, or if he sounds like me, then one of us must be very wise."

Kurt laughed.

"I'm sure that's true," he said. "All this activity—the workout I had this morning, what we did here—it's definitely helping. I feel better; I feel like I'm thinking more clearly. But I'm still not sure what any of it has to do with my business. And that's why I started down this new path."

Chou Li sat down against the tree that Kurt had used earlier.

"What new path is that?" he asked.

Kurt started to answer, then looked at his watch again.

"I don't want to be rude, but I've really got to get back to the office. Perhaps another time."

Chou Li touched his chin thoughtfully. He looked at Kurt.

"Now is the only time any of us ever has. The only time we will ever have. So *now* is the best time to do anything."

"Who said that?" Kurt wondered. "Confucius?"

Chou Li laughed.

"No! It was Steve Mariucci. You know, of the 49ers? The football team? He was the head coach."

Kurt chuckled at his assumption. Chou Li looked inquisitive.

"Why not take a moment? Explain this new path to me. Why have you chosen it? Perhaps, sharing will help you achieve the clarity you are searching for."

Kurt shrugged. He collapsed into a seated position across from his new friend and then proceeded to weave for him the tapestry of strange events that led up to that very moment.

"Ah," Chou Li interjected. "It was destined that we meet today. That's good. You are on the right path, at least for the moment. You are seeking clarity. You are seeking peace."

"Maybe that's true," Kurt said. "But I still have questions."

"But questions are the beginning of wisdom," Chou Li smiled.

"A moment ago, you asked what any of this had to do with your business. It has everything to do with it, because it has everything to do with your life and, thus, the lives of everyone around you.

"We did *tuishou* together, right?"

Kurt nodded.

Chou Li continued, "In that exercise you discovered an energy flowing through your body and mine. As the owner of a business, its energy is a direct reflection of yours. Or, at least, it should be.

"If your energy is low, the energy of your business will be low. If your energy is strong and positive, so too will be the energy flowing through your company. So it is with negative energy as well.

"If you are not aware of yourself, it will be hard for you to understand how the business is affected by you. And, remember, your employees and even your clients are connected. All of their energies flow through the meridians of your company as well.

"Perhaps you need to engage your business in a little 'pushing hands' to see it more clearly, to understand it more deeply."

Kurt thought about it long and hard. He sighed in resignation.

"That sounds great in the abstract," Kurt said, "but how would I implement it? How the hell do you even attempt 'pushing hands' with a business? I don't get the analogy."

"I can offer you the tools," Chou Li said. "But you must do the work and make the repair. Take a rest now. Don't think too much. Let these thoughts put roots in the soil. Later something will grow."

Kurt closed his eyes and took another deep breath.

"Good idea," he said. "It's been a really full day, and it's barely half over."

"I am here every day at this time." Chou Li smiled. "I hope you will consider joining me again. I think more tai chi will help you find your center."

Suddenly, the old man sprang up out of his seated position with a grace and energy that belied his age. Kurt, for his part, struggled to get to his feet. He relied on the tree for a bit of balance.

All this talk of energy, Kurt thought, *and I can barely stand up.*

The old man bowed. Out of respect, Kurt responded.

Then, as he walked across the lawn toward the parking lot, Kurt realized that he was nowhere near as sore as he had been before he did the long Yang form with Chou Li.

He had more energy, positive energy, than he'd felt in a long time. As he imagined the difficult day that still lay ahead, he hoped that new positivity would be enough.

34

Be the Change...

Returning to the office was nowhere near as bad as Kurt thought it would be. Everyone was there ostensibly doing whatever it was they were supposed to be doing.

Instead of diving into the pile of paper on his desk, Kurt decided to see if he could feel the energy flowing through and from his business. He watched everyone as they went about their respective tasks. Could he sense their energy through their actions?

He started moving around the office looking and listening. Was the energy level high or was it low? Was it positive or negative? Was it centered? Was there a discernible flow?

Whatever it was, it certainly wasn't a 'high energy' environment. In fact, the way people were moving about confirmed his sense that things were more negative than positive.

Kurt left early that afternoon locked deep in thought. It was at least two-and-a-half hours before he normally headed for the door, but he was distracted. He knew he'd likely do more harm than good if he stayed.

He was beginning to realize just how out of balance his life had become, how he had sacrificed his family and personal time to a business that was unable to provide anything positive in return. Now he was anticipating a long, restless night with too much on his mind to get any sleep.

In the middle of everything he realized he had to drop off the rental car and stop at Mushin to pick up the Corvette with no idea how long the entire process would take.

A while later, as the rental car shuttle pulled into the Mushin parking lot to drop him off, Kurt's mind was still churning.

Allie was waiting for him; the Corvette was ready. He went over the inspection results and charges, paid, left a positive review, and started to make his way home.

Damn! It feels good to be behind the wheel of my own car again, he thought. *No. It feels great!*

As traffic eased up, Kurt started to 'play' with the Corvette. The performance was different, better actually. But what could Mushin have possibly have done that hadn't been done by the dealer or his previous mechanic?

Could this boost in performance be the injector wiring and the software update alone? Can two things make that much difference?

Rationally, the vehicle shouldn't have run any better than it had before the misfire occurred. But that didn't change the fact that it was different, at least to him.

By now, he had Mushin on speed dial; he gave them a call.

What if Robert could apply the same dynamic he applied to the Corvette to my business?

The phone was ringing.

Maybe, this guy really does understand how to fix my company. But, if he did know, why isn't he doing that for everyone? It would have to pay better than fixing cars. Wouldn't it?

While the phone was ringing, Kurt's mind bounced back and forth between confidence in Robert and doubt in himself.

"Good evening, this is Allie at Mushin Automotive. I can help you."

"Hi, Allie. This is Kurt with the Corvette again. I know I just left, but I have a question for Robert. Is he still there?"

"Sure is. Let me get him before he heads for the studio. Can I put you on hold for a second?"

"Certainly."

Kurt was concentrating on the traffic and the road ahead when he realized the same peaceful music that filled the shop was playing in the background on the phone. He wasn't sure exactly what it was, but he was starting to like it.

"Hi, Kurt. Robert here. Miss me already, or have you changed your mind about attending class?"

"None of the above actually," Kurt smiled. "But I do have a question for you."

"Go for it."

"What did you do to my Corvette? It's performing better than when it was brand new. Better than when I first had it modified and 'chipped'!"

Robert laughed.

"We did the same thing to your vehicle's computer," he said, "that I hope to do for you and your business—we re-programmed it with the latest performance updates.

"You know how your computer at home automatically installs software upgrades to improve its performance? Well, that's exactly what we did for your Corvette. We tuned it up without having to change a part. Isn't technology cool?"

Kurt was quiet for a moment.

"What did you mean," he said, "this is the same thing you were hoping to do for me and my business? Are you saying there's a software 'fix' for people and companies?"

"You know," Robert replied, "I think you're starting to get it.

"There isn't a software fix, but there is a kind of re-engineering we can attempt by changing the program. And if you change the program, the operating system, you change everything."

"Have you ever given anyone a straight answer?" Kurt asked.

"That would depend on how you define straight," Robert said. "Now, if you'll excuse me, I have a class to teach."

Kurt said good-bye and ended the call. He continued down the freeway towards home.

‡

Kurt was so lost in his own thoughts he was almost home before he realized he had one more stop to make; the local pet store where he purchased his pet supplies. He turned around, headed back to the store and, twenty minutes later, found himself standing in front of the car trying to figure out exactly how he was going to fit his new, aluminum, rodent-proof container—and a forty-pound bag of kibbles—into the Corvette.

He dropped the top, placed the container on the passenger seat, secured it with the seat belt, then stowed the dog food in the trunk.

A short time later, he was relieved to finally find himself on his own street. Kurt made the right turn into his driveway, opened the automatic garage door, and put the Corvette to bed for the night.

He winced as he struggled to get out of the seat.

Damn, I forgot to tell Laurie I was coming home early. Not good.

He put the aluminum container down and filled it with food from the old plastic bin and the contents of the new bag he'd just purchased. That was when he noticed the damage the rodents had done to both the plastic container and the bag that had been placed within it. He took a long, deep breath.

One less potential crisis to deal with!

When he was finished he walked to the utility room door and punched the garage door button. As the big door rattled, Kurt glanced back to ensure it had actually closed, then he walked inside.

Laurie was standing in the kitchen staring back at him. She looked as if she'd just seen a ghost. Thankfully, she hadn't heard the racket he was making as he squared Ranger's pantry away. Now all he had to do was figure out how he was going to tell her that uninvited guests had taken up residency in their garage without her calling a realtor.

"What are you doing home?" she asked. "Is everything okay?"

She wiped her hands on a towel tucked into her apron, then moved toward Kurt—feeling his head with the back of her hand.

"You don't seem to have a fever. What's going on?"

Kurt tilted his head and stared at her.

"This is worse than I thought," he said. "I come home on time and you think I'm sick. Boy, have I screwed things up."

Laurie took a step back from her husband, reflecting on his comment, but before she could respond Max and AJ came flying in from the family room. The only thing on their minds was that Daddy was home, home before dinner.

Kurt explained to his wife that he wasn't sick. In fact everything was better than okay. He was home early because he wanted to be home early. It was a conscious decision to change his current reality. The first step in moving from where he was to where he knew he needed to be.

He remembered a quote he'd seen somewhere: 'Be the change you wish to see in the world'. And, for the first time, it made sense. If you want a better life, do what you have to do to make your life better.

Laurie stopped what she was doing and created an entirely different menu for dinner that evening. Kurt played with the kids until the meal was ready, they all ate together, then everyone pitched in to clean up. After dinner, it was playtime, a little bit of TV, a couple of storybooks, and off to bed.

Kurt gently closed the door to AJ's room and headed toward the master bedroom.

What a great evening, he thought. *This is what it's all about.*

As he entered, Laurie was in the bathroom in front of the mirror taking her makeup off. He was smiling when she caught his eye.

"Are you sure you're okay?" she quipped.

"Yeah! I'm sure. Why do you keep asking me that?"

"Because you're smiling and you don't do that very much anymore."

Kurt looked at her kind of surprised. Then started to remove his shirt. It was a long-sleeve pullover that had hidden his arms and upper body until that very moment.

Laurie gasped.

She walked over to him, and with great care reached out to touch the welts on her husband's forearms. He did everything he could to minimize how sensitive those bruises were.

"Oh, my God," she gasped. "What happened to you?"

Kurt recounted the day's events. Working out at the school with Robert, then at the park with Chou Li. He told her that he realized things could not continue the way they were. He explained that he'd experienced an epiphany and, from that morning on, things were going to be better.

He would do whatever it took to make it all happen. Only this time, his efforts would be laser-focused. He wouldn't quit until everyone agreed things had changed—changed for the better.

35

Power

The alarm went off at four in the morning and, much to Kurt's surprise, he felt good—better than he had in a long time. Better than he thought he would.

He placed his feet down on the floor, preparing to traverse the minefield of his kid's toys on his way to the bathroom. He thought about Max and AJ for a moment and smiled. He made it across the floor without incident and closed the bathroom door behind him.

He had figured it out: the secret was shuffling. Never raising your feet off the floor.

Kurt turned on the light and looked in the mirror.

There's a lot to be said for exhaustion.

He took a second look and noticed something else. Something that hadn't been there a few days before. An intensity, a fire.

He smiled. He liked what he saw. Then he proceeded to wash up and get ready.

Kurt arrived at the studio early, put his 'civilian' clothes away, set his protective gear against the wall, and bowed onto the wooden floor. He began warming up by stretching slowly and deliberately. His whole body was tight and he didn't want to pull a muscle or do anything that would interfere with this new odyssey he'd embarked upon. When he was satisfied he was loose enough, he got up and practiced the salute until class was ready to start.

He still felt awkward and uncoordinated, but he was committed to giving these new rituals all the time they needed.

Robert bowed onto the studio floor and headed directly for Kurt. Robert bowed to him, and Kurt responded in kind.

"Come," Robert said.

They walked to a far corner of the room.

"It looked like you were having fun out there," Robert said. "Were you? I hope so. Do you know where the energy you tapped into comes from? It comes from your center, the *xià dāntián*."

"I remember," Kurt said, "You said the Chinese call it the 'golden stove.'"

"Exactly. The place from which all your power originates, both internal and external. Energy resides here," Robert pointed to a place just below his navel, "until it's needed.

"We believe this energy travels from the *xià dāntián,* through the body, before being projected outward through a kick or a strike, a block or a counter.

"But, to maximize this energy, you must consider the mechanics of your body. How you move; how you make a fist; how you kick. Every detail is critically important. Repetition is good. Practice is important, but only if it's perfect practice."

Kurt tentatively held up a hand. "Perfect practice, *sensei*? I just started. I'm a long way from perfect."

"Don't get stuck on semantics," Robert said. "To maximize your power, every aspect of body, mind, and spirit must be in concert; your execution must be flawless.

"This applies no matter what your level of mastery is. That means ensuring your practice is perfect. That your technique is as good as you are capable of making it.

"To accomplish perfect practice, you must take movements that are not natural to you and make them natural. You will need to practice diligently until what feels strange today starts to feel natural tomorrow.

"This is true for what happens here in the studio, for what happens in life, and especially for what happens in your business.

"Whether you realize or not, Kerrigan Construction is the aggregate of thousands of individual actions—many of which are not natural—executed by different individuals who come from different backgrounds. They are woven together into an intricate tapestry and need to be executed perfectly every time service is rendered. That is, if you want the company to be successful."

Robert stopped and smiled. He bowed, and walked off the floor.

Looking Back

Robert sat erect and cross-legged at the center of the studio's floor, hands resting on his knees, palms up, with thumb and index finger on each hand all but touching. This was *his* time. Time to reflect, to meditate; time for a mindful moment.

It was the end of the day. The final class was over. The studio was clean, and all the students and instructors were headed home. Now it was just Robert, in the moment, sitting on the hardwood floor, trying to remain centered.

He was having difficulty letting go—something was poking at him, interrupting his measured breathing. Sitting meditation wasn't working, so he uncrossed his legs, got up, and walked to the altar at the front of the room. He knelt and bowed in front of the image of his master.

Robert lit a stick of incense, walked to the corner of the room, and took up his *bō*—an intricately carved, six-foot long, black walnut staff. He went back to the center of the floor and initiated a traditional series of movements, called *bō kata,* to demonstrate the weapon. Of the six basic patterns, he picked his favorite, *shushi no kon*, and performed it three times in succession.

Robert's first execution was slow and deliberate, with emphasis on breath control, power, and form. His second time through was focused on speed, the ability to fly through the movements while remaining in complete control of the heavy wooden staff.

On the final run-through, Robert's movements approximated what he liked to call 'combat mode'. Anyone watching would have sworn they could actually see the adversaries that surrounded him as they attacked and were systematically vanquished.

When he finished the practice he bowed, placed the staff back in the corner, and proceeded to work his way through the school's first four black belt forms. Then, he finished with the Yang long form of tai chi. First as if it was a combat practice and, then, as slowly and deliberately as he was able.

When Robert was done, he bowed off the floor, and headed for the showers. He was physically and emotionally spent. It had been a long day and he still hadn't found the peace he was searching for.

Later that evening, as he lay in bed, he replayed the past few day's events over again in his mind—first the shop, then the studio.

There was something gnawing away at him and no matter how hard he tried he couldn't make out what it was. He finally resolved to let it go, knowing that—the moment he released it—whatever it was that was bothering him would reveal itself.

His mind emptied.

It was Kurt.

Kurt sitting at the table in the employee lounge recounting what a difficult time he was having at work. Kurt sharing the problems he was having at home.

Robert could see and hear him as clearly as if the conversation was taking place once more. Only, this time in his bedroom.

He could relate all too well. He'd been through the same painful, work-related trauma. And it didn't take much for those memories to bubble back to the surface of his conscious mind.

Robert had gone out on his own in much the same way Kurt had. He found his initial success almost too easily as well.

Although, not a born natural, Robert was a great mechanic. He worked hard to be the best technician he could be. He went to all the clinics and seminars; attended off-site training when it was available; and mortgaged his soul to the tool truck drivers, and the firms they represented, for the best tools and latest technology.

In the beginning, being the 'best tech' around was good enough to ensure survival. It provided him the hint of a successful future and soon his little company was no longer just a one-man operation.

With that growth came the added responsibilities of employees, leadership, and administration. Robert remembered how woefully unprepared he was to have other human beings depend upon him for their livelihood, how personally courageous it was for them to trust him when he had no idea what the hell he was doing.

It was amazing that despite the anger and anxiety, the frustration and drama—despite his ignorance of what perils would accompany a journey like this—it all worked out.

But Robert approached running a company as he approached everything else in his life: he put his head down and pushed through it. He learned everything he could about the business of being in business.

When cash was tight, he would put it on one of the many credit cards he had stuffed into his wallet. It was a financial sacrifice he sensed was important. Resources he knew he had to dedicate, whether or not the business could afford them. Resources necessary for his future, and the future of everyone depending upon him.

Then he reflected on the important role that his Margie had played in all of it.

37

Margie

Robert smiled to himself. It was never hard to imagine Margie's face when he was lying in bed with his eyes closed.

They met when both of them were kids and knew almost instantly they were going to be together for the rest of their lives.

She was beautiful and funny; never allowing Robert to take himself or anyone else too seriously. Not 'tell-a-joke' funny, or the kind of funny that needs a prat-fall. She was observational-comedy funny—a wry kind of wit that pointed out the humor in just about everything around you.

And there wasn't a day they were together that Robert didn't wonder why someone that incredible would chose him. Especially when the 'him' she chose had no idea where he was headed or what life might have in store for the two of them.

Yet she was by his side when he decided to become the best automotive repair technician he could be, even though they both realized that decision—and the limited financial reward it implied—would have far-reaching consequences. Even when it meant there would be endless compromise and sacrifice.

Margie was there when he discovered his love for the martial arts and accepted the commitment in time and energy that would follow. She cared for the bruises and broken bones that seemed to accompany his normal practice and almost every tournament.

She was there when they took every penny out of their meager savings (and helped him borrow more), so that Robert could go out on his own. And, a few years later, she left her own career to help out in Mushin's office.

She was there, after that initial rush of success, when they were on the brink of losing everything. Margie stood by his side as they searched for help and a new way forward.

Together, they joined The Training Institute, a business coaching and consulting company that helped them, coached them through the transformation that was needed to rescue Mushin.

They were there, side by side, every Thursday for the hour-long coaching calls and for every meeting and hard decision that came after. It wasn't easy. But in the end, the business became everything they both dreamed it could be.

They saved the company and, with it, saved their 'family' of dedicated employees.

It was the only family Robert and Margie knew.

They'd tried to have children, almost from the moment they were married. They tried everything. Spent more than the cost of (what could have been) a few really nice vacations with no luck. Ultimately, the pain and disappointment was too much for either of them to bear.

So the Mushin employees became their 'kids' and they became the parents anyone would love to have: caring, generous, and wise. And unbending when it came to honesty, integrity, and character.

Margie was at the shop until the doctors told her it wasn't wise for her to be there any longer. She shouldn't expose herself to the chemicals and carcinogens. She shouldn't invite that kind of stress into her life. In fact, they said, it wasn't wise for her to work at all. Certainly, not while she was going through radiation treatments and chemotherapy.

After Margie passed, Robert was lost. The pain was exquisite, sharp, and never absent. Everywhere he looked, he could feel her presence. The pain was unbearable.

A black shroud fell over him and took its toll on the business. It was noticeable to anyone who cared enough to look, obvious to everyone at the *dojo* where he trained.

Late one evening, his *sensei* appeared at the house. The door was ajar, the living room dark. He came into the bedroom and pulled Robert, still in his work clothes, out from under the comforter.

"God dammit, Margie is gone!" he yelled, shaking Robert violently.

Robert looked away, ashamed to meet his master's gaze.

"There's nothing any of us can do," he continued. "You've lost her and all you've got left are the memories you both made. But that's all any of us have, isn't it?

"You buried you wife and no one who hasn't gone through that can have any idea what that's like. But, you gotta forgive me here, Robert… That hole was only big enough for one casket.

"She's gone, but you're still on this side of the grass.

"It just plain hurts to see a man with your fighting spirit crawl up into a ball and wait to die. It kills me to see you give up."

Robert sat down on the edge of the bed. He tried to bury his face in his hands as his teacher towered above him.

"How does this honor Margie? What would she say? I didn't know your wife all that well, but I can sure hear her tell you to quit feeling sorry for yourself, and start living again."

Robert bit down hard as he looked at his *sensei*. Maybe it was hearing someone else utter Margie's name, but suddenly the rage he had suppressed throughout her illness bubbled to the surface. His *sensei* sensed the change in Robert's demeanor instantly.

"Oh, you're angry now, huh?" he challenged. "You wanna throw me out? Go ahead. Give it a try. But you need to know I'm not leaving without a fight."

Robert frowned for a moment, then started laughing. When he looked at his master, tears were forming in the corners of his eyes.

"You will never know how close I came to throwing you out of my house just now. Or at least trying."

Robert winced, thinking about what the two of them could have done to his home, how long it would have taken to clean up the debris—the broken furniture, Margie's antique tea cups and saucers, every picture frame and shattered memory.

After that night, he didn't stop mourning; he couldn't. But he did re-engage. Robert committed himself to Margie's memory in everything he did, to everything that was important to her. He continued to treat each of his employees like they were family.

After he opened the studio in the alley behind the shop, he expanded his family to include any student, young or old, who needed an extra father or grandfather in their life.

Perhaps that was why he decided—almost immediately, and without really thinking about it—that he was going to help Kurt, if he could. If Kurt would let him.

He knew it made no sense, especially for a complete stranger. But he kept asking himself what he would do if he and Margie had been able to start a family of their own. What if one of *their* kids had come to them with the same frustration and anxiety that he observed in Kurt.

Kurt was fighting for his life, and that of his family. It sounded to Robert like Kurt knew what he was in the process of losing.

These were battles that Robert was all too familiar with, battles he'd fought and won. Victories that had come at great cost.

If he could help Kurt and didn't, what would that say about him and his values? If he could help and didn't, how would that honor Margie's memory?

Robert sat up in bed. He shook off the memories and opened his eyes. Outside the night was clear; the moon was nearly full and shone in through the bedroom window. He propped himself up on one elbow.

This is something I have to do, he thought. *Something I want to do. The only thing that can stop me from doing it successfully is Kurt quitting. And I'm not about to let that happen.*

38

Looking Forward

Kurt lay in bed, staring at the ceiling. He could barely make out the tiny motes of reflected light as they floated—illuminated by the street light out front—near the shuttered windows.

He heard Laurie's measured breathing and sensed, rather than saw, the covers as they moved up and down. He couldn't ignore the scent of her being so close. He could barely resist the urge to reach out, to wake and hold her. But he didn't.

The day before he'd shared his experience about Robert and Mushin Automotive with Laurie. He promised her things would be better. He explained why it would be different. She accepted his explanation and agreed they should move forward. After all, as crazy as the story might seem, what other options were there?

Yet he knew, even as he made that promise, he had no idea if he could actually keep his word. He perceived Laurie's skepticism and felt her still drawing away from him.

He'd reconciled himself to the fact the business might be lost. He'd already tried everything he could think of to keep it alive.

He'd gone to countless management clinics and seminars, meetings and business 'boot camps'. The results were always the same. The majority of them were filled with fluff and just enough real information to peak a person's curiosity. Always with the promise of more, if only you 'signed up'. If only you acted on their 'limited time only, special offer' that afternoon.

Lots of fluff, lots of pressure. But very little substance.

Kurt had even hired an expensive consultant to analyze the place. Someone to tell him what was broken, and what needed to be fixed. After endless meetings with the guy and hundreds of pointless questions, he received a very polished, very professional brief illuminating everything Kurt already knew needed fixing.

That's when he remembered what his Uncle Bob had told him when he was a kid. Bob was the proverbial 'rich uncle' every family seems to have, the one who'd been successful for as long as anyone could remember.

It was some kind of holiday; Kurt couldn't remember which one. But he remembered sitting at the table with the grown-ups. Everyone was there, including all of Kurt's cousins, hanging onto Uncle Bob's every word.

"Be wary of consultants," he said. "They're almost never worth what you have to pay 'em!"

Bob took off his expensive watch and dropped it on the table for dramatic effect—ensuring every eye was pointed directly at him.

"Ya' see, hiring a consultant is like loaning a guy your watch and then allowing him to charge you for telling you what time it is."

Everyone laughed, even Kurt. And he accepted his rich uncle's words as the wisdom of his elders, a life lesson he carried with him ever since. A lesson he failed to follow.

Now, as an adult, he was struggling. Looking for answers everywhere and anywhere. He'd even collected a few books on leadership theory. But, even when their content was excellent and inspiring, they never showed you how to get the results they promised were just around the corner. Even when they helped him understand what was wrong and *what* needed to be done, they never showed *how* to get it done.

Not one of them provided you with a road map. None of those books mentioned the courage you would need to get from where you were to where you needed to be.

Slowly, Kurt was moving from being hopeful to desperate, from desperation to despondency. Now his family was in jeopardy—his marriage and his kids. That was an entirely different issue.

I could always go back to pounding nails, he thought.

I could strap the bags back on and start the whole thing all over. But Laurie couldn't take that. Where the hell would I find another woman like her? What about the kids? What about Max and AJ?

Kurt couldn't deal with the thought of losing her. And, as impossible as that might have been, the thought of not having his kids close to him—physically close—was worse. It was driving him over the edge.

He tried to calm down. He tried to lay there quietly, but his mind keep dragging him back to a particularly animated argument he and Laurie had the other night.

Not an animated argument, he thought. *A battle royale.*

It was a battle that ended with Laurie storming out of the room and him sitting alone at the kitchen table wondering what had just happened. He sat there realizing that every time he thought they had reached an agreement, every time he was sure Laurie understood, it turned out he was the only one who got it.

The real problem was she was almost always right. The real problem was it was Kurt who didn't understand; he didn't get it because he really didn't want to.

Kurt remembered how he had slipped out from underneath the covers, and headed to the bathroom. He stopped when he heard voices coming from down the hallway. He changed direction and poked his head out of the master bedroom.

The voices emanated from Max's bedroom. His door was barely open, but Kurt could tell it was his son. Max was trying to console his little sister who must have slipped out of her room and into her brother's bed. Max was whispering to her as only a big brother that age could.

AJ was whimpering, but Kurt could still make out Max's words.

"Don't cry, AJ," he said. "It's gonna be okay, I promise. We just gotta be better.

"We gotta be good and not make Mommy and Daddy angry anymore. If we listen to them and don't fight. If we clean up our messes and eat our meals without a fuss, Mommy and Daddy will stop fighting. You'll see."

AJ stopped sobbing. She tried to catch her breath as she listened.

"Don't be frightened," Max continued. "Don't cry. I'm here, and I'll take care of us. I won't let anything bad happen. I promise."

Kurt remembered the rush of emotion that crashed over him as he listened in the hallway. The pride he felt in his 'little man' and the shame he felt for allowing Max to feel like it was their fault, the kids' fault, that he and Laurie were fighting.

It wasn't his son's responsibility to take care of the family. It was his. Kurt could feel all his doubts and insecurities roil to the surface as he contemplated what had just happened.

Nothing is going to destroy my marriage. Nothing.

Nothing is going to take me away from my kids. Nothing.

I'm not going to let it happen. Not now. Not ever.

Thinking about the incident in the present still gave Kurt chills. There was only one way to solve this: focus on the company.

Nothing is going to stop me from fixing my business. Nothing.

If Robert and Mushin are the answer, I'll do whatever I have to, whatever he says, if that's what it will take to make things right.

Kurt had never been so angry at himself for letting things get this far. He wasn't yet certain that things were going to be okay just because of the new relationship he was forging with Robert.

But, then again, he'd never been this desperate before either.

Force Versus Impact

It was morning again and he was back in the studio. Morning and another workout. Kurt was ready, ready to take on any challenge.

Up front, Allie and Jason were leading the class. Gender aside, the two could not have been more different. Allie was tall and slender with a dancer's kind of athletic build. Jason looked pretty much like what he actually was: a big ol' country boy. He was well over six feet and what you might describe as just plain large.

But on the studio's polished wood floor, it was different. On the floor Jason was lightning fast and far more agile than anyone his size ought to be. Faster and exponentially more powerful than any human being Kurt had ever seen.

As Jason stood in front leading the group, Allie walked up and down the lines—fine-tuning each student's movement by adjusting the angle of their hips or wrist. She helped by positioning where each foot was planted, setting its direction. She attended to every detail without uttering a single word.

Kurt had once heard coaching described as 'gentle correction,' and this was as gentle as anything he had witnessed. When Allie reached him, she bowed and then pointed to the corner of the studio. The two quietly padded over to the area she'd indicated.

"The body is capable of producing great force," she whispered. "More than you can imagine. But that force is meaningless if not directed. It must harnessed and then focused.

"The reason you're here is to learn the connection between life and art, the difference between force and impact. This is as important for your business as it is for you and your life."

Kurt nodded politely.

"You are bigger than I am," Allie continued. "Taller, broader, heavier. Stronger and more powerful. I am smaller than you are. That is the physical reality of things."

She motioned Kurt over to a 100-pound heavy bag suspended from a beam in the ceiling by a heavy metal chain.

"Let me show you something that will be easier to experience than it is to explain." She pointed to the bag.

"Punch it with all your strength, all the force you can. Now!"

Kurt punched the bag as hard as he could. He put everything he had into it, enough for his wrist to cry out in protest.

The bag barely moved.

"Was that everything you were capable of?" she asked. "Let's try again. Only this time let me help you by changing how you use your body to help direct that force."

Allie reached her arm out toward the heavy bag.

"Measure the distance to the bag with your arm extended and your fingers outstretched. Then close your fingers into a fist and move a half-step closer. Imagine your fist inside the bag up to your wrist if the bag was pliable, something easily penetrated."

She gestured down to her feet.

"Stand like I am," Allie said. "Left foot forward, right foot slightly behind, pointed outward just a bit. Both feet about shoulder width apart."

Kurt followed her instructions carefully.

"Bend your legs slightly, and drop your center. Keep your body upright. Use your toes to root yourself to the floor."

Kurt did his best to find the posture, but he felt rigid, unnatural.

"Breathe," she said calmly. "Slowly and deliberately. In through your nose. Out through your mouth. Relax.

"I want your shoulders over your hips with both directly facing the bag. Your right fist just above your right hip, fingers curled, locked in place by your thumb and facing the ceiling like this."

With quick guiding touches, Allie placed Kurt's arms and hands in the position she was describing.

"When I say 'now', I want you to bring that punch from your hip to the bag—moving your arm and wrist, so your fingers are facing the floor when you connect. I want the bones in your hand in perfect alignment with the bones in your forearm. Make contact with your first two knuckles flat against the bag.

"Do all that while shifting your weight on the ball of your left foot and pivoting your hip and body mass behind the punch. Understand? Let me show you."

Allie set herself in front of the bag, demonstrating each of the body dynamics she described. She centered herself. Took a couple of cleansing breaths and exploded into a forward twisting punch that visibly folded the bag almost in half.

The sound was deafening. Part of it was her *kiai*, the loud shout that accompanied the punch. But a big part of it was the explosion of force that caused the bag to dance on its chain. Kurt stood there staring, wide-eyed.

Now that was impressive, he thought.

"Okay," Allie commanded, "now you!"

Kurt positioned himself in front of the bag.

Feet here, he thought. *Hips here, fist here, breathe.*

There were so many different parts of his body to focus on.

"Too much mind," he mumbled under his breath.

Kurt grimaced as he realized he'd spoken those words out loud.

"Relax, Mr. Kerrigan," Allie smiled. "There's a lot to think about while on the road to not having to think about any of it at all."

Kurt took a deep breath. Allie pointed at the bag.

"Now," she said quietly.

Kurt tried to keep everything straight in his mind. He arranged his body and threw everything he had into the punch.

He could feel the difference. He could see it in the way the bag moved in response to his effort. It danced back and forth, up and down, on its heavy chain. Allie smiled proudly.

"That's the difference," she said, "between force and impact. You're the same physically—the same height and weight. Perhaps even the same strength. But, with your energy focused, the impact is multiplied exponentially because of how and where it's applied."

"That's amazing," Kurt said. "I was expending all that effort and getting nothing back in return. But just a few changes, and—"

"You get the result you want," Allie finished his thought. "The result you expect. The result you demand."

"What about my company?" Kurt asked. "Can the same principles be applied there? I feel like there's a ton of places where I'm directing lots of energy with little or no impact."

"I know Mr. Taylor is helping you with that," Allie said. "This is probably a good subject for you to explore with him. But, in the meantime, think about those examples where you're working harder, but not getting the result you're looking for. What do you think you can do to change that?"

Allie scanned the room quickly. Her eyes returned to Kurt.

"I think Mr. Taylor can help you, and I don't think it should wait. I'll tell him you need to speak with him."

40

A Compass...

Kurt was uncharacteristically apprehensive about talking to Robert. There was something in Allie's voice, in her demeanor, that caught him off guard as he stood there in the studio.

What's so important, he wondered, *so urgent that it can't wait? What am I doing wrong?*

Kurt spent the rest of the day trying to quiet his anxiety. He had been unsuccessful trying to implement any positive change at the office in the past. What was going to make these new attempts any different? Besides that, the thought of an imminent conversation with Robert revolving around some unknown topic was terrifying to him this early in his training.

Kurt was so troubled and concerned that, on his way home, he called Laurie. She was doing great as always, and that energy flowed through the phone. Maybe that's why, quite often, all it took to calm him down was the sound of her voice.

Sometimes I think that talking me off the ledge is the most critical part of her job description.

"Listen," she said, "there isn't anything you can do until you speak to Robert, right? So what's the point of working yourself into a frenzy over this? It could be nothing.

"What have you started telling us when things start spinning out of control? Isn't it: 'take a deep breath; in through your nose; out through your mouth' or something like that? So do that. Breathe."

Kurt took her advice and managed to remain calm, not just for the rest of the drive home, but for the rest of the evening.

Laurie had been acting different since he made the commitment to Mushin, since he started spending his lunch hours with Chou Li. She was positive, more supportive.

I have no idea why, he thought, *but I'm happy things are moving in the right direction.*

From Laurie's perspective, the reason for her change in behavior was obvious: it was Kurt. The recent turnaround in his attitude and behavior had been profound. After a long and painful absence, the man she fell in love with had re-emerged.

Kurt was more patient with her, more affectionate with the kids. He seemed to be more centered, less likely to fly off the handle. He listened better, and—at least according to his reports—things were starting to get better at the office.

Ironically, despite the time he was spending at the park and at Mushin, he was still physically at the office more than he'd been in a long time. In fact, he was not just physically present, but present in every sense of the word.

That night as Kurt got into to bed, he felt Laurie shift herself toward him. She snuggled under his arm and placed a hand over his heart. He kissed her softly on the forehead and fell asleep.

‡

After the morning workout, Robert walked over to Kurt.

"Morning," he said, "Allie told me that we should talk."

Kurt nodded, trying to quell the apprehension he felt inside.

"If you have a few minutes," Robert continued. "We can shoot over to the shop and catch up."

"I'd like that," Kurt said. Then he held up his hand.

"Just give me a minute? I should let them know I'm going to be a little late at work."

Robert nodded and headed out the door. Kurt walked out to the alley between Mushin and the studio. It was early, and the sun felt especially good on Kurt's face.

Not too hot. Not too cool. Another perfect October morning.

He pulled out his phone, and hit the speed dial for Kerrigan Construction.

"Hi, Rocky. It's Kurt. Can you put me through to Rick?"

"Sure thing, boss," Rochelle said cheerfully. "Let me put you on hold while I track him down."

Kurt cringed as cheesy, canned music played during the on-hold message. The prerecorded voiceover was awful. In fact, the message had nothing at all to do with who they were as an organization—nothing to do with their 'why', or who they wanted to become.

Note to self, he thought, *move changing the on-hold message higher up on the to-do list.*

"Hey, Kurt," Rick appeared on the end of the line. "What's up? How was the workout?"

"Workout was great. Listen, Rick, I'm going to be a few minutes late this morning. Maybe, more. I've got an unscheduled meeting with Robert that just came up, and I think it's going to turn out to be important. So keep things together for me until I get in, okay?"

"Sure," Rick said. "Can you do me a favor as long as you're there? Could you thank Robert and his staff for me?"

"Thank them?"

"Absolutely. Since we started taking our vehicles to Mushin we haven't had a single breakdown. And those inspections he printed for us, and the Morning Pre-Checks, are incredible. Now the drivers know exactly what to check before they leave the lot, and the guys are actually doing it."

"That's great to know," Kurt said. "I'll certainly tell him."

He finished up with Rick and headed across the alley to the shop. It was the first time he'd entered Robert's private office, and it wasn't at all what he had expected.

What an unusual place. Although, I guess that shouldn't really surprise me.

The room was filled with an eclectic collection of hot rod and stock car racing trophies, zen calligraphy, martial arts weapons, and books. Lots of books. To Kurt's mind, it was the most extensive collection on Eastern philosophy and martial arts history that he'd ever seen.

Robert was sitting quietly behind his desk moving a short, flat, three-inch diameter brass cylinder back and forth in front of him. Kurt couldn't see what it was until he sat down. Once seated, it was obvious the object was some type of antique compass.

"Know what this is?" Robert asked.

"A compass," Kurt responded.

"Correct," Robert smiled. "Know what it's for?"

Kurt took a deep breath.

It was going to be one of 'those' conversations, a talk made up almost entirely of questions, with Kurt stuck fumbling for the right answers. A literal minefield of ambiguity as far as Kurt was concerned.

"To help you find your way when you're lost?" Kurt asked.

Only after he said it did he realize how tentative he sounded.

"That's only partially correct," Robert said. "A compass can help you find your way and may even help prevent you from getting lost. But, the real answer has to do with how it does what it does.

"A compass fulfills its purpose by always pointing north. If you never lose track of north, you know exactly where each of the other points on the compass are."

Robert held the antique object admiringly in his hand.

"Do you have a compass for your business?" he asked. "I don't think we've talked about that yet, have we?"

"We haven't," Kurt replied. "How would a compass help?"

"It can help your business," Robert smiled, "and your personal life, too. But I don't necessarily mean the kind I have in my hand."

Robert set the compass back down on the desk.

"I'm talking about a moral compass, one that points the way to your better self. A compass that helps you move through the world in concert with your principles. Something by which you can measure every decision you make.

"In your marriage, the compass is the vows you exchanged.

"In business, it's a Strategic Plan—a document that helps point the way toward your vision. It ensures that your objectives and goals are consistent with that vision, and ultimately that all your actions are guided by your principles, your moral compass.

"The Strategic Plan is a road map created to help you, and your leadership team, prioritize the objectives necessary to accomplish your vision. It reminds everyone in the company of what needs to happen to maintain a competitive advantage—what differentiates your enterprise from everyone else who does what you do.

"A Strategic Plan has a lot in common with the experience you're having at the studio. You're on a journey. And, for the journey to be successful, you need three things."

Kurt found himself leaning forward in his seat.

"You need to know where you are: a starting point. You need to know where you're going: a destination. And you need to have an idea of how you're going to get there. That's the plan, your compass.

"In the case of the studio, our compass is the curriculum we've built over the years to see that our students progress as quickly as possible. It is every step we know you will need to take in order to achieve mastery, mastery over yourself and over the art.

"In the operation of a business—your business, my business, any business—it's no different. Starting point, destination, plan."

"Starting point, destination, plan." Kurt repeated.

Robert nodded and continued, "You can have goals without a plan. Unfortunately, there are too many businesses that function that way. Without a plan, there's no compass; no way to ensure you're moving in the right direction.

"I've seen small business owners confuse strategy with tactics. They bounce around from one inadequate action to the next, never understanding why they aren't achieving the results that others have. I'm willing to bet you've done that yourself."

"Sure," Kurt agreed. "We tried to focus on our web presence, thinking that was the answer. The result was increased traffic, but there was no increase in our bottom line. In fact, it actually went down."

"Exactly," Robert said. "You lost focus. You have to focus on the bottom line, right? Boom! When the bottom line goes up, what happens? Your customer satisfaction can go straight to hell. No matter which end of the balloon you squeeze, the other end falls away out of your control. It's an endless cycle.

"If you don't have a plan or if the one you have is misguided or out of date, you'll never achieve the results you're looking for. Certainly, not the results your business is capable of.

"Without a Strategic Plan, you will bounce from one inadequate solution to another. You may see some progress, but it won't be the kind of permanent, lasting success you're looking for."

Robert stopped and locked eyes with Kurt.

"A plan helps you focus. It turns blunt force into impact.

"Do you have such a plan?" he asked. "Do you have a compass? Because, without one, all the measurement and management in the world won't get your company where you want it or need it to be."

Robert pushed the compass across the desk. Kurt's eyes lit up.

"If you didn't have one before," he said, "you have one now."

Measurements... and, Progress

Weeks turned into months, with Kurt at the studio almost every morning. Even when it was impossible for him to be there for the first workout of the day, he always managed to make one of the two evening classes that night.

He was as dedicated as any student had ever been, but he was a little anxious about the progress he was making with the business.

Late on a Tuesday night, after the last class had bowed out and formal instruction had ended, Robert approached him. It was the first time in weeks. Kurt was on his knees cleaning and polishing the hardwood floor with several other students when he felt his master's presence behind him.

"If you have a few minutes," Robert said, "stop by the office before you leave. I'd like to catch up."

'If I have a few minutes?' Thought Kurt. *I've been waiting to talk to him for more than three months.*

Kurt started polishing more intensely, anxious to finish the job. Then another student kindly said she could take over. Kurt bowed off the floor, took a quick shower, and jogged across the alley to knock on the door of Robert's private office. Kurt bowed as the door opened and his teacher returned the courtesy.

"How are you doing?" Robert asked. "It's been a while."

Kurt took one of the two chairs strategically placed across the desk from where Robert was seated.

"It has, *sensei*," Kurt said. "Frankly, I was trying to be patient, knowing the opportunity to speak with you would happen when it was supposed to."

"Let's start with your training and how you think that's going," Robert said matter-of-factly. "What are your thoughts?"

"I think I'm doing well overall," Kurt replied. "I'm not sore all the time anymore. I have more energy than I've had in years. I can move around with more flexibility."

"And the forms we practice are starting to make sense. They aren't as impossible as they were at first. In fact, of all the things I'm learning, I feel the most centered doing the forms."

"Overall, I'd say I'm doing okay," Kurt shrugged a bit uncertain.

Robert looked hard into Kurt's eyes for a very long time.

"You're doing better than just 'okay', Kurt," Robert said. "Your practice is dedicated, disciplined, and determined. All the D-words we spoke about when we first met."

Kurt shifted in his seat, the slightest evidence of a smile building in the corner of his mouth.

"Overall, you're making fantastic progress," Robert continued. "Better progress than we've seen anyone make in a very long time. But there is something I find interesting.

"Most of what we teach here, especially in the beginning is considered 'hard style'; the movements are linear in nature. We find most new students exaggerate the nature of these first exercises to the point that they're choppy—disjointed, with no continuity.

"As practice continues over time, hard styles tend to become softer, just as the more circular, Chinese martial arts styles—soft styles—harden and become more direct.

"Your progress has been accelerated somehow. It's almost as if you studied a Chinese martial art before you ever got here. But, when we met, you told me that you'd never studied anythin—"

Kurt raised his hand sheepishly.

"I'm so sorry, *sensei*," he said. "I should have said something sooner, but I didn't think it would make any difference."

Robert leaned forward with interest. "Go on," he said.

"I met this gentleman at a park," Kurt continued. "It was after I started working out here. The same day, in fact. His name is Chou Li and he leads a tai chi class there just about every day. I've been taking an early lunch to get out of the office. I practice with him; I'm learning the long Yang form. It helps calm me down."

Kurt bowed his head.

"I'll stop, if you don't think it's a good idea. I didn't mean to confuse things or corrupt my practice in any way."

"Corrupt?" Robert scoffed. "Hardly. Don't stop unless you want to. Every one of the instructors here agrees that your progress is extraordinary. Now we know why."

Kurt had been holding his breath and finally managed to exhale.

"Wisdom is like water," Robert continued. "It will accommodate itself to a container of any shape. What you're doing is working and that, in and of itself, is reason enough to continue."

"That's a relief," Kurt said. "Can I ask about my business now?"

"Of course. That's the main reason I invited you here tonight."

Robert brought his hands together; his elbows on the desk.

"Do you remember where you were when you started here? I mean physically and mentally."

Kurt nodded attentively.

"You have a pretty good idea of where you are now, correct?"

"Yes," Kurt replied.

"How do you measure the difference? The difference between then and now? Can you convince me there has been *measurable* progress?"

Kurt was unsure, disoriented, similar to the first time he walked onto the studio floor.

"Well," he stammered, "I feel better. Stronger, more confident."

"We can't measure feelings," Robert countered.

Kurt sighed, then reorganized his thoughts.

"Then I would have to say the only thing we can measure is the number of drills I can complete without having to quit because I'm exhausted. We can compare the number of push-ups I could do at the start with the number I'm capable of doing right now. Or the number of sit-ups, or any other exercise we do.

"We can look at the heavy bag to see how it reacts when I kick it or punch it. We can ask whoever is wearing the 'focus gloves' if they can feel the difference in my punches or in my kicks between where I am now and where I was a couple of months ago.

"We can look at the forms. Both the ones I've already learned and the progress I'm making on the new ones I've just started."

"Excellent," Robert smiled. "We know where you were and now we know where you are. We have a starting point, and a fuzzy kind of end-point—your first-degree black belt test. So, in between the two, we can measure stuff."

"Right," Kurt said excitedly, "I started out doing fifteen push-ups and now I can do fifty."

"On your way to one hundred," Robert said. "Remember a black belt should be the beginning of a lifetime of continual study."

Kurt nodded his head in humility to the long road ahead.

"So then, how do you measure progress at work?" Robert asked. "Do you know where you are? Have you established a baseline?"

"Well, the baseline is obvious," Kurt smirked. "Make a profit every month. Make more money than you spend."

"I'm talking about goals and objectives," Robert said firmly. "Do you have those written down? Do you have a plan, a Strategic Plan, within which those goals and objectives can operate?

"When I started Mushin, the first thing I had to do was establish a baseline of optimal performance. Anyone can visualize going on a journey. But, without knowing where you are and where you want to end up, it's impossible to plan a successful route or measure your progress.

"You need a baseline. It's important to know your point of origin and your destination. It's almost as important as knowing what your Why is."

Kurt wasn't exactly sure where this was leading, but realized it was important enough to lean into. Robert continued.

"All businesses have some kind of metrics, the measurements by which performance can be determined. When those metrics are applied to strategic goals and objectives they are often referred to as KPIs, Key Performance Indicators."

Robert stood up and walked over to a white board hanging on the far wall in his office. It was empty, save a quote written along the top attributed to Taisen Deshimaru, a Zen Buddhist teacher:

THINK WITH YOUR WHOLE BODY.

Kurt smiled. The quote seemed strangely appropriate for Robert, the studio, and all of Mushin Automotive. The master mechanic picked up a marker and scribbled furiously across the board.

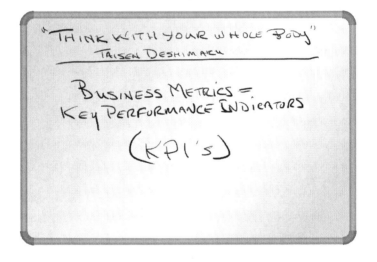

"We're interested in two kinds of KPI's," he said. "Metrics that can be considered drivers, and metrics that are outcomes. Their correlation and differences are important as well.

"But, before we go into too much detail about them, there's another question that must be answered."

"What's that?" Kurt asked.

Robert looked at him firmly and answered.

"What are you doing to measure how things are going right now? What metrics are you looking at? And, if you are not looking at anything specific, is all your anxiety about how 'bad' the business is doing really justified?"

"Bowling Ball Management"

Kurt sat quietly for a moment, contemplating Robert's questions. He glanced over at the white board again as if the answer might be hidden there. He hesitated, then began speaking slowly.

"What am I looking at when it comes to how we're really doing at the office?"

Repeat the question. It was a classic stalling technique Kurt had used in high school, a way to buy some time. Robert said nothing; he simply waited.

"Well…," Kurt said. "We look at sales, of course. Gross sales. We look at all our various expenses, the stuff that appears on the P&L. Gross profit, too. But really it feels like we're practicing 'bowling ball management' every day."

"Bowling ball management?" Robert asked, cocking his head. "I've read about a variety of management styles over the years, but 'bowling ball management' seems to have eluded me somehow. Tell me about it."

Kurt smiled.

"It's the kind of management you're forced to practice," he said, "when the whole day goes to hell. The whole day, the whole week. Maybe even the entire year.

"When that happens, it feels like all you can do is go down to a bowling alley, pick up the first fifteen-pound ball you can find, and then head to the nearest hardware store."

"Hardware store?" Robert interjected.

"Yeah," Kurt nodded, "True Value, Home Depot, or maybe even a Lowe's. You pick up a three-quarter inch garden hose—a one inch hose would be even better—then you cut off one of the metal fittings and stuff the bowling ball into that end of the hose."

Robert's eyes widened in amazement.

"Once you've forced the bowling ball deep into the hose, you wrap your lips around the end closest to the ball and spend the rest of the day trying blow the bowling ball from that end of the hose to the other!"

Robert burst out laughing.

"It never works," Kurt said, shaking his head back and forth. "But it feels like at least you're trying. Like you're doin' something."

Robert was having trouble controlling his laughter. He'd never heard management described in quite the same way. But, he had to admit, it was an effective metaphor.

"I like it!" Robert proclaimed. "I like it a lot. In fact, I can think of too many days where it felt like that was what we were practicing right here in the shop.

"The fact that you've recognized things were going incredibly wrong—and that what you were doing wasn't working—indicates an awareness that you were moving in the wrong direction. Moving away from the success you're seeking, not toward it.

"So let's dive a little deeper. I want to examine your experience with 'bowling ball management' and what it's trying to tell us."

"What do you mean?" Kurt asked.

"Well, feeling like you're shoving a bowling ball into a hose is obviously a response to frustration. Let's start with that. We can't eliminate the source of your frustration unless we can identify it, confront it, discover its origin. Once we do that, we can come up with a plan. So what's causing it?"

Kurt sat there for a minute, softly tapping his foot.

"Well, *sensei*," he said. "I know where we need to be, or at least I think I do. I even know what 'where we need to be' looks like. But I can't figure out *what* we need to do in order to get there.

"What's making me even crazier is that no one else at my company seems to even care. I mean, the people that work for me, they come in every day and do whatever it takes to get by. But there's no energy. No sense of purpose."

"It's just a job to them," Robert offered.

Kurt nodded in agreement and continued. "The problem is it isn't just a job to me. And that's what I don't get. I pay better than average wages. Our benefits are competitive with other contractors our size. Maybe even better.

"I think I'm a 'good' boss. At least I try to be. And I think what we do is important, meaningful even. So I don't understand why it always feels like I'm the only one who cares about what happens or how things turn out."

Robert was quiet. His eyes were closed; his chin was cradled in his left hand. Finally, he opened his eyes again.

"Did you watch that TED Talk?" Robert asked. "The one with Simon Sinek? It was on the resource list I gave you."

"I did," Kurt nodded.

"Did you find it meaningful? Enlightening in any way?"

"Yes."

"Was the importance of having a powerful and compelling Why revealed to you?"

"It was."

"Good," Robert said. "Then I have one more question. However, I don't want your answer now. I want you to take some time to think about it first. Is that okay?"

"Sure," Kurt said. "What is it?"

"Actually," Robert smiled, "my one question is really five or six questions. The first is: What's your Why? What's your personal Why? The second is: What's your company's Why?"

"Is it okay for those to two to be different?" Kurt interjected.

"They could be," Robert said. "Which leads me to my third question: If they're not the same, are they at least consistent with each another? Are the two compatible?

"Finally, my fourth and fifth questions—which may be the most important of all—are: Do the people you work with agree with the company's Why? Does it resonate for *them* like it does for you?

"Have you communicated the company's Why to everyone? Can they articulate it, clearly and concisely, to a person outside of the company, someone who does not work there?"

Kurt sat there pondering Robert's questions.

My answer to all of these is a definite 'I don't know'.

Robert started to get up from his chair. It was obvious their meeting was about to end. He smiled at Kurt.

"Let's discuss your answers," he said, "after you've had a chance to think about them for a while."

First, the Why?

Kurt could hardly wait to get to work. Days had gone by, and he'd thought a lot about his last meeting with Robert, enough to finally come to terms with the first three of his master's questions. But he realized that his answers alone were not going to be enough.

He needed to know where his employees were with regard to the company's Why. Whether they understood it. Whether they could explain it to someone else. And, perhaps most important, whether or not they embraced it—even if they didn't agree with it.

Over the past few months Kurt had made progress compared to where he'd been when he started. But, after talking to Robert, he knew there was a lot more to be done, and it all seemed to revolve around answering Robert's Why questions.

Kurt arrived in the company parking lot, entered the building, and walked toward his office with purpose. It was great to see that everyone was there on time and working. The first thing he did as he sat down at his desk was call Rick in.

"Close the door, Rick. I need a minute."

Rick was a little apprehensive. While there were more sightings of the 'old Kurt'—the enthusiastic, passionate building contractor he once knew—daily life at Kerrigan Construction had been hard, almost unbearable over the past couple of years. As a result, Rick was no longer 100% confident that whatever new suggestion Kurt was about make would stand a chance of working.

"What's up, boss?" Rick asked.

"Have a seat," Kurt gestured to a chair. "I know that you and just about everyone else around here thinks I've lost my mind. Maybe you think I've taken too many hits at the studio."

Rick tried to suppress his smile.

"But there has to be a better way to run this business than what we're doing now," Kurt continued. "Because what we're doing now isn't working for the most part. And, even when it does, it doesn't give the consistent results we need or deserve."

"I know," Rick nodded. "There are times I feel like I'm banging my head against the wall."

"Think about Robert for a moment," Kurt said. "I believe we both respect what he's done at Mushin. And a lot of the things they practice daily at his shop make sense. At least, they do to me. That's why I think we should examine their 'playbook' and incorporate some of those things here."

"We've started trying some things already," Rick said. "And, so far, it's making a difference. But aren't you afraid that if we do too much, too fast, we won't know which things actually helped?"

"I'm not afraid and I'll tell you why," Kurt replied. "Because before I met Robert we were playing Whac-A-Mole around here. It was all damage control and crisis management—putting out the hottest fire first, then moving on to the next disaster."

"I agree," Rick said. "It seemed all we were doing sometimes was patching holes in the wall, creating cosmetic fixes that didn't do a damn thing to improve the foundation of the company you built."

"The company that *we* built, Rick," Kurt said emotionally.

He looked at Rick, realizing how long this man had been at his side, all the hours he'd put in. He thought about how passionately Rick believed in the same dream, how much he believed in his boss.

"It's crazy," Kurt shook his head. "I'm a contractor, yet I framed this business without a basic set of building plans. I changed things around here all the time with nothing more than the hope it would, somehow, make things better. Then, even worse, I'd find the next thing to fiddle with, before I even knew if what I had just finished screwing around with was working."

Rick reluctantly nodded in agreement. That was pretty much it.

"There has to be a better way," Kurt continued. "Robert says I need a compass, an overarching set of plans that can point us toward the future we want. He wants us to create a Strategic Plan. Not some dead report to file away, but a living document to help guide us."

"That sounds great," Rick said. "But where do we start? *How* do we start?"

Kurt reached into a desk drawer to grab a book.

"We start," he said, "by figuring out our Why. Because, without that, we've got nothing. No reason to exist."

Kurt placed a softcover copy of *Start With Why* by Simon Sinek on the desk. Rick sat back in his chair, frowning; it was obvious he wasn't excited.

"C'mon, boss," he said. "Everybody watched this guy's video at the team meeting months ago. You're not going to make us read the book now, are you? We know how important a powerful Why is."

Kurt thoughtfully considered his manager's words.

"Okay, then," he said. "What's our Why? Why are we here doing whatever this is that we're doing? Do we build stuff? Renovate? Are we remodelers? Is our Why all about installing windows and doors? Solar panels? Tell me, Rick, what's our Why?"

Rick leaned forward in his chair and smiled.

"Jeez," he said, "this isn't some deep philosophical debate. We're a construction company. We build stuff. Good stuff. We build it to spec, to last a long time. That's our promise. We finish each project on time and on budget. Or at least we try. That's our Why."

"Then we're in trouble," Kurt said. "Because that answer is not powerful enough, not compelling enough, to take us where we need to go. It's not going to take us where I know we need to be."

"How else can I say it?" Rick shrugged.

Kurt passed his thumb along the pages of Sinek's book multiple times, absent-mindedly, as if an answer might slip out from between the pages.

"I'm not sure," he said. "Maybe our Why is to make people's lives more beautiful, to create functional work environments and living spaces that delight them. Maybe what we do is bring dreams to life. Maybe our Why is all about helping them fulfill their dreams."

Kurt sat back, looking over at Rick. They were both surprised by the sincerity of Kurt's statement. Rick cleared his throat.

"That sounds a whole lot more meaningful than just building stuff," Rick said sheepishly.

"Yeah," Kurt agreed. "Building stuff is what almost every one of our competitors does. I'm going to suggest that 'just building stuff' isn't good enough for us anymore."

"Damn," Rick smiled. "That's a great Why. Everyone here should be able to understand and get behind it. Where did that come from? What made you think of that all of a sudden?"

"It wasn't all of a sudden," Kurt said. "It's the reason I started this company. It's the reason I put the bags down, stopped pounding nails for somebody else, and went out on my own. I just haven't been able to put it all together and articulate it until now.

"But, before I ram my own Why down everyone's throat, I want to call a meeting. I want all of us to get together and talk about this. Maybe someone else on the team has something to contribute. Maybe they have an even better Why.

"I think it's important for everyone to participate, because it'll have to be their Why as well as yours and mine. We need everyone on board to propel the company forward. Let's schedule a meeting for next Thursday morning, and see where this takes us.

"After we nail down our Why with the team, you and I can move on to that Strategic Plan. I think a good plan should help us clarify the What and the How of where this company goes next."

Rick agreed. He stood up, shook Kurt's hand, and got to work. Thursday came and went. The meeting was a success, even if there wasn't as much direct participation as what Kurt had hoped for.

There were times the silence was eerily uncomfortable. Too many times he had to challenge one of his team members just to prime the pump and get things started.

Trying to get his people to raise their hands was frustrating, especially since it was obvious—at least, to Kurt—that this process was about improving *their* future as well as his own.

He realized their reluctance was caused by three major issues: a lack of confidence, a lack of trust, and fear of an unknown future. All of which Kurt could easily relate to.

Each person might have their own reason for remaining silent, but he was certain that trust, confidence, and fear were central to the problem. So he focused on sharing his own insecurities.

In the end, as the troops filed out of the meeting room, Kurt knew that honesty and empathy had triumphed. Everyone was excited about the company's new Why, and where it would lead.

The "Dirty Dozen"

Kurt had started this journey of discovery with a new sense of conviction. He knew he had to dig himself out of the hole he'd fallen into. Not just for himself, but for Laurie and the kids. That much was clear. No more hiding, no more games.

He had to right this ship for all his employees as well. They had families of their own to take care of. They trusted that Kerrigan Construction would be there for them. They trusted Kurt.

Things had been getting better slowly. Too slowly. Profits were still not where they should have been. Not where they needed to be. Kurt knew he had to accelerate the progress he'd been making somehow. He just didn't know how.

During his next late night meeting at Mushin Automotive, Kurt sat down with a yellow legal pad on his lap ready to take notes. He was anxious. Prepared to get some answers.

"*Sensei,*" he said, "I appreciate everything you've done to help me to this point. I really do. But, honestly, I'm frustrated. I feel like we've hit a plateau at work. Good things have happened, they jut haven't happened fast not enough.

"We've never really talked in specifics about the turn-around you accomplished here at Mushin. I can't remember how long ago it was since I first asked you about this, but it's been awhile."

"It has been awhile," Robert offered.

"It may have been one of those, 'I'll share that when you're ready' kind of things," Kurt said, "But, the fact is, I'm ready now.

"How were you able to turn things around here? When did you turn the corner and become profitable, consistently profitable?"

Robert leaned back in his chair and glanced over at a shelf near his desk. Among the stock car models and racing trophies was a small black-and-white photo of man in a mechanic's uniform.

"It started with my mentor," he said.

"Your mentor?" Kurt interrupted.

"Yes. The turn-around started with what my mentor, my coach, referred to as his Dirty Dozen—a dozen KPIs he always tracked. Twelve KPIs guaranteed to make a difference, guaranteed to work, if you 'worked' them.

"You see, I figured out early on that I couldn't do this by myself. I didn't have the skills, knowledge, or experience to run a business. So I searched for someone who'd already made the journey from under-performing to success.

"Once I found him, I sat at his feet and soaked up anything and everything he was willing to share with me. Convincing him to help me was probably one of the best investments of time and effort I ever made in business."

Robert stood up and made his way to the white board.

"It looks like you came prepared to take notes," he said, eyeing the legal pad on Kurt's lap.

He erased everything except for a definition at the very the top:

KAIZEN = CONTINUOUS IMPROVEMENT INCLUDING EVERYONE

Robert picked up a marker and started writing so quickly that Kurt could barely keep up. Beneath the definition, he put down 'Dirty Dozen' and then, under that, twelve indicators.

"In my business, automotive repair," Robert said, "the Dirty Dozen are: Total Sales, Gross Profit, Gross Profit Margin on Parts, Gross Profit Margin on Labor, Car Count, Average Repair Order...

"Hmm, lemme think for a minute. It's been awhile."

Robert stopped and pulled away from the white board to ponder. He smiled, then continued writing.

"There's Labor Mix, Labor Content per Job, Technician Efficiency, Service Bay Productivity, Total Sales per Service Bay, and Total Sales per Technician."

He stepped back, and surveyed his writing once more.

"One, two, thr— Yep, that's twelve."

"The Dirty Dozen," Kurt said, as he finished writing on his pad.

"I tell you what," Robert chuckled. "I'll make it a Baker's Dozen at no extra charge. Thirteen KPIs to track. The extra one is called Effective Labor Rate. I'm not sure what the correlation might be in your world, in construction. But there has to be something.

"In fact, some of these—Car Count, for instance—are not going to match at all. You'll need to get creative and translate them into Key Performance Indicators that mean something in your industry. I can walk you through that later. But, first, you need to understand why they're important, and how they work, in *my* world.

"There are more than thirty other Key Performance Indicators that we measure now. But, back then, when all I was interested in was survival, it was these thirteen. Checking them, on a regular basis, made the difference between success and failure.

"I realize that construction has other numbers, but I'm willing to bet that some of the KPIs Mushin focused on in the beginning are similar to ones that you should be looking at right now."

Kurt took a deep breath, then pushed the air out until his lungs were empty. So many questions forming in his head.

"Like what?" he asked. "What kind of KPIs?"

"I'll bet one is your Closing Ratio," Robert said confidently. "The relationship between the number of proposals you present to prospects compared to the number of contracts you execute.

"That's something I think would be a critical ratio to know and understand, because it can tell you a lot about your advertising and marketing—whether you're attracting the right people. It tells you about your estimates as well—how accurate they are.

Most importantly, the Closing Ratio is a measure of your sales effectiveness—whether or not your sales people are showing how, and why, your company is different. They need to communicate why price should not be the prospect's only consideration when making a purchasing decision.

"I'm not sure, but I think that ought to be a critical factor requiring timely, honest, and accurate information."

Kurt nodded enthusiastically and started writing on his pad. He was anxious to learn everything he could about the magic Robert had worked at Mushin.

His *sensei* seemed to know, almost intuitively, that Kurt needed to understand the material completely if he was going to have any chance of implementing it with any success.

"Don't stop now," Kurt said. "It's getting late, but I'm sure we can get through at least a few of these KPIs before we have to quit."

"Then let's dig in," Robert agreed.

He walked around his desk to the antique oak filing cabinet tucked away in the corner of the office, pulled open a drawer, and removed a rather thick hanging folder marked 'Financials.'

Robert opened it, and pulled out a smaller manila folder with a group of papers neatly stapled together. He grabbed one, folded the cover page back, and walked over to where Kurt was sitting. It was a Profit and Loss Statement. He pointed to the top.

Ordinary Income/Expense	
Income	
Labor	52,988.11
Parts Income	44,513.09
Hazmat Income	405.28
Sublet Pass Through	5,094.89
Tire Sales	2,035.27
Total Income	105,036.64

"The first KPI is Total Sales and it's the easiest one to understand. It's Total Sales for any period you'll be measuring. That number can be called by many names: Total Gross Sales, Total Revenue, Total Income. They're all different ways of saying the same thing.

"So, if the snapshot you're taking of the business is at the end of last month, your Total Gross Sales would be the total revenue you received for all the products and services you sold that month."

Robert pointed to the document in Kurt's hand.

"This is one of our old P&Ls," he said.

"Sure," Kurt nodded. "I get financials back from my accountant every quarter."

"Not enough," Robert said, shaking his head. "Especially when things aren't going right. Accounting information qualifies as historical data. It's about things that have already transpired; things that happened in the past. Three months is too long to go without knowing what went wrong. But we can talk about that later."

"Getting back to the P&L, like Total Sales, it can have a lot of different names. Our accountant calls ours a 'Statement of Revenue and Expense'. But it's still a Profit and Loss Statement, regardless of what it's called. If you look at the financials your accountant does, you'll find Total Sales right up at the top.

"If it was for last year, the same rules would apply. Only you would want to look at both the Total Sales for the year and then, maybe, break that number down by month depending upon what you're trying to figure out. With me so far?"

"Yes," Kurt said, nodding his head. Robert continued.

"Total Sales is an important number, but despite what most people think—and, in the beginning, I was one of those people—it isn't the most important number you need to be focusing on. For my money, the most important KPI is margin, and I'll show you why as we move through the rest of the KPI's we cover tonight.

Ordinary Income/Expense	
Income	
Labor	52,988.11
Parts Income	44,513.09
Hazmat Income	405.28
Sublet Pass Through	5,094.89
Tire Sales	2,035.27
Total Income	**105,036.64**
Cost of Goods Sold	
Tech Costs	22,106.96
Parts (COGS)	21,164.98
Hazmat	0.00
Sublet Expenses	2,859.82
Tires	1,340.00
Service Advisor Cost	8,035.85
Total COGS	**— 55,507.61**
Gross Profit	**= 49,529.03**

"The next one, Gross Profit, is the easiest to figure. Sometimes it's shown in dollars. Sometimes it's identified as Total Gross Profit Margin and shown as a percentage."

"I don't want to sound dumb," Kurt said raising his hand, "but what's the difference? Profit, Profit Margin… Aren't they the same?"

Robert smiled. "There's no such thing as 'dumb' if you're seeking knowledge, and you don't honestly know the answer. Gross Profit is the difference between your Gross Sales and—in our business—Cost of Goods Sold. It's calculated in dollars."

Robert pointed out the numbers on the P&L.

"Your Gross Profit Margin reflects your Gross Profit in relation to Gross Sales as a percentage. You get it by dividing your Gross Profit by your Total Sales and converting it into a percentage."

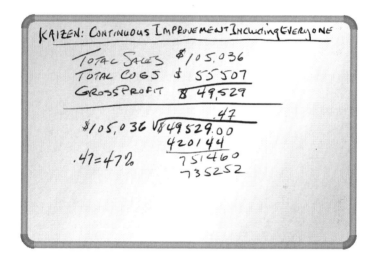

Robert wiped the white board clean. He picked up a marker and started writing again.

"Gross Profit and Gross Profit Margin are considered Outcome KPIs. That means they're indicative of past activity, something that happened already. Something you no longer have any control over.

"On the other hand, a Driving KPI measures something that can —and, often does—have a significant impact on an Outcome KPI. We can take a look at this later if you want to."

Kurt nodded anxiously. He knew what Gross Sales was about and he understood where the number came from. Gross Profit was more elusive; it had too many variables to wrap his head around.

"Take a look back at your notes," Robert said. "See how I broke Gross Profit into two more KPIs? Let's dig into that further."

"In my business, auto repair, we track a cumulative Gross Profit but it's often more effective as a management tool if you break that number down into its core components: Gross Profit on Labor and Gross Profit on Parts.

"Gross Profit Margin on Labor is defined as Hourly Labor Rate less the Cost of Direct Labor. The Cost of Direct Labor, in my case, is the cost of the technician's wages or salary per hour associated with making that Labor sale.

"We can report this KPI one of two ways. It can be 'loaded,' reflecting taxes, benefits, and costs—things like sick or personal days, health insurance, vacations, and uniforms. Or we can report that number without the load.

"We can look at it in dollars as Gross Profit on Labor or as Gross Profit Margin on Labor, whichever is easier for you to use. The point is the KPI should be a tool, a number you can compare to whatever are 'best practices' in your industry.

"I'm not going to calculate that number for you now, because I don't want to confuse you. We can come back to it another time.

"Just know that in our business—for independent repair shop owners like me—we're looking for a Gross Profit Margin on Labor of about 70% unloaded, and about 60% calculated with the load.

"That means if you're charging $100 per hour for your labor, it shouldn't cost you more than somewhere around $40 with the load built in. Or about $30 unloaded. Of course, that can vary. But, all things considered, it's a great rule of thumb.

"You calculate Gross Profit on Parts or Gross Profit Margin on Parts using the same principles. The math is pretty much the same.

"You start with the Parts Price, the price the customer pays for what you're selling, then subtract the Cost of Goods Sold (the cost to acquire that part). The result is your Gross Profit on Parts.

"You know, I just explained Gross Profit on Parts by starting with the Sale Price and working backwards. But, once you know the margin you need and your cost, you can calculate the other way to make sure you actually achieve the margin your business requires."

Robert walked to the white board, erasing it again.

"Calculating Gross Profit Margin on Parts is straightforward also. You take whatever that number is and divide it by whatever you sell that part for.

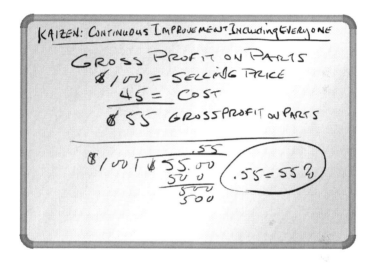

"If we're selling a part for $100, and it cost us $45, we'd subtract $45 from $100 and our Gross Profit would be $55. To figure the percentage, we divide the Gross Profit by the Selling Price."

"It's critical that you understand your Gross Profit and Gross Profit Margin on Parts, if you want to be successful.

"Changing the number in either direction, up or down, will have a profound impact on your Gross Profit. And Gross Profit impacts your bottom line. It's really your Net Profit—what you've got left in the register at the end of the day—that's important anyway.

"After all," Robert smiled, "it isn't how much you make that counts. It's how much you get to keep."

Kurt looked at the clock on Robert's desk. It was a large, ornate timepiece encased in a sculptured Chinese dragon. He knew that Laurie might be starting to worry. Robert noticed the distraction.

"Are you sure you want to continue?" he asked. "It's starting to get late, and I don't want to hold you up."

"You must be a mind reader," Kurt smiled. "This is all fantastic. And exactly what I needed to hear. But… I'm taking a lot of time away from my family right now. Is it okay if we pick up on the rest of the Dirty Dozen after I finish working with these?"

"Absolutely," Robert said. "The white board can wait. Get home. Your wife and kids are waiting."

45

Hard and Soft

Kurt struggled to get his gear on. It was always a struggle. As much as he enjoyed the contact and challenge of sparring—of putting everything he learned into practice—he didn't enjoy getting his clock cleaned quite as often as seemed to be the case.

He wasn't a big fan of the protective gear either. He understood its purpose, that it probably saved him from hospitalization and acute bodily injury more than once. He recognized that these were martial arts gloves, with the fingers removed at the first knuckle. But, as far as he was concerned, they were still awkward—perhaps because he still had to wrap both hands.

More than anything else, the helmet reduced his visibility enough to make a well-thrown hook, or quick round-house kick, all but invisible. Something both Jason and Allie were delighted to demonstrate every time they sparred with Kurt.

But there was no sparring without gear. At least not until you reached the highest levels of skill and ability.

Kurt got himself together just in time to walk to the blue corner of the studio floor. Everyone else—except for Mr. Taylor, Ms. Knox and Mr. Widham, who stood in the center of the floor—formed a perfect geometric square around the designated combat area.

Allie tucked a blue scarf into the back of Kurt's belt, then tapped him on the shoulder. Kurt's opponent got a red scarf from Jason. Then both would-be warriors walked to the center of the square.

Robert stood in the center and reminded both fighters of the rules—no contact to the neck or throat or groin; controlled contact to every other strike zone. The object was to simulate combat and to demonstrate mastery, not to harm another student.

Robert was the senior referee, while Allie and Jason acted as the back and side judges.

"Hajime!" Robert shouted. "Ready!" He raised his right arm up between the two fighters. Kurt and his opponent bowed formally, touched gloves, and assumed their 'ready stances.'

Robert's arm dropped. "Begin!" he said.

‡

That was the last match of the evening and, when it was over, Kurt was pleased with how he'd done. First off, he didn't embarrass himself. He'd won two of the three points—holding his own against a more experienced opponent. As far as Kurt was concerned, that was far more than 'good enough'.

He did better than he had in most of his previous matches; it was obvious his skills had improved. Although, he always managed to walk off the floor hurting.

When Kurt reached his corner, Jason was waiting for him.

"Can you stay for a few minutes after class?" he asked.

"Sure," Kurt replied. "What's up?"

"Nothing to worry about… Just leave your gear on."

Leaving his gear on told Kurt there was something to worry about. Jason was an accomplished martial artist who loved to spar and relished the physical contact.

When class was over, and the other students had left, Jason called Kurt to the center of the floor.

"I've noticed somethin' I think I can help you with, but it will be easier for me to show y'all than it will be for me to explain."

Kurt peered out cautiously through the protective grate of his padded helmet. Jason hadn't suited up.

"Aren't you going to put your helmet and gloves on?"

"Hell no," Jason replied. "No need."

The big man's face lit up in a wicked grin. Kurt wasn't sure if he should be hurt or just insulted. Jason took a step closer.

"What happens if y'all were to take a stone and smash it against the sidewalk?" he asked.

Kurt hated conversations like these—ones that were meant to deliver a point that always seemed to elude him somehow.

"Something is bound to give?" Kurt replied. "That something is going to break?"

"Why?" Jason asked.

"Because they are both solid? They're both hard?"

Kurt's lack of confidence confirmed his insecurities.

"How're your hands feelin' about now?" Jason asked.

Kurt opened and closed his fists; he rotated both wrists.

"They hurt," he shot back. "My knuckles are sore, and both my wrists hurt like hell. My shins are bruised, too. But they're always bruised are after a controlled contact practice, or when we spar."

"Have y'all ever wondered why they're so sore?" Jason asked. "Why you're gettin' so badly bruised up all the time?"

"I'm not sure I have," Kurt smiled. "I just thought that's the way it's supposed to be. That, after a while, I'd stop hurting."

"Well, that's a fact," Jason nodded. "You will stop hurtin' after a while, but not because you get used to it, or your knuckles or your shins toughen up. Although, I'm guessin', they will.

"It gets easier, and y'all will stop hurting, because of what I'm gonna share with you. Something Robert shared with me when I first started here. That's the concept of 'hard and soft'.

"Here's a question: If y'all know that takin' a hard, possibly brittle object and smashin' it into another hard object will result in somethin' breakin'—somethin' we already know is not productive and makes no sense—why would you do it?"

Kurt made two fists and looked down at his sparring gloves.

"What's the alternative?" he asked. "All I've got as weapons are my arms and legs. That's what I've been taught, right?

"My fists are hard, at least as hard as I can make them. My shins are what they are. I can kick with the knife edge or the ball of my foot, with my heel, or I can use a chop or a knife-edge strike or a punch. But to be effective they have to be hard strikes, don't they?"

Kurt was confused and unsure of where all this was going.

"I thought 'hard' was what our style was all about, anyway."

Jason bounced up and down in front of him, shifting his weight from one leg to the other, shrugging his shoulders and pumping his arms. It was obvious the big guy was warming up. The question was: Warming up for what?

"Well, let's see," Jason said, shooting a jab in Kurt's direction.

Kurt noticed that his teacher's fists weren't closed. Jason had his fingers lightly curled, but that was about it.

He closed his fist at the last possible moment and the jab landed right below Kurt's right shoulder, in the soft tissue just below the collar bone. The pain was exquisite and sharp—almost electric.

Kurt instinctively covered the aching spot with his hand. Jason continued to bob and weave in front of him.

"What happens if y'all take somethin' hard, almost brittle, and crash it into somethin' soft? Somethin' like the space just below your collar bone?"

Kurt rubbed the point of contact.

"It hurts like hell!" he said.

"What's the hardest part of the body?" Jason asked.

"The head."

"Yep." Jason nodded. "Are the bones in your hand harder'n the bones in your head?"

"No. Not even close."

"Then why in the world would y'all attack somethin' harder'n your hands with your hands—knowin' that your hands are the most likely thing to break? It doesn't make any sense, does it?"

"No, it doesn't," Kurt agreed. "But what else can I do?"

"The alternative is selectively targeting hard with soft, and soft with hard."

Kurt dropped his arms to his sides in frustration.

"You're talking in riddles," he said. "Honestly, I don't get it."

Jason was still moving on the floor, clearly enjoying the mild workout this was providing.

"I'm not gonna hit your forehead with my fist," he said, mock gesturing toward Kurt's head.

"If I do, I might break my hand. At the least, I take the chance of badly bruisin' it. Maybe even breakin' it and losing it as a weapon.

"But I can place a targeted strike with one of my fists to your nose, the soft tissue around your eyes, the area above and in front of your ears on your temple, or where your jaw attaches to the skull."

He smiled at Kurt.

"Y'all get it now? Hard against soft."

Kurt nodded slowly, taking it in—hoping that Jason's hypothetical example wasn't about to become reality.

"Or I can use the heal of my open hand to attack the front of your face. Soft against hard.

"It's yin and yang; soft and firm; givin' and receivin'; full and empty; male and female."

Jason gestured for Kurt to engage with him.

"Come on! Spar with me 'n I'll show you."

Kurt shook his head. "You don't have any protective gear on," he said. "But I do. I don't want to hurt you."

Jason smiled wryly. He winked at Kurt.

"I'll try'n be as careful as I can."

Then he gave Kurt an object lesson in hard and soft, targeting and hitting him anywhere he wanted—whenever he wanted—with deadly precision.

Open hand to the side of the head or the front of the helmet; closed fists to various parts of the body; kicks demonstrating the same principals whenever Jason chose to make contact.

As quickly as the big guy had come at Kurt, he backed away.

"Now you," Jason shouted.

He danced around the polished wooden floor, shifting his large frame one way or the other to deflect the energy of each kick or punch. Kurt tried his best to employ the techniques he'd just learned. Jason let him make light contact, enough to drive the point home into Kurt's muscle memory. Then he motioned the session was over, that he'd made his point. Jason smiled.

"Y'all started learnin' here with the goal of fixin' your business," he said. "These principals apply there as much as they do here.

"In a difficult situation, when someone, anyone, y'all are dealin' with is hard, unyielding, it makes no sense to position yourself the same way. If y'all do, no one is gonna win and somethin' is bound to break.

"However, if your approach is soft—if y'all are unwillin' to contend, if y'all are flexible and yielding—you're more'n likely to draw that person in and prevail.

"If someone is in your face yellin' and screamin', how far you think y'all are gonna get if you meet their force with the same or a greater force of your own?

"You don't have to go to war to get what you want or need.

"Just somethin' to think about, somethin'll work in life and in your trainin.'"

With that, Jason bowed deeply and backed off the floor.

46

Blending

A week had passed since Jason demonstrated the power of 'hard and soft'. It was a powerful lesson, one that Kurt worked diligently to master and practice every day. Like everything else he'd learned from Robert and Mushin's staff, it made a profound difference.

Difficult situations seemed somehow less difficult. Yet Kurt knew the only thing that changed was him, his level of awareness about what he was confronting. Now he had the tools to evaluate whether a situation was hard or soft; he knew what the appropriate response should be.

Kerrigan Construction was showing signs of growth again. The phones were ringing. Kurt's long-time employees seemed to be more focused, both in the office and on the job. Some were even showing up early to participate in Kurt's early morning practice of the Yang short form in the company's yard.

His progress at the studio was undeniable, even to him. He was there almost every day and—in the process of working out at the studio and in the park—he'd dropped more than twenty pounds of 'excess' and converted another twenty pounds into muscle.

He had more energy, was more focused and more confident than ever. He was infinitely more patient and understanding.

More than that, Kurt was self-aware perhaps for the first time in his life—aware of his actions, aware of his reactions, aware of the impact those actions and reactions had on everyone around him.

He had achieved a level of self-control he had no idea was even possible. He seemed to practice it every day in almost everything he did, and his world reflected that.

It was just past noon at the office, and Rochelle had gone out for lunch. Kurt was eating a salad at his desk, manning the phones, when it happened—a challenge to all of his new-found serenity.

The client, on the other end of the line, was extremely aggressive —disrespectful to the point he wouldn't allow Kurt to say much beyond, 'Kerrigan Construction. Kurt here. I can help you.'

In the past, Kurt would have reacted badly. He would have responded to the customer's verbal assault in kind, with an attack of at least equal force. Instead he took a deep breath, composed himself and allowed the customer to vent until the tirade ended.

It had been so intense and had come with so much force, Kurt wasn't even sure what the caller wanted. So he decided it would be best to counter the customer's 'hard' attack with a 'soft' response.

He allowed a number of seconds to pass in complete silence before responding. Finally, the customer shouted in frustration.

"Is anyone there, dammit!"

"Yes, there is someone here," Kurt answered calmly.

"Then why the hell didn't you answer me?"

"Because I wanted to make sure you were finished. Interrupting you before you were done would have been rude."

The customer grunted.

"Now," Kurt continued, "it seems like something bad happened. I'd like to understand what that was, so I can get to the bottom of it and fix it for you."

Time seemed to stand still until the irate client responded. When he did, it was obvious he had calmed down enough to carry on a normal conversation.

By the time the call ran its course, the problem was identified, and a solution was in place. In the end, the client apologized for his rant and earlier behavior.

‡

Kurt was feeling pretty good when he arrived at the studio that evening. He couldn't wait to tell Jason about his experience—how understanding 'hard and soft' had made such a difference in the outcome of what could have been a very bad situation.

Jason smiled and gave Kurt a high-five.

"So, y'all blended with this guy on the other end of the phone, saw the world from his point of view and managed to find a solution you could both live with. Very cool!"

Kurt stared at Jason, dumb-founded.

"Blended?" Kurt asked. "What's blended?"

Jason's eyes lit up. He rubbed his big hands together.

"Ah! We've never been over blendin' before, have we?"

Kurt shook his head.

"It's what y'all did today with that upset customer," Jason said.

"We do it here all the time. When we have someone with a problem, someone who isn't givin' us a chance to explain at the desk or out in the shop, we move around to where they are and sit or stand right alongside 'em... You know, shoulder-to-shoulder, facing the same way.

"That allows us to see the world from where they're standin'— literally. It helps them know we care, that we see the importance in understandin' how they feel and what they're experiencin'.

"Y'all have felt this in your training, only no one has ever called it by that name.

"If y'all think about it and look at the combat applications of tai chi or some of the other Chinese forms, ya'll see it a lot because they're all so soft and circular by nature—especially the forms that result in a take-down, a joint-locking technique, or a throw. In Japanese martial arts, the best examples are *aikido* and jiu jitsu.

"Think about it for a minute. Y'all facin' off against a potential enemy, someone who pulls the trigger and decides to come straight at you. Whaddya do?

"Do ya plant and hold your ground, or do ya allow them to enter your space and then find a way to deflect their energy?

"If ya can, you deflect it, right? You don't face it head on.

"If ya do, you have hard against hard. And somethin'—or more'n likely someone—is surely gonna break.

"So ya allow 'em to enter your space. Ya move closer to 'em, in fact, you move into their space—blockin' or deflecting their attack, whatever it might be—without changing the vector of their attackin' force, without changin' its direction.

"When that happens, y'all are blendin' with 'em—and ya may even find yourself side-by-side, facing in the same direction. Then ya can exercise a variety of options.

"Ya can 'help' them follow-through on the path they've chosen by multiplyin' their force with your own energy—takin' 'em off balance and throwin' 'em well away from you.

"Ya can use a joint-lockin' technique or a throw, or both, to disable or incapacitate 'em. Or ya can exploit any vulnerability ya can find, any openness ya uncover when y'all are inside their defenses.

"But, to accomplish any of those options, the first thing y'all gonna have to do is become one with your adversary. Ya gotta 'blend' with 'em until, for that moment in time, y'all are one.

"The coolest part of blendin' is knowin' what it can do for ya when ya aren't on the floor, when ya aren't using it in combat.

"Y'all done just that at work today with the guy on the phone."

Kurt nodded in agreement.

"He came straight at ya with all the force he had. His goal was to knock ya off balance, to take ya down."

As if to demonstrate, Jason slammed his fist into his open palm.

"Wham! Now if y'all had come straight back at him, war woulda broken out. Somebody woulda walked away injured, if they walked away at all. Someone woulda 'won' the fight.

"But ya didn't do that. Your gut instinct to not react caught him off guard. The fact y'all wouldn't take the bait and face him directly caught him unprepared.

"Instead ya allowed the silence to create an opportunity for ya to move alongside your adversary. Being in the same place, lookin' at things from the same perspective, allowed ya to see what he was seein', to experience what he was feelin'.

"How cool is that?" Jason grinned a huge smile.

"While ya'll was doing that, ya both became one and as one found a solution ya both could live with. A peaceful solution that didn't raise one of ya up to the position of winner or relegate the other to loser. Y'all found a solution that worked without insult or injury to either of ya.

"If ya think about it, there's no more powerful tool to create a successful relationship. That's what I'd recommend ya continue to do at work—stay calm and blend.

"Don't allow ya'self to get suckered into playing someone else's game. They're probably better at it anyway. Ya don't have to hurt the other guy; sometimes it's enough to help them on their way. A guy like that can do a pretty good job of hurtin' himself anyway."

Kurt smiled and extended an open palm to Jason. His instructor took a firm grip with his massive hand.

"Thanks," Kurt said. "It's good to know there's a name for what I did, and a theory behind it. Blending. I need to work on that more."

47

Flexibility

Kurt remembered how hard it was to warm up and stretch before each class was just over half a year earlier. He recalled the discomfort in trying to swing a leg up onto the lower of the two barre bars at the rear of the studio. It wasn't any less challenging as he did it now, but thankfully it was easier.

The difference in his body was dramatic. Where once he had difficulty getting the tips of his fingers within six inches of the floor he now could touch his toes.

His waist, back, arms, and legs had a new resiliency that he hadn't experienced in years. He enjoyed the fact that the difference was measurable—obvious to anyone who had watched his progress.

That resiliency acted as a barometer, reading the pressure Kurt experienced at any given moment. The greater the pressure—the more impossible things were at home or at work—the more difficult it was for him to loosen up and release his tension.

That made it easy for Allie to notice there was something wrong when she padded across the floor in Kurt's direction. She put her hands on his shoulders.

"What's up?" she asked. "You're all locked up. Everything okay?"

In truth, everything wasn't okay. It had been one those of those 'take one-step back' days.

"I'm fine," Kurt replied. "just stuck with nowhere to go and no options. And it's driving me nuts."

Allie kept both hands gently placed on Kurt's shoulders.

"Are you sure, Mr. Kerrigan? Are you positive there's no other way to approach your problem? No alternatives?"

Kurt shrugged.

"I saw you warming up," Allie continued, "trying to stretch. I realized immediately there was something wrong. Do you know why we encourage everyone to get here early and loosen up?"

"To avoid injury, I guess," Kurt said. "To ensure we don't pull or tear anything."

"That's one of the reasons," Allie nodded. "But there's more to it than that. Flexibility offers you a greater range of motion. It allows your body to move differently. It offers you a wider field of vision. When you're flexible you're able to bend without breaking. It's a willingness and ability to change direction.

"From a business perspective, it's the ability to see compromise, to see different alternatives. On the studio floor or on the street, the ability to remain fluid offers you more choices—more ways to defend yourself against an opponent's attack, more ways to respond and eliminate a threat or disable your opponent."

Kurt was dialed in to what Allie had to say. She was the most flexible human being he had ever encountered, capable of a perfect vertical side kick and incredible extension.

"I'll bet you locked up at work," Allie said. "You lost your resiliency and went rigid. When that happens, your vision narrows. All you can see is what's in front you. You miss the infinite universe of possibilities you might have if you had remained flexible."

Kurt sighed slowly. She was right, of course.

"It happens at the shop," Allie continued. "When a technician slams into a difficult diagnostic problem and loses perspective. His focus becomes too narrow; the obvious, correct solution is lost.

"What did you miss today at work Mr. Kerrigan? Can you loosen up enough to see it?"

Kurt thought on her question for a moment. What Allie was saying is there are always alternatives, but you must be willing and able to see them; remain flexible enough to respond. To do that, flexibility had to be a priority, both physically and mentally.

Goals and Objectives

Robert and Kurt started meeting on a more regular basis: one evening every few weeks. It wasn't easy, especially for Kurt. It meant missing dinner with Laurie and the kids, and generally resulted in a very long day. But Kurt was certain the potential for improvement was there, and that more than warranted the sacrifice.

Their meetings became a ritual. They would get together after class and move across the alley to the quiet of the deserted shop and Robert's private office. There his teacher would prepare a fresh pot of green tea and, after a few quiet moments, the meeting would begin. This time Robert broke the silence.

"Have you established a set of written goals yet?" he asked. "Goals and objectives for your business? How about a set of goals and objectives for you personally?"

"Yes," Kurt replied.

"Which? Business or personal? Ideally both."

"Well, as far as the company goes, we had an all-staff meeting. It was pretty good really. Although, I wish more people felt they could speak up. But I think we made progress overall.

"I shared what I think our Why should be going forward. What it's always been, actually."

"That's a great start," Robert said. "But I think we need to take the next step. Your Why has to be stated in terms of actionable goals and objectives. That's where the Strategic Plan comes in."

"Yeah," Kurt said enthusiastically. "I talked about that with my manager and it's something we'd like to get started on."

"Good," Robert said. "It's important to have your personal goals and objectives written down. It's important to carry them with you.

"It's just as important for everyone in the business to be aware of what your shared goals and objectives are as a company, so they can articulate them as well."

"I'm not sure I can over-state this, but you want your people on 'your side.' You want them to know where you're headed as a company and why. You need them to share your vision for the future, to understand how they will benefit if you're successful."

"I know," Kurt nodded. "We've started to meet regularly and the next time we come together as a group, I'll make sure everyone has the opportunity to contribute. I need to hear what they have to say and they need to know I'm listening. I think that's the only way they'll ever get the kind of employee 'buy-in' I'm going to need to make this work."

"Great," Robert said. "But you realize that you don't really have 'employees', right? You understand that no one there works for you."

"Huh?"

"They work for themselves, Kurt. They have their own goals and objectives—and they had them long before they started at Kerrigan Construction. Your company is merely the means by which they've chosen to accomplish those goals and objectives."

Kurt frowned. That was something he'd never considered before.

"Do you know what their personal goals and objectives are? Each and every one of them? You probably should. It'll help a hell of a lot more than any 'team-building' exercise will."

"I care about my people, Robert," Kurt said. "You know that by now. I try to be fair.

"I want them to have a good life. I don't want to see them struggle like I have. Geez, like I *still* am. But there's a lot going on all the time. A lot of balls in the air and I'm not the best juggler.

"I want my people to deliver the best products and services we're capable of delivering. I want our customers to be happy working with us instead of one of our competitors.

"No, actually, I want them to be blown away. I want our customers to be absolutely delighted. I want them to stop people on the street to brag about the work we did for them.

"But, after all these years, I shouldn't have to worry about making payroll anymore. I want a business that works for me at least as hard as I'm willing to work for it."

Kurt leaned back and took a deep breath. Robert's demeanor was composed, empathetic. He spoke softly.

"What you described are hopes and expectations. They're the components of a vision, yes. But they're not actionable. Not really."

Kurt pursed his lips in frustration.

"They're not goals and objectives," Robert continued. "Goals and objectives need to be written down. They need to be SMART."

"Smart?" Kurt asked.

Robert nodded. He got up, walked over to the white board, and took the cap off of a marker. He wrote the five letters in a column.

"It's an acronym," he said. "Your goals have to be Specific."

He filled in the word 'specific' next to the letter s.

"They have to be Measurable," Robert continued, "Achievable, Results-Oriented, and Time-Based."

As he finished writing, Robert turned to Kurt.

"What you shared with me," he said, "doesn't fit any of those criteria. More importantly, If you can't explain to me what your goals and objectives are, how can you expect your people to know? How can you expect them to get on board? You're asking them to get on a bus without knowing where it's headed."

"I haven't made it clear enough, have I?" Kurt said. "And if I haven't, why should they hop on my bus?"

"They shouldn't," Robert said. "Would you?"

Kurt put his hands on top of his head. His silence was answer enough.

"I was in the same place, not that long ago," Robert continued. "And I realized I'd made a mistake. I took on the responsibility of owning a business without knowing anything about running one.

"I was miserable and unhappy, and it impacted everything and everyone around me. Then I understood that I was the one who had to fix the company, because I was the one who broke it.

"But, to do that, we had to establish a starting point for the journey ahead, a 'snapshot' of that moment in time. We had to measure everything. Though that wasn't much at the time.

"Remember the KPIs? Key Performance Indicators? Back in the day, at Mushin, we looked at ones like efficiency and productivity.

"When we were done 'taking the snapshot', getting it all down on paper, I had to come to grips with the reality that the business was under-performing. Well below industry levels, in fact. Barely break-even. In other words, the result of all that measurement and effort was depressing as hell.

"That's where SMART goals and objectives came into play. The snapshot was certainly specific and measurable. So the plan to get out of the hole needed to be as well."

Robert leaned against the edge of his desk, close to Kurt.

"Believe me," he continued, "with as bad as everything looked, I certainly didn't want to write down my goals or publish them. What if we failed to reach them? Then I could be held accountable.

"It was the last thing I wanted to do, because once I shared them with everyone at the shop, I'd have to find a way to get everybody excited, get them on the bus. I'd have to make a plan to reach those goals, and live with whatever happened next…"

Robert stopped, drifting away into his own thoughts.

"So what did you do?" Kurt asked. "How did you turn things around? How did you go from where you were to where you knew you needed to be?"

"All good questions," Robert said. "We'll get back to them when you're ready. When you truly need the answers and are able to really understand them."

49

Lizards Lurking

Rochelle sat quietly staring at her employer until you could cut the silence with the knife Kurt carried in his back pocket. It seemed like forever, certainly long enough to make Kurt uncomfortable.

When he could no longer handle the silence, he burst out.

"C'mon, Rocky. What's bothering you?"

"You're a hot mess, Kurt," she replied. "and you're driving everyone around here nuts and that isn't good. Not for you. Not for me. Not for any of us!"

There was no arguing. He knew he was frustrated and anxious and he knew he wore those emotions on his sleeve.

"I know," Kurt replied. "But what am I supposed to do?"

"You've just gotta get past your fear," Rochelle insisted. "The fear that whatever it is you're trying to do *isn't* going to work. Recognize that fear for what it is. Embrace it. Then dance with it."

Rochelle leaned back and crossed her arms. She was done. Kurt stared at his trusted admin, trying to remember a time when she hadn't been an integral part of Kerrigan Construction. Yet, he still wasn't at all sure where this was coming from.

"Rocky, what are you talking about?"

She shook her head, then started again.

"I'm talkin' about the Resistance! That's what I'm talking about."

Kurt was lost. He had no idea what she was trying to tell him, but knew it had to be important.

Rochelle kept shaking her head back and forth. Kurt had never seen that look of consternation before.

"Okay," she said. "You just sit here. Don't move. Don't get busy with anything else either! I'll be right back."

She stormed out of Kurt's office on a mission. When Rochelle barked instructions like that, regardless of to whom, everyone listened. She returned five minutes later with a handful of printouts, closed the door, and spread the papers across Kurt's desk.

"Let's try this again," she said. "These are blog posts from a guy named Seth Godin. I started following him a while ago—right after you decided it was time to get this place back on track.

"I mentioned what was going on here to a friend one night over dinner, and her husband—who really didn't seem like he was at all interested in our conversation—looked at me and said, 'You really *need* to read Seth!' And I'm all like 'Seth' what? Seth, who?"

Kurt's expression hadn't changed. He was still lost.

"I didn't know who or what he was talking about. Then he tells me he'll send me a couple of blog posts and a link to Seth's site.

"He said, 'Trust me on this one'. He said this Seth person would provide the understanding I would need to manage 'the storm that's coming'. He meant here at work. You know, with all the changes. Anyway, by the time I got home, there was an email with the link and attachments waiting for me.

"I read it all that night. Stuff about marketing and leadership, about fear and overcoming what Seth calls the 'lizard brain'—what others call the Resistance.

"At first I didn't get it either, but then I got hooked on what he had to say. Especially the simple, straightforward way he went about saying it. It was like he was writing to me personally.

I found examples of what he was describing everywhere. All through my life. Here at work. Everywhere. All the things I was convinced were holding me back from getting what I wanted. Things I thought were coming at me from the outside—."

"But… But…" Kurt tried to interrupt.

"No 'buts', Kurt," Rochelle responded. "Just listen. Please."

Kurt smiled and let her go. It was obvious she was on a roll.

"The Resistance, this 'lizard brain', is all about something called the amygdala, the prehistoric brain. That's the brain we had when we crawled up out of the ooze. The 'simple' part of the brain at the base of the skull. Back here…"

Rochelle pointed to where her spinal cord entered her head.

"The part that existed before we could speak. It has no capacity for language, no capacity for conscious thought. It's all about basic stuff like survival. You know… Hunger, sex, comfort, and fear.

"It's the part of the brain concerned with keeping you safe, keeping you out of harm's way. The part that uses fear to stop you from doing anything that has even the slightest shred of risk associated with it.

"I started reading his stuff figuring, 'What the hell? What could it hurt?' And know what? It didn't hurt anything. In fact, it did the opposite: it helped. It helped me understand that the only thing holding me back was me."

Rochelle stopped to catch her breath. She surprised herself with the torrent of words she'd released. Kurt was surprised, too.

"Go on," he said.

"Listen, boss. We're all dealing with a lizard brain. It's that little voice you hear inside your head that keeps saying: 'Don't do it. You're gonna fail and look like a fool. They're gonna laugh at you.

"The truth is everyone here at work is watching you. Everyone is hoping you succeed. Me included.

"But I can see that lizard sitting on your shoulder trying to subvert your efforts to fix this place. I can see him trying to cripple your ability to make a decision and then stick to it.

"So here! I'm gonna do what my friend's husband did. I'm gonna turn you on to Seth Godin. Here's some of my favorite posts and a link to the site. I've even written down a bunch of his books for you.

"This is no magic bullet. It isn't going to make the bad man go away. But, once you know what it is that's holding you back, I'll bet it will make it a hell of a lot easier to get past it and move forward.

"That's it. I said what I had to say. If I was out of line, I'm sorry. It may not be what you want to hear, but I know it's what you need to hear. What all of us here *need* you to hear."

Kurt realized the courage it must have taken for her to corner him like she did. He recognized how difficult it must have been for her to confront him with something he certainly didn't want to deal with—at least, not at that particular moment.

"Thank you, Rochelle," he said, smiling. "This is obviously really important to you—and if it's important to you, it's important to me. I'm going to work my way through this stuff right now. I promise.

"If it's the 'lizard brain' and the Resistance that's getting in my way, we'll just have to find a way to break through it. That should be easier now that we know what we're dealing with."

The meeting ended as abruptly as it had started. But the change that followed was continuous and a lot smoother.

50

Calendar Impaired

Dinner was great. The kids had gone to bed without a fight. In fact, Max even read a story to AJ. Laurie settled down to one of the cable dramas she cherished, and Kurt spent the better part of an hour satisfying his own addiction—a hard, fast workout in the 'man cave' he carved out of the garage.

The house had come with an attached three-car garage: one large double, and a smaller single on the outside. He kept his work truck in the driveway, or on the street when he wasn't driving it, and Laurie's SUV and his Corvette inside.

The third garage had been a depository for all things unwanted until he decided to build a place just for him. To save money, he dedicated a couple of hours to its creation every weekend. After all, building stuff is what he did. He finished the walls, epoxied the concrete floor, re-did the lighting, and filled the space with weights.

After he started at Mushin, he added two one-hundred-pound heavy bags: one hanging from the ceiling joists he'd spent days reinforcing, and the other a round-bottomed bag tethered to a plywood foundation with bungee cords and bolted to the floor.

He detailed the 'cave' with a killer sound system, hung an LCD TV on the wall, and pointed his bicycle trainer at the screen. The only thing missing was a shower.

When Kurt finished his work out, he threw a towel over his shoulders, then headed inside to clean up and get ready for bed.

Dripping with sweat, he walked past Laurie to the bathroom. She looked up from the TV and shook her head in mock disgust.

"Ew, gross," she said. "Go take a shower, clean yourself up, and come to bed. This is almost over."

Kurt smiled, flexing his abs and biceps.

"Here I am," he said playfully. "You can have your way with me if you want. I promise, I won't resist."

He took a step toward the bed. Laurie giggled, pulling the covers up to her neck. She shook her head.

"No! You can't have your way with *me*. Not until you shower."

Kurt smiled, then turned toward the bathroom.

Fifteen minutes later, they were side by side in bed watching the news. Kurt was tired, happy that another full day was ending. He leaned over to kiss his wife lightly on the forehead.

"Love you," he said. He hesitated then started again, "Just wanted to remind you about the end the of the month, the last Saturday. I have the exhibition at the studio. It's my first time going to it, and I'll probably be tied up until two in the afternoon. The good news is I should be free after that."

"Exhibition?" Laurie asked. "At the studio? You never told me. The end of the month? That's only three weeks from now."

"I did tell you," Kurt said firmly. "Twice, in fact. We talked about it a couple of months ago when I first found out. Then I checked in with you again a few weeks ago."

Laurie sat up in bed, visibly upset.

"You do this all the time," she said. "Did you write it down on the calendar? Because if you had told me you'd be part of some special event at the studio, we both know I'd remember. I'd remember because I would write it down on the calendar. But I'd still tell you to write it down."

Kurt knew he hadn't done that. He rubbed his eyes in defeat, then looked up at his wife.

"No, I didn't write it down. I thought you did."

"Really, Kurt?"

Laurie pushed the covers away, and reached for her iPhone charging on the side table. She quickly navigated to her calendar.

"You got lucky," she said, scrolling through that Saturday's agenda. "There's nothing going on with the kids. The only thing we have is dinner with Sean and Denise later that evening."

Laurie set the phone down. She propped a pillow up against the headboard and settled back against it.

"Now what's going on at the studio? What's this exhibition thing all about?"

Kurt could feel a sigh of relief welling up from deep inside, but he stifled it. He'd dodged a bullet, and he knew it. But he didn't want Laurie to know that.

"Evidently, it's something they do every year," he said. "It's for the students, their families, and the community. The ticket sales go to support a few local charities that Robert cares about.

"It's donation-based. You give what you can at the door. There's kind of a potluck lunch and dessert after, that's supplemented by pizza and stuff from Nick's Italian down the street. Whatever money is raised goes back into the community."

"That sounds nice," Laurie said. "What time does it start?"

"Nine o'clock. There'll be demonstrations. You know, traditional weapons, forms, stuff like that…"

Kurt's voice suddenly lowered.

"I'll be participating, too."

He tried to gauge Laurie's reaction, but she was impassive, impossible to read.

"No," she shook her head. "You never told me about any of this. I'd remember if you did. Especially since you'll be a part of it."

Kurt scanned his memory.

I did tell her, he thought. *Twice. Didn't I? Maybe I did forget. No point in making a big deal out of it… Even if I won, I'd lose!*

He shrugged his shoulders.

"Come on, Laurie. If I didn't say anything, it's because I honestly forgot. Besides, I know how busy you and the kids are all the time, especially on the weekends. I wasn't sure this was something you would be interested in anyway."

Laurie's demeanor softened.

"Honey," she said, "of course it's something I'd be interested in, because I know it's something you're passionate about."

Kurt smiled. This wasn't going to be as bad as he thought it would be. He was relieved and could feel her reaching out as well.

"Not to mention," Laurie continued, "what it's done for all of us. Working out at the studio and Robert helping you with the business has changed your life. My God, it's changed all of our lives.

"Just promise me that the next time something like this comes up, you'll write it down on the calendar. Promise you won't keep it a secret."

Kurt shook his head affirmatively. Then he rolled over and took Laurie in his arms.

Show Time – The Exhibition

Kurt was excited. It was the Saturday morning of the exhibition and he was awake, out of the house, and in the studio's large training room helping to set up long before the sun came up.

He positioned rows of chairs along the sides and at the back of the room, along with the tables the caterers had left the day before.

He was nervous.

This would be the first time he'd be able to share what he was learning in public and he didn't want to look awkward or foolish. More than anything, he didn't want to embarrass the studio or anyone associated with it—especially in front of an army of strangers. And they were expecting an army.

Anticipation at home had started to build almost immediately after Kurt and Laurie's late night conversation. It was at a point where all AJ could talk about at home or at pre-school was the coming exhibition.

"Is Daddy going to wear a costume like I did in my recital?" she asked. "Is he going to dance and be a prince?"

Every time his little sister asked questions like that Max, who was two years wiser, would groan.

"No, AJ," he chided. "Dad's not going to wear a costume. He's gonna wear his karate stuff. He's gonna be a dad in karate suit."

That's when Laurie had to intervene: before the conversation slid into to a debate, and the debate escalated into a war.

"Listen up, you barbarians," she said. "Your father is going to be your father."

Max smiled and gave a triumphant side-eye to AJ. He'd won.

"We're going to support him," Laurie continued, "just like he supports you at soccer, Max. And you at ballet and gymnastics."

She tenderly touched AJ on the tip of her nose.

Inevitably, that ended the discussion with the children, but not without Laurie herself wondering what this exhibition would be all about. Other than his admission of 'I'll be participating', Kurt had remained rather cryptic about the nature of his role in the event.

‡

People started to arrive just after eight-thirty and one of the other students reported the seats were already filling up quickly. Kurt was in the locker room when Jason asked him to check and see what was going on outside—whether or not they needed to tend to any last-minute details.

Kurt opened the locker room door, took two steps and stopped cold. Laurie and the kids were sitting in the first row, right in the center. His wife was holding a large bouquet of flowers. He walked over to where they were sitting and kneeled down in front of Laurie who was bracketed on each side by Max and AJ.

"It's so great to see you're here," he said. "You all look great. And those flowers… Wow!"

AJ shrieked and jumped into her father's arms.

"Daddy," she said, "you look great in your karate costume."

Max rolled his eyes. Even now, with him almost seven years old, he felt it was his responsibility to clear this up once and for all.

"It's not a costume, AJ," he admonished. "It's a uniform."

Kurt stood up and spread his arms outward.

"You're right, Max," he smiled. "It's a uniform. So, whaddya think?"

Max tried hard to not display any emotion.

"You look okay, I guess" he admitted. "I jus' wanna know what's going on? What are we gonna see? What are *you* gonna do?"

Kurt crouched down and hugged both his children.

"You know, Max," he said, "You're going to see what you're going to see. And when you do, you can tell me. How's that?"

Max shrugged. Kurt thought about Max's questions and stood up again.

"What you're gonna see" he continued, "is all about breaking barriers. About doing things you never thought you could do."

As Max pondered this, Kurt leaned forward to kiss his wife, first on the forehead and then on the lips. Both kids groaned, and Max wiped his lips with his forearm. Then, almost as if they'd practiced, the two children spoke in unison.

"Stop it! That was gross!"

Kurt kissed Laurie again almost as if to taunt them.

"It's great to see all of you here," he said. "The only problem is now I'm really nervous."

"Don't be," Laurie said lovingly.

Kurt glanced at the clock on the back wall.

"We should be starting any minute now. I have to get back. Hope you enjoy!"

Laurie leaned forward and gave her husband a hug.

"Break a leg," she said.

AJ's eyes nearly popped out of her head. She looked horrified, almost in tears.

"Mommy," she cried. "Why do you want Daddy to break a leg?"

"No, honey," Laurie said. "It's just an expression. What it really means is: good luck."

Laurie looked at Kurt and gave him a wink.

"Do well," she said. "Have a great show."

Kurt waved good-bye and walked over to the 'staging area,' a space temporarily curtained off in front of the door to the locker room. He was met there by Allie and Jason. Allie smiled and looked over at Jason, then back at Kurt.

"Wow," she said. "Is that your wife and kids? Beautiful family."

Jason nodded in agreement.

"This has 'ta be the first time we've seen 'em," he said, "since ya started here. How cool is that? They get to see what ya been up to all this time."

Kurt smiled uneasily, lost in his own thoughts. Allie sensed his apprehension. She touched him on the shoulder gently.

"All you have to do is stay focused and show 'em," she smiled.

Kurt took one last look at the crowd before the program started. That's when he noticed an older gentleman quietly enter the studio and make his way toward the back. Kurt gasped not realizing the sound of his surprise could be heard by Allie and others nearby.

My God! he thought. *Chou Li is here. What the hell do I do now?*

Five Fingers

The exhibition began with the children who practiced at the studio. They were arranged by age and then rank, demonstrating the basics of what they had learned: kicks, blocks, strikes, and a number of the beginning forms.

Robert acted as the event's master of ceremonies, introducing each group along with an explanation of what the audience was about to witness. After the little kids, some of the higher-ranked teenagers showed their stuff with more advanced combinations, forms, and weapons.

Finally, it was time for Kurt to take the floor with his group of adult students. They were still behind the artificial barrier the curtain provided when Robert walked up to Kurt.

"Now is not the time for distractions," he said. "You'll need to focus or you're likely to hurt yourself. What's wrong?"

"It's Chou Li," Kurt said, his eyes closed. "My tai chi instructor from the park. He's here!"

Robert placed his right hand on Kurt's shoulder with enough pressure to get his attention.

"That's wonderful," he said, genuinely pleased. "Aren't you excited for him to see what you've been up to here? You should be proud of what you've accomplished, not concerned.

"Do you really think we would allow you to do anything out there today you're not capable of?"

Robert reached up and placed his left hand on Kurt's other shoulder. His grip was significant.

"You've got this," he said. "You've been working toward this moment since the morning you started here. Now it's time to show everyone what you can do. What you've already done."

Robert left the staging area and walked over to a large mound covered by one of several blue construction tarps that Kurt had donated. He grabbed the tarp and pulled it away with a flourish.

Underneath were three rows of bricks, separated and stacked. Each row started with a one brick and incrementally increased to ten. Each brick was separated by a small spacer at each of its corners.

Then Robert headed over to a second mound and pulled that tarp away, revealing stacks of wooden boards. Each board was an inch thick, eighteen inches long, and twelve inches wide.

Kurt walked out to the center of the floor with six of his classmates. Among them there were three brown belts, and four white belts (including Kurt). Behind the group of students stood Allie, Jason, and Robert; each of them with a black belt securing their *gi*.

The crowd grew silent in anticipation.

Until that moment, the Kerrigan family had been only mildly interested in what was going on. Laurie had found the younger students adorable, the music interesting.

She had noticed that Max and AJ tried to mimic a few of the blocks and punches as they sat in their seats.

But now their father was on the floor, gleaming under the lights in his white uniform. Laurie noticed how serious Kurt looked. She spied her children on either side. They were quiet, leaning forward in their seats.

Kurt was the center of attention. Kurt and stacks of bricks and boards. It was obvious that something big was about to happen, something that had to do with focus—with the consolidation of force—with power.

He approached the first stack and settled into a fighting stance. He eyed the bricks. The room became eerily quiet.

Kurt extended the fingers on his right hand, bent the first and second knuckles slightly, and tucked his thumb in tight alongside his index finger. A configuration known as 'ridge hand'.

Unbeknownst to him, Max had risen to his feet and was standing at the edge of the polished wooden floor. The boy started to imitate his father's stance with his right arm extended. A few folks in the audience looked on with mild amusement.

Kurt was too deep in concentration to notice. He was focused on two things and two things only. One was his breathing. The other was force versus impact.

He placed the outer edge of his 'ridge hand' against the center of brick. He lifted his hand and dropped it twice—measuring the distance in his mind.

He inhaled, focusing on a spot two inches below the brick.

He gathered his *qi*, his energy, as both Robert and Chou Li had shown him. Then Kurt raised his arm and struck through the brick releasing all that pent-up energy with a mighty a *kiai*!

The brick shattered on impact as the explosive sound of his yell reverberated around the room.

Laurie gasped. AJ jumped out of her seat.

Max swept his arm down in a chopping motion and let out a mighty *kiai* of his own.

A few people chuckled as Laurie ushered her son back into his seat.

From there, Kurt and his classmates—along with Robert, Allie and Jason—attacked the remaining bricks and boards. When all was said and done, Kurt had broken first a single brick, then two.

He went on to the boards, breaking a total of three at one time with his fist. As for the single boards, he dispatched them with a series of kicks: first a snap kick, then a roundhouse, a crescent, and finally an axe kick.

As that portion of the exhibition came to a close, Kurt and the other white belt and brown belt students cleared the stage. Only the masters remained. Robert, Allie and Jason each took their turn destroying stacks of eight, nine, and then ten bricks at a time.

The next segment showcased students performing advanced *katas* and weapons forms.

Finally, the exhibition appeared to have reached its conclusion when Robert walked to the center of the floor. He bowed to his students, performed a salute, and then addressed the crowd.

"I sincerely hope everyone has enjoyed this morning's exhibition as much as I have. It represents countless hours of effort, hard work, and dedication on the part of the individuals who participated.

"Now, I hope all of you will stay and join us for lunch."

With the exhibition complete everyone began to migrate to the tables covered with all kinds of food, both catered and contributed, set up in front of the mirrors at the back of the room.

Kurt joined his family. Before he could say a word, Laurie grabbed his right hand and rotated it in front of her. His knuckles were visibly irritated, and the knife edge of his right hand was swollen slightly. But, all in all, he seemed to be in one piece.

AJ locked her arms around Kurt's neck in a death grip, while Max just stood there, in awe, staring at his father.

Laurie gave her husband a hug and a kiss.

"That was impressive," she said proudly. "Truly impressive."

As Kurt kissed Laurie's forehead, he realized that Chou Li was standing beside them. He turned to face his *sifu*, his master, and bowed. Laurie looked at the two men curiously.

"This is Chou Li," Kurt said, "the leader of my afternoon tai chi group. Chou Li... this is Laurie, my wife; Max, our son; and AJ, our daughter."

Chou Li bowed deeply.

"I am honored," he said. "Kurt is a willing and conscientious student; we have shared many wonderful conversations in the park after class. I am really pleased that I was able to witness this moment."

Kurt returned the bow.

"I'm so glad you came. Will you stay and have lunch with us?"

"No," Chou Li said, "I'm sorry, but I shouldn't. You have a beautiful family and this special time is for you."

Chou Li started to back away, then stopped.

"Will I see you tomorrow at the park?"

Kurt nodded. He took the old man's hand in his. Chou Li smiled, then turned to leave. At that moment, Laurie called out.

"Chou Li, perhaps you will be able to join us another time. I'd like to properly thank you for helping keep my husband centered and sane."

Chou Li nodded and waved his good-bye. Max watched the old man with interest. Then he took a step forward toward his father, placed his left hand over his right fist and bowed, just like he'd seen everyone on the floor do.

"Are you going to teach me how to do that?" he asked. "Are you going to teach me to do what you just did?"

AJ jumped into the conversation.

"Me too! Me too!" she squealed.

Kurt reached down and messed up Max's hair. He didn't have to reach that far anymore; Max was getting so tall.

"Well, I may not be the one to teach you," Kurt said. "But we can enroll you guys in the studio. If that's okay with your mother."

Laurie smiled. It wasn't going to be a problem.

Max took his father's right hand, examining it with curiosity.

"How did you do that, Dad?" he wondered. "How did you break that brick with just your hand? Without hurting yourself?"

Kurt laughed.

"You know those *Peanuts* specials we watch on TV?" he asked. "The ones that come out every Christmas and Thanksgiving? Well, there was also a play—kind of like the ones you have at school. There's a scene in the play, maybe my favorite scene, and it included everybody: Snoopy, Charlie Brown, but the funniest one was Lucy.

"Do you remember Lucy? And her younger brother Linus?"

Max nodded enthusiastically.

"Lucy got real upset with Linus," Kurt continued. "Kind of like when you get mad at AJ and she threatened him with her fist."

Kurt raised his right hand until it was positioned right in front of his own face. Max's eyes widened.

"She looked at him with her fingers spread open and wide like this. Then she said, 'See these five fingers, Linus? Individually, they're nothing.'"

Then Kurt curled his fingers into a ball.

"'But when I curl them together like this into a single unit, they form a weapon that is terrible to behold'.

Linus gave in. But when Lucy started to walk away he looked at his own fingers, shook his head, and started talking to them, 'Why can't you guys get organized like that?'"

Max laughed. He got the point.

"Well," his father continued, "When I started here my fingers were kind of like Linus'. Now they're organized like Lucy's!"

Max looked down his right hand.

"Daddy, I'm hungry!" AJ insisted.

"Okay, honey," Kurt said, "there's plenty to eat over here."

He took her hand and started toward the tables of food at the back. Laurie followed, looking back over her shoulder for Max.

The little boy was still rooted in place, staring at his right hand, opening and closing his fingers. First he made a fist, then he formed it into a 'ridge hand' like his father.

"Okay, guys," Max said, "I think it's finally time for you to get yourselves organized."

A Thousand Words

Kurt was sitting at his desk on a Monday morning looking out into the office. The immediate excitement of the exhibition had passed, but the pride remained. He was thinking that things were starting to look pretty good, both at home and here at work.

The door to his office was always open—even in the midst of what must have felt like complete chaos to his employees. Change was occurring daily.

Everyone seemed to agree that access and transparency were critical to the success of what Kurt was trying to accomplish at Kerrigan Construction. As far as he could see, the only way to get there was through an 'open door' policy. That meant, quite literally, that Kurt's door remained open just about all the time.

Consequently, it wasn't much of a shock to find a stream of people bouncing in and out of his office in the course of a normal day. And, for the most part, Kurt didn't mind. He felt that feedback and honest communication were essential to ensuring that all of them were on the same bus, headed in the right direction.

More than anyone else, Rick, as general manager, was Kurt's eyes and ears. So it wasn't unusual for Kurt to look up and find Rick standing at the door, or at the foot of his desk, patiently awaiting his attention.

Today was no different with one possible exception: the wad of crumpled papers Rick held tightly clutched in his right hand.

Kurt could see that he was agitated, and that wasn't generally a good thing. Especially since Kurt's normal response to chaos was an admonition to 'Calm down and take a deep breath'. It was obvious Rick hadn't done that. At least not yet.

Kurt motioned for his GM to come in and take a seat.

"What's up?" he said. "You look stressed."

"I am," Rick insisted. "Got a minute?"

Kurt could feel the tension in his own body start to build.

"Sure. What's going on?"

Rick spread out the papers he'd been holding across the polished surface of the desk.

"I'm gonna ask you a question," he said. "But it's one of those questions I already know the answer to. What are they called again? Questions I already know the answer to?"

"Rhetorical?" Kurt offered.

"That's it," Rick said. "Do you remember 'before'? Before you found Mushin and started working out every day at the studio? Remember when we did the Hamilton job? The old Victorian out in Deer's Point?"

Kurt winced and visibly pulled away from the desk.

"Do I remember it?" he asked incredulously. "That job cost us more than $20,000. It's hard to forget losses like that. Especially when things are tough to begin with. But that's ancient history. Why are you asking about it now?"

Rick leaned forward, covering the papers he had placed in front of him with his hands.

"Do you recall what went wrong?" he asked. "Why we went in the hole on that job?"

"Of course I do," Kurt said, rubbing his eyes.

He sat back in his chair, and took a long breath.

"It was a massive remodel," Kurt continued. "Interior walls to the studs, hardwood floors, 'popcorn' off the ceiling. It started out as a good project, a profitable job that we—"

"That's right," Rick interrupted. "We got past all our inspections and the walk-through with the client. But this was before we had the checklists and punch cards we use now, before we documented everything we do at every stage with digital images."

Kurt nodded, still unsure where the conversation was headed.

"We finished the job on time," Rick continued. "Got everyone and everything signed off. Then, a few months later, one of the water lines running through the family room started leaking. It wiped out the wall and ruined the new hardwood flooring."

Kurt's brow furrowed at the memory.

"The client insisted it was our fault," Rick said, "that we'd missed something. Even though he and his wife were at the walk-through to sign off on that part of the project, we had no way of proving everything was fine when it was inspected."

"We had to protect our reputation," Kurt chimed in. "We just went back in and fixed it all."

"Exactly," Rick said. "We fixed the plumbing, repaired the walls, replaced the flooring. We took it in the shorts. Then we licked our wounds and went on to the next project."

Kurt's eyes were squinted half-closed. He had his elbows on the desk with his fingers interlocked. He tried to breathe. He looked at all the papers that Rick had spread out on the desk trying to make out what they were.

"Please tell me" Kurt sighed, "that all those papers aren't your way of telling me that it happened again. Especially now, with all the new safeguards we've got in place."

For the first time since he'd entered the office, Rick smiled.

"No, boss!" he said, beaming. "I'm not gonna say that, because it didn't happen. What I am gonna do is come across the desk and give you a great big hug, because everything we've been doing since you figured out these new procedures saved our collective ass."

Kurt let out a sigh. Rick was vibrating with excitement.

"You know the Principe remodel we finished a while ago?" Rick asked, not waiting for a 'yes' this time. "It was one of our first jobs after integrating the inspections and digital images into the daily operations. We were still figuring out how to do it without scaring the hell out of our clients or making fools of ourselves."

"The Principe's," Kurt interjected. "Weren't they the couple that kept thanking us for documenting the job so thoroughly? The ones who thought it was so cool that we 'recorded' the entire project in the album we gave them."

Rick bounced up and down in his seat like a school boy.

"That's right," he said. "They were so grateful that we kept them involved. They left one of the first reviews talking about how great the inspections and images were. How they'd never experienced anything like that before. They said it was an integral part of the process, an important part of their project."

"Okay," Kurt said, "that was a fun trip down Memory Lane. But what's this all about?"

Rick wasn't done with his Q&A yet.

"What else do you remember about that job?" he asked. "Anything special? Anything odd? There was something that came up in two of the project team meetings we called."

Kurt shook his head back and forth. Then it dawned on him.

"I'm not 100% sure," Kurt's face brightened, "but wasn't there evidence of corrosion on some of the copper pipes headed to the master bath? Some of the lines going to the tub and the shower?"

Rick moved his hand from the pile of papers, revealing four digital images of the bare walls and copper lines running to the stall shower and the tub that clearly showed a residue of corrosion.

The photos were accompanied by the project manager's notes indicating his suggestion to replace those lines in order to 'quality control' the job. Taking this action, his notes indicated, would prevent future damage should those lines fail and begin to leak.

There was also a note about installing a main water shut-off valve in the garage—either automatic or manual—to allow the client to close down the water supply to their home when they were traveling (something they did quite often).

Both the repair and the shut-off valve had been declined. Both were signed off and initialed by the project manager and the client.

"See that?" Rick pointed to inspection sheets.

Kurt stared at the papers Rick had thrust in front of him.

"What?" Kurt asked. "I see the notes and the images. What are you showing me?"

Rick pointed to the client's signature and initials.

"See those initials?" he insisted. "That's forty thousand dollars worth of initials right there!"

"What the hell are you talking about?" Kurt asked, puzzled.

"I'm talking about the Principe's," Rick said. "They were Europe on vacation when the master bath plumbing on the second floor went to hell and started leaking."

Kurt looked up from documents and smiled. He got it.

"Two weeks' worth of water damage," Rick continued. "That's what I'm talkin' about. Walls, hardwood floors, carpeting and mold.

"I'm talkin' about us probably having to eat all of it in the old days. If we didn't have the images and inspection sheets signed and initialed—proving that the client saw the potential for damage, and declined to address it on a change-order—we'd be sunk.

"You hav'ta call Robert and thank him. Tell him he just saved us a small fortune by introducing us to those new procedures."

Kurt smiled in agreement.

"From the first moment I received their vehicle report," he said, "I knew we should make it a part of our workflow process."

"You know what's even better?" Rick asked. "Better than the inspections and the fact there is no question that we're not liable?"

Kurt looked at Rick, curious about what he might have to say.

"The Principe's realize they should have listened to us. They know they should have issued the change-order and paid the extra money to have us take care of the plumbing before it ruined the work we had just completed.

"They were so happy with what we had already done and the way we did it—and so sorry they didn't listen—they told their insurance company they weren't going to let anyone else touch the house but us.

"Instead of it costing us money, like that other nightmare did, we're scheduling the remediation work and the rest of the repairs. Kurt, you're a damned genius."

Kurt finally felt like he could breathe.

"Thanks," he said. "Maybe I'm a lucky genius. Lucky that I met Robert."

"You're the one who made it happen *here*," Rick smiled. "I've called everyone together for a team meeting. We're going to talk about both projects, Hamilton and Principe. I want to reinforce the policies and procedures you've laid out... Because they work."

Rick gathered up his papers, came around the desk, locked Kurt in a bear hug, then headed out the door.

Kurt took another deep, relaxing breath.

There was no better feeling than what he was experiencing. He had been exposed to something new, accepted it, rolled it around in his head, and figured out how to make it work.

He used that wisdom in a different way than Robert had, but it still worked. And making it work resulted in everything he could ever hope it would and more.

The only thing he could compare it to was taking something he'd learned in the park with Chou Li, and then applying it successfully when he was on the floor in the studio.

Things are back on track, he thought. *Damn, it's about time.*

54

The Unity of All Things

Robert had once described himself as a 'thinking martial artist.' When pressed, he explained that there were plenty of martial arts practitioners who learned the movements and actually achieved some degree of aptitude without ever mastering *bushidō*, the way of the samurai warrior—a combination of Zen, physical conditioning, martial prowess, philosophy, and art.

He contended that some of those individuals (perhaps most) never achieved an understanding of how all the aspects of *bushidō* are connected. And how, without that level of understanding, their journey would never be complete.

One evening, in Robert's office, Kurt was pushing his teacher for more information about the metaphysical nature of training in the martial arts. Robert reached behind his desk and handed Kurt two yellowed, dog-eared, and well-read books.

One was *Zen in the Martial Arts* by Joe Hyam and the other was *The Tao of Jeet Kune Do* by Bruce Lee.

"Here," he said. "I recommend you read these two books as you start this new segment of your training.

"I think they will help you achieve a new and different level of self-awareness—an understanding of who you are, where you are, and how you are an integral part of a much greater whole.

"It's the part of your business management training that will go way beyond the numbers."

Kurt bowed his head in appreciation of the gift.

Upon seeing Kurt's reaction, Robert smiled. It was apparent he would need to clarify his intent.

"This is meant to help get you get started. They're the two books that formed the cornerstone of my library, and my hope is they will serve as the cornerstone of yours. However, these two books are especially meaningful to me; I'd like them returned when you've finished with them or have purchased your own copies."

Kurt bowed again, this time in recognition of the conditions his *sensei* had set forth with regard to the loan of the two books.

‡

Kurt was excited to get home and crack open at least one of the books. He waited until the kids went down for the night, then found a place for himself on the couch in the family room—his left arm on the bolster, positioning the book so the lamp could illuminate it better. It was the one by Bruce Lee.

Laurie was beside him, curled up on the other side of the couch, using his right thigh as a pillow.

What Kurt realized almost immediately was the extent to which he found himself comfortable with everything Lee had chronicled within its pages.

Kurt's understanding was accelerated by Robert's handwritten notes in the margins—his questions and interpretations of the text. Kurt found Robert's musings and analyses strangely consistent with his own, as his own personal philosophy began to emerge.

Laurie tapped Kurt on the knee.

"I'm not thrilled about seeing you come home with welts and bruises all over your body. You know that, right?

"But I do like the new you, the you you're becoming. You're different, Kurt. Better in so many ways."

Kurt closed the book and looked deep into his wife's eyes.

"Here's the 'new and improved' Kurt Kerrigan," she announced, imitating a TV ad pitch man. She continued sincerely. "Patient, giving, caring, and available. You're home more. And you're more present when you're here. Whatever you're doing at the studio, don't stop. I like what it's done to you. I like it, and the kids love it!

"So, thank Robert for all of us. If seeing you bruised is the price I have to pay for having you back… Well, then, I'll gladly pay it. Besides," she chuckled, "you're the one in constant pain!"

Kurt smiled, and brushed her hair back with his hand.

"I am at that," he laughed.

Laurie snuggled back into the crook of his leg. Kurt returned to *The Tao of Jeet Kune Do* to learn more about the philosophy of the iconic martial artist.

He was unaware of the importance this loan from Robert was to have, an importance that would go beyond the content contained in each volume. Soon the books would become a catalyst for Kurt as he replaced Robert's books with copies of his own, forming the foundation of own library.

‡

Things were moving in the right direction at work as well.

The communication between the front office and the rest of Kerrigan's workforce had never been better. What started with Kurt and Rick meeting on a regular basis to ensure the company was heading in the right direction, radiated out to all the employees in the organization.

Everyone was informed. Everyone had a chance to contribute and voice their concerns. The consensus that formed around the company's new Why made a profound difference as it was adopted. There was something magical about having a purpose everyone in the company believed was transcendent, almost noble.

It transformed the mundane, mechanical explanation for what the company did into something everyone there could get behind, something they could all be proud of. It was something they began promoting in all their marketing and advertising efforts, in print and on the web.

To enhance our clients' lives by creating beautiful and functional living spaces and work environments that delight them, adding our expertise and experience to their ideas in order to bring their dreams to life!

Along with the Strategic Plan Kurt and Rick were building, this powerful new Why gave them a standard by which to judge all their corporate decisions.

Everyone from the receptionist to the project managers to the folks actually doing the work knew what they were there to do.

If something failed to meet the high criterion of their new Why, it probably wasn't going to happen. If it did not result in something beautiful or functional, something that did not bring their clients' dreams to life, someone had better be able to explain why they were doing it to begin with.

This gave everyone at Kerrigan Construction a clarity rarely experienced by their competitors—competitors perfectly happy to build just about anything for just about anyone.

In addition, this powerful new Why attracted a different quality of clients—people who were more interested in fulfilling their dreams than in just having something cobbled together. It relegated those individuals more concerned with getting a deal—than in the creation of a dream—to look elsewhere.

All this allowed Kurt and the rest of his leadership team the chance to be more discerning in their customer acquisition efforts.

Better clients translated into better projects.

With a new focus on Key Performance Indicators and the information they provided, better projects translated into better margins and higher profits.

It was a virtuous cycle. And every day, with each little action, it was transforming Kerrigan Construction into a better, stronger, more resilient, and more responsive company—a place that functioned in harmony with Kurt's new philosophy in which everything was connected, an integral part of a larger whole.

It was the new way he was beginning to see business. The way he was experiencing his home life, and the way he knew he would be interacting with the world, both now and in the future.

There were still problems. Lots of them. And the change Kurt yearned for wasn't happening as fast as Kurt would have liked, but —however slowly—it was still happening.

The Tempest

Kurt had been feeling pretty good about himself. Slowly, but surely, things were coming together at work. He was able to start paying down a small part of the credit card debt he'd amassed.

It felt like things were coming together. But then Laurie decided to take the kids shopping. There wasn't much choice. It was winter and the kids had outgrown just about everything in their wardrobe.

She didn't like taking them along. With the financial pressure of the last couple of years, the simple act of shopping had become nerve-wracking enough. But that, coupled with the fact that guiding Max and AJ through the mall was like herding cats with a stick, made it almost impossible.

She found that shopping with a girlfriend or two gave her the illusion it was actually doable. So she made arrangements with her two closest friends, Jessica and DeDe, to accompany her with their little broods as well.

Now Laurie waited in line at the check-out, a stack of clothing in her left arm. She clutched AJ with her right hand while scanning the children's department for Max. Her girlfriends were behind her.

As she reached the counter, she set down her load and searched her purse with her free hand. Her wallet emerged with a stack of coupons rubber-banded around it. She dug out her credit card and passed it to the sales associate across the counter.

The young woman tallied each piece of clothing in the register, along with the appropriate coupons, then swiped the card.

Laurie sensed something was wrong. The clerk was suddenly uncomfortable. The young woman swiped the card a second time. Then she leaned forward and quietly spoke.

"I'm sorry, but your card has been declined."

"Impossible," Laurie replied. "That card has a zero balance. It just came in the mail yesterday. It's never been used."

The clerk looked at her sheepishly. She was only the messenger.

Laurie thought about the possibilities for the card's denial.

Maybe I forgot to authorize it. You have to call in and give an initiation code before it can be used.

For a moment, she was frustrated by this stupid mistake. Then she remembered calling. No, it had to be some other reason.

Laurie was embarrassed. Standing right behind her—watching the entire scene, waiting patiently for their turn to check-out—were two of her closest friends. This could not be happening.

Laurie dug in her wallet and pulled out a second card.

"Here," she said. "Use this one. I'm sure it will be okay."

The clerk smiled, and ran it for her. The credit card terminal responded with the same message, a single word: declined.

Laurie felt her face flush. She wanted to turn invisible and disappear. Jessica touched her gently on the shoulder.

"I'm sure it's just a mistake on their part," she said. "It happens all the time. Don't worry about it."

Jessica smiled and handed her credit card to the sales associate.

"We'll put this stuff on my card," she continued. She glanced at Laurie, "You and I can sort it all out later."

Laurie was mortified, wounded, utterly defeated. She wanted to cry; she wanted to scream; she wanted to hide.

She thought about grabbing Jessica's credit card back from the clerk. Returning all the clothes. Running out of the store with the kids in tow as fast as she could. But she knew she couldn't.

She was in shock. She watched in slow motion as the transaction went through. The sales clerk smiled and handed the card back to Jessica, then bagged up the clothes and offered them to Laurie.

It took a moment before she realized the bag was for her.

‡

On the way home, she fought back the tears. The kids were very quiet. They knew something was wrong and they didn't want to make it worse. But slowly Laurie's pain turned to anger.

Things like this never happen, she thought. *Never!*

She was careful about money. But what about Kurt? Something was wrong, very wrong. And she was going to get to the bottom it as soon as she got back to the house.

Soon she was ushering the children into the family room. She found something decent for them on public TV, then got to work.

The first card was maxed out with a balance of $15,000.

How is that possible? she thought. *We never use this card.*

She checked with the bank that issued the second card she had tried at the store. The company representative told her that card was close to its credit limit.

"How much has been charged?" Laurie asked.

"The limit is ten thousand dollars," the rep said. "The card shows a balance of just under that amount."

"How long has it been like that?" Laurie wondered.

"Let me check," the rep said. "The minimum payment has been made for each of the past five months."

Laurie thanked the person and got off the phone. She sat there with her hands on her knees. She was crushed.

She and Kurt were at least $25,000 in debt.

At least that much, she thought. *What else don't I know about?*

Her questions plunged her even deeper into despair.

How close to bankruptcy are we? How could he keep something like this from me? Aren't we supposed to be partners?

Her first thought was to call Kurt at the office. Ask him what the hell was going on. But she decided this was something that needed to be addressed in person. Aside from that, she knew she needed to cool down before confronting her husband.

‡

Kurt came in through the door two hours later. He hugged and kissed the kids first, then walked to where Laurie was sitting on the couch in the family room. He leaned down to kiss her 'hello'. She turned her head, raised her arm, and pushed him away.

Kurt backed up, surprised.

"What's up?" he asked. "Did something happen today that you want to talk about?"

Laurie glared at him for a long, uncomfortable moment.

"The kids have already eaten," she said curtly. "There's stuff in the fridge if you want dinner. I'm not hungry."

Kurt knew from her tone and body language that all he could do was wait, wait to find out what had gone so terribly wrong.

"You sure you don't want anything?" he offered.

"We'll talk later, after the kids are in bed," she said.

Kurt made himself a sandwich and ate alone. He got the kids ready for bed, tucked them in, then returned to the family room.

Laurie hadn't moved an inch.

Kurt was concerned. Even when she got angry, this wasn't like her. He grabbed one of the kitchen chairs, brought it into the family room, and sat down across from Laurie. He reached out to touch her knee, but she brushed his hand away.

"What's going on?" he asked. "Why are you acting like this? Did I do something wrong?"

Laurie's hands were closed; her fists clenched tight.

"I took the kids shopping today," she said slowly. "We were with Jessica, DeDe, and their kids."

Kurt nodded. That seemed reasonable.

"I had to," Laurie continued. "Max has outgrown or destroyed everything he has and AJ's too big for most of what's in her closet."

She stopped. She was done. The answer he wanted should be obvious by now. But Kurt stared back at her blankly. He really didn't seem to get it.

"Is there anything you want to tell me?" she asked. "Anything you've been hiding from me?"

Suddenly, Kurt felt his heart rate take off. He could tell Laurie was barely in control of her anger, but he had no idea why.

What the hell is this? he thought. *Does she think I'm with another woman? That's ridiculous. What kind of man does she think I am?*

Laurie kept staring at him waiting for an answer. Kurt was beginning to feel indignant. He felt his own anger rising. It didn't matter what the hell happened, he didn't deserve to be treated like this. She had to be crazy to think he'd ever cheat on her.

"What the hell's going on with you?" he barked. "What do you think I'm up to? And when? When would I have the time? I go to work every day. I come home every night.

"I work hard for you and the kids, dammit."

He tried to take a deep breath to calm down. It didn't work.

"I'm tired of playing these little guessing games. There's no way I can win, so just stop," he said. "It's all crap anyway. If you have something to say, then say it, dammit!"

Laurie was fuming; she was as angry as Kurt had ever seen her. She felt betrayed... by their marriage, by his vows, by his lack of honesty. She felt exposed by the terrible situation they were in.

"What's going on?" she asked sarcastically. "How about having two different credit cards declined while I was checking out at the mall with my closest girlfriends standing right behind me?"

Laurie's eyes glistened in the light as they filled with tears.

"How about using a card that should have had a zero balance? A card we never use. Only to have it declined because it was maxed out. How about finding out the other card I tried was close to being maxed out as well!"

Kurt looked down. He hadn't cheated on her with a woman. This betrayal was far worse. This was a betrayal of trust. Tears streamed down Laurie's cheeks.

Laurie had the two credit cards clutched tightly in hand. She had cut them up hours ago. Now she hurled the pieces across the family room.

Kurt felt his heart stop. He had been trying desperately to keep the business going. He was desperate to make payroll and pay his suppliers. He was stuck. Trapped.

He couldn't sell the business. There was nothing to sell. He had to keep it going—and using the cards seemed like the only answer at the time.

He knew he should have discussed it with Laurie beforehand, explained it all, but he didn't. In all honesty, he had been afraid to. And he knew it.

He was afraid of how it would make him look in her eyes. Afraid she would say 'no'. Afraid that all the hard work of the last few years, and a lifetime of effort, would go up in smoke.

56

And, the Teapot

Kurt got up from the chair and walked into the kitchen staring at the floor. What he did was wrong. There was no question about that. He had betrayed Laurie's trust, a sacred trust. He didn't know what he could do to fix that, or even if it could be fixed.

He went to the cupboard, took out two of her favorite herbal teas, filled the teapot, and started boiling the water. Laurie was in the family room sobbing quietly.

Kurt fixed the tea the way she liked it, with honey and a little lemon. He grabbed two coasters, brought Laurie's cup of tea to the family room, and placed it on the table beside her. He sat down across from her with his cup cradled between his hands.

"I screwed up, Laurie," Kurt said, his voice a whisper. "I've been trying to keep the business going. I thought I could float payroll and the bills just a little bit longer while we were recovering.

"Things have been getting better. But not as fast as I thought they would. Not as fast as I would like and I didn't want to lose it all. So I started paying stuff with the cards."

Laurie glared at him.

"When were you going to share this with me?" she asked. "While we were in bankruptcy court? You know what you did was wrong. You knew it was wrong because you were afraid to tell me. How could you do this? Don't you trust me? Didn't you think I would understand?

"I thought we were partners. I guess I'm just the nanny. A live-in housekeeper with benefits. Well, I'm turning in my notice. I quit!"

Kurt was shaking. He got off his chair, and placed his cup of tea on the table alongside Laurie's. He knelt in front of her. His voice started to crack.

"Please, Laurie," he said. "Stop talking like that. I know I blew it, but don't talk about leaving. I need you. The kids need you. Please."

"Who are you trying to con?" Laurie retorted. "If you really you needed me, you never would have deceived me.

"What do you always say, Kurt? 'Never bullshit a bullshitter'? You lied to me. There's nothing else to talk about."

Kurt shook his head as tears ran down his cheeks.

"No, Laurie. That isn't true. I didn't lie. I just didn't tell you. That's not the same. I was going to tell you. But, I didn—"

"Really?" she interrupted. "And that's supposed to make me feel better? The fact that you kept something that important from me? That you were afraid to tell me how bad things had really gotten?"

"No," Kurt said. "It isn't better. But it isn't lying either."

Kurt stood up and tried to pull Laurie into his arms. But instead she beat her fists against his chest. She had been betrayed by the one person she was sure would never do that. Her husband had proven her wrong and she couldn't bear that.

Kurt wrapped his arms around his wife and buried his face in the crook of her neck. He held her as each of them tried to catch their breath between sobs. He dropped to his knees, begging.

"Please, honey. Forgive me. I know I don't deserve it. I know how disappointed in me you are. I swear, as God is my witness, that I will never do anything like this again. I see how much I've hurt you. And that's killing me!"

Kurt took a deep breath. "Please don't leave me," he said softly.

"I know I don't deserve a second chance, but I'm begging you. I'd rather die than lose you!"

Laurie looked down at her husband. She could feel the truth in his words. She believed him when he said he loved her. She believed he was truly sorry for what he had done.

She knew that, despite the embarrassment and disappointment, she loved him. Despite everything he'd done, she still loved him.

She placed her hands under his arms and pulled him up.

"We need to talk," she said sternly. "We need to talk if we're going to make this work."

Kurt nodded his head slowly.

"No more hiding stuff," Laurie continued. "No more secrets. You and I have to sit down and figure out what we owe. We have to get rid of the debt you've piled up. We have to do it now. And we have to do it together. Otherwise, there's no point in going any further."

Kurt's sense of relief was overwhelming. He started to breathe normally again. He held his wife tightly in his arms.

"I love you, Laurie," he said. "I love you so very much!"

She took Kurt's hand and led him to the kitchen table. Then she grabbed the notepad she kept by the kitchen phone, and sat down beside her husband. She was quiet for a moment. When Laurie finally spoke, she did so with authority.

"Okay. Let's figure out how we're going to get through this."

Communication

At the next one of their recurring meetings Kurt asked Robert what he thought his single biggest mistake was when he first began the process of transformation at Mushin Automotive.

"Communication!" Robert exclaimed without hesitation.

"Communication?" Kurt repeated. "That's it? That's the biggest mistake you made. How?"

"When you're trying to accomplish something," Robert said, "it doesn't really matter what... You know it's going to take more than just *you* to get it done. So you start bringing other people in.

"You know where you are. You know where you want to go. You know what you want to accomplish. And you know it will be good for everyone if, and when, you can actually make it all happen.

"You're excited. The team is excited because they know—or, at least, they believe—that you know what you're doing; that you're trying to fix wherever it is that's broken. You're all headed out to conquer the universe. Your little corner of it anyway.

"Everything is ready. And, believe me, I was ready. I had everything in place to make the journey a success, a journey that required the support and cooperation of everyone involved.

"There was only *one* problem, and it turned out to be a big one. I failed to tell anyone anything about the journey they were about to embark upon. I didn't share anything with anyon—."

"I don't get it," Kurt interrupted, looking puzzled.

"You just said everyone was onboard. That they were excited. Then you said your biggest failure was not telling them anything about what you were doing or where you were going. How is that possible? How could they buy into the dream, and still be in the dark? It doesn't make any sense."

"You've got kids, right?" Robert asked. "I've seen them here."

Kurt nodded proudly. Max and AJ loved the weekly sessions.

"Did you ever have a Saturday where you told the kids to load their stuff up and get in the car? That you were headed out, but you didn't tell 'em where you were going.

"They were still excited, right? They had no idea where they were headed or what might be in store for them. They just knew the alternative was staying home and that would be torture—because there's nothing to do there on a Saturday morning that's any fun!"

"Okay, I get it," Kurt said. "At least I think I do. But now I have another question."

"What's that?"

"Why?" Kurt asked, his head tilted to the side. "Why didn't you tell them? There has to be a reason."

Robert suddenly laughed, then composed himself.

"Sorry," he said. "This isn't funny. At least not funny 'ha ha.' But, as long as you're asking, there were two reasons. One I was aware of, and one I wasn't. The first reason was: I thought they knew. I thought everyone 'got it'. But they didn't. I didn't communicate the why, the where, the what, or the how of what we were doing.

"My people didn't know what our goals and objectives were. As a result, they didn't have any idea whether or not I knew how we were going to make this journey. They didn't know if I had a plan. They couldn't know, because I hadn't shared it.

"In fact, they were totally in the dark with regard to just about everything involved in this little adventure of mine."

"And the second reason, the one you didn't know?" Kurt asked.

Robert shook his head slowly, then took a deep breath.

"Honestly, I didn't know *how*," he said. "I didn't know how to communicate at that time, how to share something that critically important. Worse yet, I didn't even know where to go or who to ask in order to learn."

Robert was as sincere as Kurt had ever seen him. Instinctively, Kurt leaned forward to be sure he didn't miss anything.

"I didn't know a lot of things then," Robert continued. "I didn't know that—like you and me and every other business owner in the country (in the world, maybe)—the people on our team, the folks who work with us, have needs of their own to satisfy.

"When you first get started in business, your people assume you are the one to help *them*. They look to you to meet their needs and expectations. In fact, by jumping on the bus with you, they assume you're the one who can help them achieve their own personal goals.

"But over time, my lack of communication, my inability to share, allowed members of my team to lose interest in everything associated with me, my company, my vision, and my dreams.

"Nature abhors a vacuum and—in the absence of shared goals— my people substituted their own. And their objectives didn't always align with mine. I'd be willing to bet the same thing is going on at Kerrigan Construction, and has been for some time.

"The biggest mistake I made when I went into business was my failure to realize just how important it was to communicate, often and honestly, about everything. All the time. People close to you, in your personal and your professional life, can handle the worst kind of news as long as it's communicated— clearly, honestly, and often.

"Nothing's as bad as *not* knowing. Nothing is worse than having to fill in the blanks yourself."

Robert took a sip of tea. Kurt sat back in his chair and sighed.

My God, he thought, *I'm guilty of this at home. The debt I was hiding from Laurie. When I need to communicate the most, I stop speaking all together. No wonder she gets crazy.*

Robert watched Kurt sink deep into his thoughts.

"You okay?"

"Yeah," Kurt said, "I learned a lesson about communication in a pretty painful way with my marriage. I was too guarded about sharing 'bad' news and it came back to bite me."

"Then you know what I'm talking about," Robert nodded. "You just need to apply the same principle with your employees.

"With regard to Mushin, I can tell you things started to turn around after I started sharing what was going on with the company —not only the truth about the present, but my plan for the future.

"In all honesty, that new approach didn't suit everyone. Some of the folks we started with are gone. And that's okay, because the ones who stayed did so because they liked what they were hearing. They liked knowing what was happening, even if what was going on wasn't always great.

"The result is what you see now: everyone working together to achieve a set of common goals and objectives that benefit the entire company. That means employees, leadership, vendors, and most of all our clients.

"My lack of communication was the biggest, single mistake I made. But, once I corrected it, it turned out to be our single most powerful asset, our secret weapon."

Kurt smiled with sudden realization. In one blinding moment of clarity, he realized that he was guilty of the same thing.

Kurt had felt like he was battling his employees to get them to do what needed to be done, without realizing that he never clearly communicated exactly what that was. He never said what it was he expected from them. Even more critically, he never explained *how* his vision would benefit the team.

He was functioning on the edge of a black rage, fueled by the frustration of trying to move his company forward. Yet it seemed no one else in the company was even remotely interested in making that journey with him.

This is on me, he thought. *Every time something bad happens at work, every time there's a problem, I disengage. Rocky tried to tell me that and I barked at her insisting that she was 'out of line'.*

Kurt winced at the memory. *I owe her a big apology.*

But if I'm doing it at work and at home with Laurie... Where else? Am I doing that with Max and AJ? Oh my God, I bet I am!

Kurt found himself overcome with emotion. He realized how remote he'd become from almost everyone in his life—even those he loved the most. He shook his head, then looked at Robert.

"What you just said about failing to communicate. It hit me like one of Jason's round-house kicks to the head. I'm doing it at work. I'm even doing it with my wife. But, worst of all, I think I've failed to communicate to my kids how important they are to me."

Kurt quickly gathered up his notebook and jacket.

"Is it okay if we finish this conversation another time? I want to get home and see if I can start to rectify things."

"Of course," Robert said. "Don't worry. There's always time for positive change."

"I know," Kurt agreed. "It sounds like communicating better—more openly, honestly, and often—changed your life. I promise you it will change mine as well. First at home, and then at work."

Kurt bowed deeply, saluting his teacher, his mentor, his friend. Robert smiled and bowed in return.

‡

Kurt drove straight home. All he could think of was the anguish he must have put Laurie through over the years by having to guess what was on his mind. The hell he put her through by not communicating what was going on while he was running up their credit card debt.

She was in the laundry room when he came through the door. Dirty clothing waited on the floor to be washed, stacked like a three-dimensional map of the Himalayas.

"Honey, I am so sorry!" Kurt exclaimed as he moved toward her, stepping between the piles of clothing.

"What have you done now?" Laurie asked, surprised. "What are you sorry for?"

He held her for a moment, kissed her on the forehead, and then explained his conversation with Robert. He apologized again for his inability to share what he was thinking, or what was going on with the business, or where they were headed as a family.

He promised things would be different from that moment on— different at home, and at work. The kids heard them talking. Kurt gathered up Max and AJ, hugged and kissed them tenderly.

"I'm sorry, guys. Really, really, sorry."

Max was the first to respond. "For what, daddy?"

AJ parroted the same question. Kurt tried to keep his response simple. After all, Max was barely seven with AJ two years behind.

"For not always letting you guys know how much you mean to me. How important you are in my life. In Mom's life, too."

Max looked confused. "But you're a grown-up and a dad, and grown-ups and dads don't have to apologize."

Max's response stopped Kurt in his tracks.

"Oh, yes, they do!" Kurt replied. "Or, at least, they should. Grown-ups are people just like dad's are people and people make mistakes. Everyone makes mistakes. Even you guys, right? And, when you make a mistake and have hurt someone, someone you really love, what are you supposed to d—"

Before Kurt could finish his sentence AJ interrupted, certain she had the right answer.

"You 'pologize," she said. "You tell them you're sorry and that you will try never to do that again."

Kurt smiled. He could hear Laurie in AJ's words.

"That's right, my little princess. And, that's what I'm doing right now. I love you guys more than anything and I need you to know that. I'm not sure I've shown you how much I care often enough. I'm going to fix that by showing you all the time from now on."

AJ jumped back into her father's arms. Max followed. Everyone seemed to realize how important what had just transpired was.

Kurt's Numbers

"Okay. So, let's go through this again so I can be sure I understand this correctly," Robert said, "because there are too many similarities here to ignore."

Kurt was sitting in Robert's office, desperate to accelerate his turn-around efforts. He was still having difficulty creating a set of Dirty Dozen KPI's for his own business. Robert sighed as he placed two steaming hot cups of green tea on the table.

"Like most small independents in my trade," he said, "I'm guessing that contracting businesses like yours fail to track their numbers. At least, not the right numbers. According to what you've told me, they simply figure out their 'hard costs,' and then add a twenty percent margin to that number—ten percent for overhead and another ten for profit. Is that, right?"

Kurt brought the cup to his mouth with both hands, ready to take his first sip. He stopped and nodded.

"That's pretty much the way it's done," he admitted.

Robert took a long sip of his tea.

"That's suicidal," he said. "I know how hard it is to estimate accurately in *my* business. And I'm willing to bet it isn't any easier in yours. In fact, it's probably harder.

"There are things that will be forgotten, and won't ever make it to the estimate. There are things that will make it to the estimate, but the quantities will be wrong—maybe you measured incorrectly somehow and need more of something than you thought."

Kurt nodded in agreement as Robert continued.

"There are things that will get used on a job that will never be accounted for—that will never find their way to the estimate or the final invoice. Things you will never know are gone, unless you do a physical inventory. Things you just aren't willing to burden your client with—especially if you're close to, or over, your initial bid.

"Most of us are guilty of the same sins, the same failed business practices. Guilty because we were never exposed to 'best practices' when we were learning our respective trades."

Kurt looked into his cup. "I'll add an 'amen' to that," he said.

"But once the truth is revealed," Robert continued. "Once you know there is a different way, there are no more excuses. In the end, success isn't really that hard because most, if not all, small business owners fall into the same predictable traps.

"They're too busy practicing crisis management and damage control—too busy putting out the hottest, most dangerous fire—to consider what needs to be done to ensure the next crisis is avoided.

"But, from what I've read and experienced over the years, there are enough similarities in all small businesses to help formulate a set of general solutions that just might work.

"Consequently—if you're willing to do the work—it's not hard to differentiate yourself from everyone else who is struggling out there. And, with a modicum of effort, you will succeed by default."

"I get that. The only question is," Kurt said, "what should I be doing?"

"Focus on strategy," Robert answered. "Focus on achieving your mission and realizing your vision—instead of bouncing from one problem to another—and you'll find it won't take long before you're on the right path.

"Recognize that for tactics to be effective, they should be focused on achieving your goals, but only those goals that are an integral part of your Strategic Plan.

"Concentrating on your margins is something that is critical for every business owner. But not if it comes at the expense of quality or customer care. You can focus on your margins so long as you continue to serve one of the universal truths in business.

Kurt looked over more curious than ever as Robert continued.

"There's something that Stephen Covey once said: "No Mission/ No Margin, No Margin/No Mission." It means without sufficient margin, there can be no mission. And, without a powerful and compelling mission—a meaningful Why—you will never be able to attain adequate margins.

"He was right, you know. You need to develop a pricing strategy that works for you, your business, and your customers. One that focuses on margin and not just chasing your tail for higher revenues. But one that is true to your mission as well.

"You'd better understand the true nature of marketing—what it's all about, and what it's truly capable of accomplishing. That it's more than just the means to drag more warm bodies to your door. It's more than increasing Car Count in my world, and it's more than lead generation in yours.

"It's getting the 'right' people interested in you, your story, and what you do. It's about AIDA. Creating Awareness, Interest, Desire, and then Action. And, as far as your internal operations are concerned, it's all about managing the kinds of jobs you accept."

Kurt looked up, more than a little surprised.

"That's right," Robert continued. "You have to manage the mix of work you accept. You have to choose the work you will do."

Robert reached into his pocket, pulled out a folded wad of bills and tossed it on to the table alongside his cup.

"Admit it, Kurt. There are times it would be cheaper to reach in your pocket and pay to have certain people and certain kinds of jobs just go away."

Kurt laughed. He knew exactly what Robert was talking about.

"I'll tell you something else," Robert said. "It's about plugging the dike. Eliminating or at least reducing the problems we have with shrinkage and breakage—with leaks, losses, and recidivism.

"It's about quality control as well. And quality control is really all about process and preventing comebacks, preventing 're-dos.'

"In the end, it's about a lot of things: risk management, safety training, internal communications, and even providing the right benefits. You need inspired leadership and a management style that provides more than just gentle correction."

Robert sat back. He took a deep breath, then reached for his tea. It was almost gone; what was there was cold. He grimaced.

"Okay, Kurt. Let's take a look at some of the things you can continue to do to monitor and better manage your business. Let's see if we can dig some Key Performance Indicators out of your industry that will work for Kerrigan Construction.

"But, before we start, I'm going to heat up some more water."

Kurt smiled as Robert got up from behind his desk.

A Weak Moment

Robert picked up both cups and refilled them. He placed one in front of Kurt, then maneuvered behind his desk and sat down with the other artfully balanced in his hand.

He took a long satisfying sip, then focused on his student.

"Why did you leave the security of a good job with a decent salary to go out on your own? Staying where you were certainly would have been safer and infinitely more predictable."

Kurt shifted uncomfortably in his chair for a moment.

"Because I wanted to be out on my own," he said. "To be my own boss. I wanted the mistakes I was dealing with to be *my* mistakes, not someone else's. I wanted to make a profit, and I wanted that profit to be mine."

Robert smiled. It was a smile that Kurt recognized.

"Great!" Robert said. "So now you're in business and the profits are yours. Here's the first question: What *are* you making now?

"Perhaps more important: How much *should* you be making?

Because, if you're like most entrepreneurs, you haven't got a clue, or an answer, for either.

"Oh, and one more thing: Are those profit numbers before or after you've compensated yourself?

"There's a concept I'll be sharing with you a little later on that's all about planning backwards. I generally refer to it as reverse budgeting and it's all about building those rewards in up front.

"Profit is be your reward for the risk, courage, and discipline it takes to run your own business. It's not compensation for the work you do while you're there. It's what you pay yourself to be there and get all that work done. What you'd have to pay someone else to do the work if you weren't there."

Kurt nodded, and smiled a 'got ya' smile.

"Before we started this journey," he said, "before I learned from you and Chou Li, I wouldn't have been able answer any of those questions. At least not honestly. Mostly because I didn't know. But I can answer them now—even if I'm not happy with all the answers.

"Before I met you, the profit at Kerrigan Construction, if there was any, *was* my compensation. If there was anything left after we paid all our expenses, it was mine to keep. If there wasn't anything left, then it was my problem. I was the one who had to figure out which credit card was going to take the hit and how I'd eventually have to pay that debt off.

"Now I've started to pay myself first. I've built that number into our overhead. It's a part of our estimating."

Robert sipped his tea with an approving smile.

"Before, when I was struggling even more," Kurt said, "I had no idea that there was a generally-accepted industry number for profit.

"Now I know I shouldn't settle for anything less than nine to eleven percent Net Operating Profit. In fact, twelve percent would be better. And that's after taxes. After I've taken my salary. If that nine to eleven percent isn't there, I need to work backwards to find out why it isn't. Then fix it."

"That's a great start," Robert said, still smiling.

"All things considered, those numbers aren't that different from the ones most shop owners should be focused on. Although, in mine, we'd like to see them even higher than eleven percent.

"But, just like in construction, most shop owners start out as craftsmen: laborers, workers, mechanics, or technicians. They know plenty about practicing their trade, but little or nothing about running a successful business.

"Inevitably they start out by cheating themselves, believing that it's okay to ignore their own needs. That it's normal, maybe even to be expected. They project their own experience outward, assuming their reality is shared by every other shop owner in the country.

"In other words they think, 'If I'm struggling, everyone else doing what I'm doing has to be struggling, as well. And if they're not, then chances are they're taking advantage of someone—their suppliers, their customers, or maybe their employees.'

"But that doesn't have to be the case. As we've discussed, the two most critical numbers in our business are Gross Profit and Margin. It's the well from which everything else springs.

"If we do everything right—if sales are adequate, and we're managing the business correctly—Gross Profit will be sufficient to ensure all our other numbers are where they ought to be.

"But, realistically, you already know the converse is what you really need to concentrate on. That is, if all the KPIs are where they ought to be, if you understand Outcomes and Drivers, your Gross Profit should meet or exceed all your needs and expectations.

"Now I'm going to give you some advice you weren't expecting to get. At least, not from me."

Kurt looked up, puzzled. "Really?" he asked. "What?"

"I want you to take a break from the numbers for a while, Kurt. I think you've been trying to do too much, too fast, for too long.

"There's a secret to all of this, especially when it comes to working with the numbers…"

Kurt leaned forward, waiting for his teacher to continue.

Robert got up from the table and walked to the white board, then held up three fingers.

"Three things," he said. "That's it. No more."

He erased the board and drew a large red circle with the number three dominating the center.

"Pick three things—the three that will give you the greatest 'bump,' the most positive result—and leave the rest for later. They'll still be there, and you can always go back to them.

"Three things. Period."

Kurt repeated his new mantra slowly, "Three things. Period."

Small Contractor Metrics

Kurt closed the door to his office and settled in behind his desk. It was nice having company in the middle of the day even if it was business related. It was time for his regular meeting with Peter Summerville, one of Chou Li's tai chi seniors.

He wasn't at all sure how or why they connected. The only thing he could be sure of was that it was at the park. But somehow Peter opened up to Kurt in ways that surprised everyone who knew him.

Until that time Peter had been considered a loner by everyone at the center. He rarely participated in anything with the exception of Chou Li's tai chi group; otherwise he kept to himself. That was until Peter heard Kurt mentioning to Chou Li that he had to leave a few minutes early one afternoon in order to make a client meeting at the construction company to discuss a large renovation project.

The next week Peter got up the nerve to speak with Kurt, saying that he had been an independent contractor before he retired. Kurt had smiled, and immediately invited his fellow tai chi student out to coffee so they could explore their oddly similar backgrounds.

Kurt discussed his frustration and angst about the difficulties he was having getting his company back on track while Peter shared his grief at the loss of his wife of over fifty years and the sense of loss he felt no longer being connected to his business.

It was exactly the 'medicine' that Peter had been needing. He'd found a compatriot, someone who listened and understood him.

Peter welcomed himself into his young friend's life, and Kurt was more than happy to oblige. Now every Tuesday afternoon the senior center's shuttle drop him off at Kerrigan Construction for what transformed itself into a weekly management and strategy session—an hour that Kurt had come to appreciate and enjoy.

Kurt was leaning back in his chair staring at the ceiling when he heard Rocky knocking on the door with Peter by her side.

"Kurt," she said with a grin. "You have to do something with this man. He keeps asking me to leave my boyfriend and run away with him. I keep telling him I can't; that I'm afraid with all his charm and experience he's gonna be too much for me. But he's almost got me convinced it would be the right decision for both of us."

She turned and gave Peter a little peck of a kiss on his cheek as turned to go back to her desk. Peter came in and took a seat. Kurt smiled and shook his head playfully.

"Are you trying to poach one of my most valuable employees?"

"Just trying to help that young lady," Peter said with an impish grin. "I want her to experience what life could be like in the care of a real man. A man who knows how to treat a woman properly."

Kurt pondered his friend's response.

"Hmm… That'll be fine as long as she stays here in the office."

Kurt got up from behind his desk and fixed Peter a cup of coffee just the way he liked it—a drop of Half&Half and one packet of organic brown sugar.

The meeting began as a conversation with Kurt sharing what his concerns were for that week. This time it was numbers. Again.

Peter took a small sip of his coffee, smiled, and pointed his index finger directly at Kurt's nose.

"Listen," he said, "the first thing you need to know about any of your numbers is that almost all of them are historical in nature. They report the results of something that already happened in the past, and that leaves you with three choices.

"You can choose to ignore them, because whatever happened is already over. You can react to what you just learned already happened a month or a quarter ago. Or you can use what you've learned to get out in front of the problem and manage proactively.

"I'm not a big fan of ignoring a problem, hoping it will go away."

Kurt chuckled in recognition. At one time, that had been his biggest issue: his preferred choice.

"I mean, really," Peter continued. "When was the last time you saw a problem fix itself? That's about as common as watching a rock roll itself up a hill."

Kurt laughed even more heartily as Peter went on.

"I'm not a big fan of 'reactive management' either—waiting for something bad to happen so you can figure out what you need to do to fix whatever it was that just broke.

"Once a problem shows up, it's too late to take effective action. It's always better to ensure the problem doesn't have a chance to manifest itself in the first place. To my mind, the most effective action is managing pro-actively."

Kurt had been taking a few notes on a yellow legal pad when he raised his hand to get Peter's attention.

"This sounds great, Peter," Kurt said. "But can you be more specific? How do you get in front of a problem?"

"Great question," Peter replied. "The way I tried to get in front of an issue before it turned ugly was to monitor the numbers."

"You mean your Key Performance Indicators?" Kurt asked.

"Absolutely. That's the only way to be sure everything is on track. But you have to monitor the *right* metrics."

"What's an example of 'right'?" Kurt asked.

"If you ask your friend Robert," Peter said, "or any of his mechanics, why there are warning lamps and chimes built into every vehicle on the road, he'll say they're there to alert you to a situation you shouldn't let get any worse, an imminent danger.

"I'm pretty sure he'd tell you the best way to avoid having a warning lamp come on—or a gauge move into the 'red'—is to practice preventive maintenance and remain aware of what's going on with the vehicle at all times."

"That's actually how we met," Kurt said. "I was on the freeway when a warning light came on. Robert's shop was nearby."

"Then you understand," Peter said. "Your KPIs do the same thing. They're the warning lights for your business.

"One of the reasons KPIs are important is that they can indicate present and future performance, rather than just something that happened in the past you can no longer do anything about.

"There are lots of KPIs in contracting, too many for just an hour. But there are a few we can go over to get you started."

Peter looked around the office. To the side was a white board similar to the one Robert had. In fact, Kurt had bought this one because he found it so useful when he was meeting at Mushin.

"Mind if I use the board?" Peter asked. Kurt nodded. The old man got up, grabbed the eraser, and wiped the board clean. He started writing terms while Kurt copied it all onto his notepad.

1) TOTAL REVENUE
2) AVERAGE GROSS MARGIN
3) GROSS PROFIT DOLLARS
4) MARGIN — IN HOUSE LABOR
5)   - SUBCONTRACTOR
6)   - MATERIALS
7)   - CHANGE ORDERS
8) PRODUCTIVITY
9) JOB MIX
10) OWNER HRS WKD TO GPD
11) TARGETED LEAD GENERATION
12) CLOSING RATIO
13) CUSTOMER SATISFACTION RATING

"Let's start at the top," Peter said. "The most obvious KPI is Total Revenue—or Sales, if you're more comfortable calling it that. This number will almost always appear at the top of your financials. Sales are a measure of what you've done, the jobs you've already completed and have been paid for and it's a critical number.

"I think you can tell by the number of times I've written 'margin' on the board, just how important I think it is."

"I noticed that," Kurt smiled.

"Yep," Peter nodded and continued. "There's Average Gross Margin, the margin on In-House Labor, Sub-Contractors, Materials and even the margin on your Change Orders."

"So what influences these numbers?" Peter asked rhetorically. "Sales and Margins are the result of a number of actions and efforts. Sales are the result of things like lead generation, which is a function of your advertising and marketing. What you have to do to generate pre-sale prospects.

"But Sales are also a function of your Conversion Rate—the number of pre-sale prospects, or leads, you convert into bids. And the number of bids that actually become projects. Each of these can be looked at as KPIs."

Peter stopped for a moment. He was thinking, trying to decide whether or not to share something he felt might be important.

"Let's stop for a second," he said. "Language is important and words matter. They have power. We talk about 'bids'. We use that term because we both know what it means. But you should never use 'bid' when you're talking to a client. 'Bidding' suggests multiple contractors each submitting estimates for the same project.

"Your job is to set the bar so high there's no doubt you're the right choice for someone's project. That includes everything you do: every phone conversation, every piece of printed material, every meeting, and every contact point. Your job is to see that all your competitors are compared to you.

"One of the best ways to do that is to separate yourself by your actions and by the language you use. I suggest substituting the word 'proposal' whenever you're tempted to use 'bid'."

"You know," Kurt said, "that's something I've never thought of in all these years. My general manager Rick and I always talk in terms of bids without really thinking about it. That's going to change."

"Good," Peter said, smiling. He turned back to the white board and erased the initial KPIs he'd written, replacing them with a new set that he entitled 'Additional Metrics.'

"Let's get back to the KPIs," he continued. "You told me how Robert shared the first few of his Dirty Dozen with you, his most important numbers to track. Think of these as additional KPI's to help fine-tune the business.

"The first is Client Acquisition Cost. This number represents the true dollar cost you incur to acquire a customer.

"It's the dollars you spend on sales, plus your advertising and marketing costs, over a specific period of time in relation to the number of new customers that materialize.

"Acquisition Cost can lead to another KPI, and that's Retention Cost. This is what it costs to keep a client.

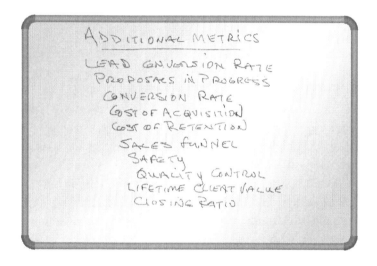

"It's what it costs you to stay in touch with a client and keep your company's name alive in their frontal cortex, so they will either choose you for their next project, or refer you to one of their friends, colleagues, neighbors, or family members.

"Another set of important numbers for contractors like us, or anyone who has an involved sales process, is anything that is Sales Funnel related. Functions tied to what's going on in the 'pipeline'.

"You need to know how many proposals are in the pipeline, as well as where they are in the process. Are they complete? Are they 'dead'? Or are they still in the works?

"Keep that pipeline filled—and your people are busy—and your business will expand. Allow the flow of potential work to dry up, and you'd better be ready to face some pretty lean times going into the months ahead."

Kurt was trying hard to keep up, hoping he would be able to decipher his furiously scribbled notes later on.

"There are others," Peter continued, "like Safety for instance. What we do is dangerous. The potential to get hurt is always there. Thus, Safety has to be a 'top of mind' priority for everyone. If you get complacent or lazy, bad things happen. And when they do, your Experience Modification Rate and Worker's Comp skyrocket.

"You should be monitoring your Quality Control. It's critical to bottom line profits. Didn't you once mention that Robert's shop has a sign somewhere saying 'MAD'? Meticulous Attention to Detail. That's what Quality Control is really all about."

"There are a host of other KPIs you should be looking at. Some every day. Some every week. But all of them at least once a month.

"You should know what the Lifetime Value of a typical client is. You should know what kind of revenue stream they provide.

"It would be nice to know who is responsible for the 'lion's share' of your referrals as well as why they're referring folks to you as much as they are. That's how you expand your referral base."

Peter pointed toward the bottom of the board.

"And you want to know what your Closing Ratio is. What your ratio of proposals to contracts is."

"What about Customer Clumps? Do you know where your current and past clients are located on the map?"

Kurt wrinkled his eyebrows.

"What difference does that make?" he asked.

"To target your marketing more effectively," Peter responded. "So you can focus on specific geographic areas where friends or neighbors of your current clients live. Who knows, they might have seen one of your Kerrigan Construction signs on a neighbor's lawn, and then asked what they thought about your services."

Peter surveyed the board. For the first time, he appeared to be befuddled. He scratched his head.

"I swear I wrote down Owner Hours," he said.

Kurt scrolled up through his notes.

"Here it is," he said. "It was in the first set you gave, number ten. Owner Hours Worked to GPD."

"Thanks," Peter said. "Okay, so even though I erased it… Owner Hours Worked to GPD, Gross Profit Dollars, is important. This is the number of hours you're working *in* and *on* your business, and the relationship that has to your gross profit.

"Now there are choices here. Two very different directions to consider. And you get to choose. Do you want to focus on high volume and low margins like everyone else in our business? Or will you take the road less traveled?"

"The road less traveled?" Kurt asked. "You mean do the opposite of that? Like high margin, low volume?"

"That's exactly what I mean," Peter said. "Think about it. Just about everyone else is focused on high volume/low margin. It takes a lot more hours to manage low-profit projects. That means more 'hands-on management'. And, remember, those are your hands.

"But a high margin/low volume model almost always results in the reverse. It asks less of you. Fewer Owner Hours are required to manage a smaller number of higher-yield projects.

"All things considered equal, which would you prefer?

Kurt made a face. He was unconvinced.

"This sounds good in theory, Peter," he said. "But I can't double my prices and turn away half my customers."

Peter set down his marker, and laughed out loud.

"In all honesty," he said, "that may not be such a bad idea. But, listen, maybe a more 'real world' example will help make my point."

Peter erased the white board again. Then he drew a horizontal line, splitting the board into two sections.

"Imagine that you and all your resources are stretched to the max. You're working five projects simultaneously over a four-week period. That means that you, personally, are either at work, or on a job site, or in your home office just about every minute of every day. I'm talking like sixty-five to seventy-five hours a week, or more.

"Let me flesh this out."

Peter scribbled numbers and percentages in a few columns.

"The total Average Gross Profit for those five projects at, let's say, twelve percent, turns out to be approximately $16,034. And it took two months—or approximately 560 hours—which translates to just over $28 Gross Profit Dollars for every Owner Hour invested.

"Let's change the Gross Profit Margin and see what happens. Of course, it's likely we will have changed lots more. Same five projects. The difference is that we've increased our Margins by ten percent. Each project returns a Gross Profit Margin of twenty-two percent."

"Is that realistic?" Kurt asked. Peter ignored the question.

"Let me finish. The total Revenue involved in four of those projects was slightly higher. But one of those projects was a 'stinker'. That's something we realized, but ignored, in the previous model. And it resulted in a bit of a loss."

"Loss," Kurt piped up. "That's a four-letter word in my world."

"In mine, too," Peter agreed. He pointed to the board.

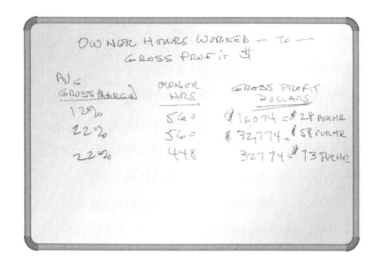

"So with our Gross Profit Margin ten percent higher, our Gross Profit in Dollars turns out to be $32,774. Even if we assumed that it took the same effort—and it would not because we walked away from the one project that was guaranteed to cost us money—if you divide the higher GPD number, $32,774 by 560, you wind up with just over a $58 Return on Effort. That looks a lot better than the $28 ROE we show above.

Peter sat back down and smiled.

"Realistically," he said, "it's even better than that because we eliminated one entire project, which should result in at least twenty percent fewer hours without doing anything else.

"Given that, you're left with 448 Owner Hours. That's a ratio of about $73 Gross Profit Dollars per Owner Hour invested. When you come down to it, Kurt, it's all just a matter of where you focus your attention.

"You've got to look at your business to see what's working and what isn't. Then educate your employees. Demonstrate to them the importance of a 'lower workload' model. Get them to buy into the process and have them actively participate with you.

"You know, someone once told me that great leadership was all about enlisting the active and voluntary participation of others. The key words are 'active' and 'voluntary'—both are action verbs.

"Sure, you can try to force everyone to do what you know needs to get done. But if their participation is *not* active and voluntary, I can almost guarantee you that your efforts will go down in flames.

"There's more that we could cover, but I think this is enough for one week. There's plenty here to digest."

Kurt nodded his head. He'd reached his limit. He was exhausted. His temples throbbed and the pain he felt behind both eyes was exquisite. He smiled at Peter.

"I'm good with stopping here. Thanks, Peter."

Sun Tzu

Kurt was sitting on the grass in the shade under is favorite oak tree. Chou Li sat cross-legged across from him.

It was the time Kurt had come to cherish, the few minutes after completion of the long tai chi form when Chou Li would answer questions—any questions Kurt had—about the life, about the Tao, about elements of the form they had just completed and its applications on the street.

But this afternoon Kurt's mind was evidently elsewhere.

"You seem distracted," Chou Li said. "You're not focused today."

Kurt chuckled. There were times he was convinced his master was from another planet. He was the most perceptive, sensitive, and intuitive human being that Kurt had ever encountered.

"You're right," Kurt admitted. "It's something we've talked about before: my company. I'm trying to re-engineer it and Robert, the head instructor at the studio, has been helping me. He and I have talked a lot about the different elements of what I should be doing. But something isn't quite right."

Chou Li leaned forward with interest.

"I've made a number of changes," Kurt continued. "And we're seeing improvement in many areas. It's just that sometimes, some of the things we're trying to execute seem counter-productive to other things we're already doing. I guess there are times it feels as if we're all over the place."

Chou Li smiled, leaning back as he sat on the grass.

"What you need is a plan," he said. "Has anyone sat with you to help create a Strategic Plan?"

Kurt smiled. It seemed somehow incongruous that his tai chi instructor, the old man sitting across from him—no matter how extraordinary Kurt found him to be—would be the second person to broach the topic of strategic planning with him.

"Not step by step," Kurt said. "Robert's talked about it some. And my GM and I have started working on a Strategic Plan, but we haven't gotten very far."

Chou Li took a deep breath and gathered his thoughts.

"Sun Tzu had much to say about the importance of planning. In almost all cases, it was within the context of war. But much of what he said applies to life and business as well. Of all his thoughts on the subject, this is perhaps my favorite:

> *Those who are victorious plan effectively and change decisively. They are like a great river that maintains its course, but adjusts its flow. They have form, but are formless. They are skilled in both planning and adapting and need not fear the result of a thousand battles: for they win in advance, defeating those that have already lost.*

"Can you see his wisdom, Kurt? Can you describe what Sun Tzu is trying to tell us?"

Kurt scanned the field, thinking a moment. He looked up.

"We have an expression that goes: 'If you fail to plan, you plan to fail.' That's pretty much the same thing, isn't it?"

"No, I don't think so," Chou Li said, shaking his head. "Sun Tzu has gone far beyond that simple statement."

Kurt pulled at some grass in frustration.

"Both statements address the importance of planning," Chou Li continued, "But only one addresses the critical element of change, for all things change. The general who is unwilling or unable to recognize change for what it is—and adapt to it—is certain to fail.

"There's another quote from Sun Tzu that might help:

Strategy without tactics is the slowest route to victory. Tactics without strategy is the noise before defeat.

"Does that make sense?" Chou Li asked. "Perhaps I can help you with this planning exercise."

"That'd be fine," Kurt said. "But is that something you'd be, ah… comfortable doing? It isn't something we've ever talked about."

Chou Li laughed, loud and hardy.

"Ah, you're wondering what this old man who has been helping you with your tai chi practice could possibly know about business and strategic planning. You are thinking to yourself: 'How is Sun Tzu, Lao-Tzu, or the *I Ching* going to help me here?'"

"I did not retire from tai chi, Kurt. Before I came to the park to teach the long form, I owned a fairly large small business and experienced what you are going through now.

"While much of what is in *The Book of Changes*, and the wisdom of both Sun Tzu and Lao-Tzu, guided me, the degree I earned at Cal Berkeley in Business certainly didn't hurt. Nor did the MBA from Stanford."

Kurt laughed. It was an embarrassed laugh fueled by his presumption.

"Well, then, I'm sure you can help me." Kurt said smiling.

Chou Li rubbed his hands together in delight, nodding.

"A Strategic Plan," he said, "is not as difficult to understand as most people make it. In fact, it can be straight-forward and simple because, in truth, all strategic planning includes the same elements.

"At its most basic, it's a problem-solving document, a statement of where you are now and where you'd like to be in the future. It's your vision, a discussion of how you get from one place to another.

"The plan should start with a summary of your current business model—meaning what you do and how you accomplish it, what's working and perhaps what is not—."

"This sounds awful close to a Business Plan," Kurt interrupted. "I tried that once. How is this any different?"

"One is operational," Chou Li said. "The other is actionable. A Strategic Plan puts ideas into action."

Chou Li cocked his his head to one side.

"You know," he said, "in all this time, I've never asked what exactly you do. What business are you in, my friend?"

"I'm a contractor," Kurt said. "I own a construction company."

"What kind of construction?"

"Well, we operate in a number of different areas. Our primary focus is new home construction. However, we do a lot of residential remodeling and restoration work as well."

"Very good," Chou Li nodded. "Then you'd start by describing each of those elements of your business in detail and the percentage each is of the whole. This should include the positive and negative aspects of each. Have you ever done a SWOT analysis?"

"No," Kurt replied. "I've heard of it. What's that stand for again?"

"Strengths, weaknesses, opportunities, threats," Chou Li said. "It's important that you are honest with yourself here. You will need to confront your weaknesses openly. And you will need to illustrate your strengths without exaggeration.

"You will need to assess your opportunities in the market, places for growth and expansion. And, finally, you need to understand whatever obstacles may threaten the future you seek to create.

"The more honest you are, the more valuable the analysis will be. Because, in the end, this tool helps you define the terrain, the marketplace and the very nature of your plan. It's a manifestation of your vision."

Chou Li paused to let everything sink in. When it was obvious that Kurt was waiting for more, he continued.

"Have you already established your goals and objectives? This is important as the Strategic Plan is the mechanism through which you will achieve them. You need to break your goals and objectives into tactics, individual actions, that help you get there.

"You need to think hard and carefully about everyone involved in your company. What are their strengths and weaknesses? Are the people you have surrounded yourself with the same ones who can help on this new journey?

"Perhaps you will need to hire additional people to accomplish specific tasks that either are not being realized at the moment or are not being done well. Or make the difficult choices required if someone is to be left behind."

Kurt shrugged his shoulders.

"It seems like there are a lot of difficult choices here," he said.

"There are," Chou Li agreed. "All choices are difficult because they demand that you prioritize, that you actively decide what gets carried forward and what gets left behind."

"When you mention additional people," Kurt said, "I think of our marketing efforts. Sometimes we're so busy doing the projects we've brought in-house, I don't think our outreach is good enough."

"Marketing is a very important piece," Chou Li said, "Asking yourself: Is what I'm doing today bringing me the tomorrow I seek? Have you established an ideal client? Do you really understand them? Who they are and what they want. What their fears are. How they feel.

"What do you have to offer them that's valuable, unique? Something that only you and your company can provide. Do you know what it is that makes your company different?"

"You're talking about our value proposition," Kurt said.

"Yes," Chou Li nodded. "Have you determined what that is? You have to be able to complete one simple statement: 'I know we may not be your least expensive option, but…'"

"'But' what?" asked Kurt. "What's the rest of it?

"The unfinished part is what makes you special, unique, and exceptional," Chou Li replied. "Until you can state that sentence consistently and with confidence, you're lost.

"That's your true value proposition. Once you know it—once you feel it deep down in your bones—how do you communicate it to your potential clients, to your qualified leads and sales referrals?

"Are your internet efforts working for you? Are they generating the right kind of leads? The right kind of traffic? Are they helping to prequalify potential clients? Are they eliminating distractions?

"Where do you want to be next year? In five years? In fifteen? How will you make the journey from your current reality to your vision? How will you deal with the creative tension that is the natural result of a journey like that?

"What are your financial targets? What is your schedule for achieving them? What is your schedule for accomplishing each and every element of this plan, these goals and objectives of yours?

"And, if you're successful, what will that future look like? Your vision must be bold enough to fuel the journey and power your Strategic Plan through good times and bad, so craft it carefully."

Chou Li sat quietly while Kurt stared in awe. He'd just received a micro-course in business management while sitting in the park, under an oak tree, after an hour of tai chi.

"That was great," Kurt said. "How can I possibly thank you?"

"How?" Chou Li asked. "That's simple. Be generous with your time and knowledge. Live a life of service. Honor others and yourself, and in so doing you will honor me."

The 15-Question Business Plan

Kurt pulled his notebook out of the Corvette's glove compartment. He felt like his head was about to explode.

So many things to capture, he thought. *So many things to write down so they are not forgotten, so they don't evaporate.*

He was so excited after his conversation with Chou Li that he couldn't wait to share his experience with Robert.

When they were finally able to sit down and talk, Kurt literally exploded into an animated account of what had transpired. Robert confirmed that Chou Li had started Kurt off in the right direction.

"I've got something for you I think might help you on this journey. It's a tool I picked up years ago, something I actually pull out of my business management tool box every couple of years just to ensure I'm on track.

"It isn't quite the same as a Strategic Plan, but I depend on it as one of the fundamental planning elements for our business. It's a 15-question planning tool and here's how it works."

Robert reached behind his desk and pulled open the printer's paper tray. He counted out fifteen pages and handed them to Kurt along with a pen.

"Okay, here," he said. "Each page will have its own question that I'd like you to write at the top of the page.

"I think you'll see very quickly how this little exercise will help reinforce what Chou Li shared with you at the park.

"The first question at the top of the first page is: What business are we in?

"There are lots of possible answers, but I'd like to suggest that—unless your answer addresses fulfilling your Why—it will not only prove inaccurate, it will prove itself inadequate as well.

"Take Mushin, for instance. If we didn't account for our Why, ours would simply state something about 'fixing cars and trucks'.

"Instead, our answer states that:

> *Mushin Automotive assures the personal freedom and mobility of our clients through the care, maintenance, and repair of their passenger cars and trucks. We do this by understanding and anticipating their wants, needs, and expectations almost before they do. And then, by meeting or exceeding those wants, needs, and expectations each and every time service is delivered.*

Kurt nodded. He knew those were more than mere words. He had experienced it personally. Robert continued.

"The question at the top of the second page is: Who are our customers? Or, more appropriately, who is our ideal client?

"Can you describe them in any kind of detail? Who are they and what are they looking for when they start searching for a contractor?

"Third page and question: What do they want, need, and expect from us? What do they want need and expect that we can provide better than anyone else?"

Kurt was trying desperately to keep up. Finally, he raised his hand to indicate he needed some time to write everything down. Robert waited for a moment, then continued.

"Fourth: Who is our competition?

"One of my early teachers had the best answer to that question I've ever come across. His answer was:

> *I'm the competition. I'm the one everyone has to watch out for. I'm the innovator. I'm the one committed to understanding*

my customer's wants, needs, and expectations better than anyone else in my market.

I'm the leader. They're the followers. By the time they have imitated something I did yesterday, I've already evaluated whether or not it worked and gone on to something else. I'm always moving forward, while they're always trying to catch up, at least one step behind.

Since I'm out in front by myself, I have no competition.

"That's a great answer, but you'll still have to identify the other players with whom you are competing for clients and contracts.

"The fifth is: What advantages do we have over our competitors?

"And the sixth is: What advantages do they have over us?"

Kurt raised his hand again. He felt like he was drowning. Robert paused for nearly a minute, then went on.

"Seventh and eighth are: What are our competitors doing that we're not doing? What are we doing that our competitors are unable or unwilling to do?

"Ninth and tenth are: Who are the owners of this business and what are their roles and strengths? Who are the managers of this business and what are their responsibilities?

"Eleventh and twelfth are: What financial information do we have available and when? What financial information do we need?

"Thirteenth: What changes will take place in our industry and in our marketplace over the next two years? Five years? Ten years?"

"Yeah," Kurt chimed in. "Wouldn't it be great to know that."

"It would," Robert agreed. "And, as the leader of your company, knowing what's coming is a big part of your job description.

"Back to the questions: What are our company's problems and/ or desired goals? As you can see, that's really two questions. So it counts as fourteen and fifteen.

"Answer those—and use what Chou Li suggested—and you'll be well on your way to creating quite an effective road map for the re-engineering process you've begun.

"Couple that with a powerful, compelling vision and an effective mission statement and there is little I can think of that could stand in your way."

The meeting kept going after that. When it was time to go, Kurt was convinced he had what he needed to complete a Strategic Plan —and with it a 15-Question Business Plan—that would be effective, compelling, and successful.

63

Planning Backwards

Kurt clipped a pen into the spiral binding of his notebook as Robert erased the white board. A lingering thought still nagged at Kurt.

"There's one more thing, something I've been struggling with."

Robert walked back to his desk and sat down.

"What's up?" he asked.

"I'm working on all the things we've talked about," Kurt said. "And I'm pretty sure I get it. I understand the importance of all of it, but I'm having trouble with getting there—getting from where my company is now to where we need to be."

"Be more specific," Robert said.

"I see the goal," Kurt continued. "I understand the objective. I just can't seem to figure out the steps in between. I can't figure out what to do first and, to tell you the truth, I think I'm being too tentative—too tentative and insecure.

"I guess it all boils down to not feeling sure about where to start. And that sucks. It sucks because I try really hard not to be like that anywhere else in my life. It's driving me nuts."

Robert sat quietly, lost in thought. Finally, he looked at Kurt.

"I think I have something that might help. You have a problem with getting started, right? Specifically, not knowing *where* to start. Perhaps, more to the point, you're not convinced that where you want to begin is the *right* first step. The problem may be that you're starting at the wrong end."

"Huh?" Kurt said. "How can you start at the wrong end? I mean, if you're going from here to there, don't you have to start 'here'? I'm sorry, *sensei*, I'm lost."

Robert smiled.

"Your insecurity revolves around not knowing *where* to start. Too many paths, too many choices, coupled with the knowledge that some of them will certainly turn out to be wrong.

"Let me share what's worked for me, because in the beginning I found myself stuck, paralyzed in precisely the same situation you find yourself right now.

"I couldn't see a direct route looking forward, so I turned the whole 'execution/implementation' thing on its head. I had to start at the finish line looking back to where the race started."

Kurt was still lost, and now a bit frustrated.

"Stay with me," Robert said. "Let's say you started with a goal that was unfocused and unmanageable—something like 'increase my bottom line.' Does that meet the SMART guidelines we've talked about before?"

"No," Kurt said, shaking his head confidently.

"Of course not," Robert agreed. "It's too big and too sloppy. No deadline. So we tighten it up, modify the goal to fit the guidelines: Specific, Measurable, Achievable, Results-Oriented, Time-Based.

"We lay it out this way: Increase bottom line performance to a minimum of ten percent Net Operating Profit by year end, December 31. Today is March 2, right? That gives us ten months to make something happen.

"So the goal has a deadline—a tight deadline—but a deadline, nevertheless. It's specific, measurable, hopefully achievable, and results-oriented."

Kurt nodded. He was beginning to understand.

"Remember the result is to increase bottom-line profit," Robert continued. "And it's time-based: by year end. But none of that tells us where to start, or what we have to do first. And that's okay, even though it doesn't feel like it's okay.

"But, before I go any further, there's something I think needs to be addressed and that is 'what if'."

"What 'what if'?" Kurt asked.

"Well, 'what if' we miss our goal?" Robert said. "What happens if we only get to seven percent net profit, and not the ten we were shooting for?

"If we started at break-even or, worse yet, at a loss, would you really want to throw yourself off a bridge if you missed your goal—but still managed to double or triple your net profit?"

"No," Kurt smiled, shaking his head.

"I didn't think so," Robert said. "In any case, there are times when working backwards from the positive vision of an imaginary future makes the most sense. At least, it did to me. So let's look at this backwards."

Robert reached over the desk and grabbed Kurt's wrist. Then he shook his hand vigorously.

"Congratulations!" he said. Kurt stared back, confused.

"You just achieved your first goal," Robert continued. "You just hit a ten percent NOP: Net Operating Profit. Strong work."

Kurt's eyes brightened; he figured out Robert's game.

"Now all you have to do, Kurt, is look back over the past year—hypothetically, of course—and tell me what steps you had to take in order to make that happen. What would you have had to do?"

Robert paused, waiting for a response. Kurt cleared his throat.

"Well," he said, "we'd have to get a better handle on our costs—both fixed and variable. Control our expenses more intelligently.

"But I'd say the first thing we did was move from being revenue-driven—constantly hustling to increase our sales—to working to improve our margins."

Robert leaned back in his chair, crossed his arms, and smiled. Kurt picked up on his approval and continued.

"We did better at selecting the jobs we bid on. Our marketing effort ensured that we were getting the right kind of clients, ones who appreciated us and were willing to pay a little bit more for the quality and care we bring to a project."

Kurt's confidence increased as he saw the steps more clearly.

"We screened them better. We upped our presentation skills to make the value we bring to a project compelling, that it's worth the few extra bucks."

"You've got the idea," Robert said. "What else did you do during the 'last year' to achieve your goal?"

"We took a long, hard look at the bidding process," Kurt said, "to ensure that our estimates were more accurate—with sufficient margins built in to earn the kind of profit we're looking for.

"We managed our 'buy outs' better. That means we chose our sub-contractors more carefully, and worked with them to ensure there were no screw-ups at their end that impacted us, the job, or our profit picture in a negative way.

"We examined our on-the-job performance to be sure we were as efficient and cost effective as we could be. We did everything we could to eliminate unnecessary waste and shrinkage."

Kurt's excitement was contagious.

"And, 'last year', we did a better job providing value to our customers. That ensured we got great reviews and higher referral rates. And we did a better job of following-up and maintaining a link with our clients long after the job was signed off."

Kurt stopped and took a moment to breath. Robert smiled.

"So then," he said, "it would be safe to say you *do* know where to start, wouldn't it? You just came up with an almost comprehensive list of things that need to be done to accomplish your goal of a higher net.

"Within each one of the steps you identified, there is a series of sub-steps that will need to be taken in order to achieve those goals and objectives. We call this process 'planning backwards', and it works—or at least could work—for almost any type of outcome.

"When you get a better handle on your numbers, you can even use the same process to determine your 'take home', if you choose to. And, that's even more fun than it sounds like it could be."

Kurt's mouth dropped open.

"You can determine your 'take home' at the beginning of the process and not at the end?" he asked.

"Sure, you can," Robert said, "if you understand your KPIs. You know what kind of net you want. Ten percent, right? Ten percent net after everything else has been paid and accounted for. So you figure that in.

"Then you decide you want another hundred thousand dollars —just for you. You don't need a reason. Just because. Figure that in.

"You know what your costs are, and you can extrapolate those numbers out along with a projection of what your sales would have to be in order to have that hundred grand drop out at the other end of the process—the other end of the 'sausage grinder.'

"We call that 'reverse budgeting.' It's simple math, really.

"We know what we know, and we know what we need. It's just another equation. The good news is that we already have a lot of the information we're going to require and can figure out what would have to happen in order for the numbers to work out the way we want them to, the way we *need* them to.

"What do you think, Kurt? Things still seem hopeless, or is the idea of working your way backwards through the process starting to make sense?"

Kurt reached across the desk and grabbed Robert's wrist and hand and shook it vigorously. He smiled.

"Makes a lot more sense than what I was struggling with a half-hour ago. At least, now, I have a starting point. I'm going to give this a try. I think it's what I needed to bring all of this together and get the results I need."

Kurt smiled and shook his head in disbelief.

"I don't know, Robert. I just don't know what would have happened if the Vette hadn't acted up, but I'm grateful for that misfire every day. I can't thank—"

Robert lifted his hand, indicating that Kurt had said enough. He could sense his student's gratitude and his sincerity. Nothing else was necessary. The conversation was over.

Drivers and Outcomes

Weeks went by, transforming themselves into an undefinable blur punctuated by work, lunch workouts with Chou Li and his tai chi group, mornings and evenings at the studio, and evenings and weekends with Laurie and the kids.

Work was starting to come around. Too slowly for Kurt, but the progress was undeniable. Kurt attributed whatever changes he saw as much to his own metamorphosis—which was profound, and duly-noted by almost everyone Kurt came in contact with—and to his work on the Strategic Plan.

What started out with concern as, 'Hey, Kurt… You okay?' had transitioned into silence and an attitude of, 'This is better, and we'd better not say or do anything to send us back into the abyss!'

For Kurt, it was simply a matter of living the principles of the two new environments he'd immersed himself in.

He was in better shape than he'd ever been; he was calmer and more centered. He didn't fly off the handle like he'd done thousands of times in the past. He would simply assess the situation, discuss possible solutions with Rick and the rest of his staff, come to a decision, and then act.

More than that, he was communicating effectively with his staff every day—reinforcing the company's objectives; explaining how they were doing; and constantly emphasizing the motivational Why of Kerrigan Construction.

The results were undeniably better for everyone—employees, customers, and vendors. And, especially, better at home.

But there were still plenty of things Kurt needed to understand. Things that left Kurt with a hole at the bottom of his stomach.

A few minutes after Kurt arrived at the office one morning, he received a text message reminding him that he had an appointment to get the Corvette serviced at Mushin that Thursday.

Great, he thought. *Another chance to discuss KPIs.*

He was especially having problems with this idea of Driver KPI's and Outcome KPIs—what they meant and how they might be used as a tool to help 'fix' the business.

Kurt resolved to take Thursday morning off so he could bring the Corvette in for service and confirmed the appointment.

‡

Kurt arrived at Mushin Automotive a full hour before they opened. He parked the car, got out, and started stretching. He was tempted to head across the alley and join the last half of the morning's workout, but decided against it.

Don't disrupt the class, he thought.

Instead, he found himself slowly and quietly moving through the long form and the *qigong* exercises that preceded them.

He was deep inside his moving meditation when he overheard several of Mushin's employees arriving at work from the studio, congregating at the entrance to the shop. Six or seven clients had arrived as well. The strangers had been watching him closely as he gracefully flowed through the long form.

Allie opened the front door and walked over to him. Suddenly, Kurt stopped, embarrassed that he had been on display.

"That was impressive," Allie said, pressing her palms together. "Robert mentioned that you were working your way through Yang-style tai chi. The movements are beautiful and flowing. But you can sure see how they can be applied in combat. I like that. Would you consider sharing what you've learned across the alley some day?"

"Sure," Kurt said softly, eyeing the nearby crowd as it dispersed.

Allie grabbed the Corvette's mileage, then extended her arm toward the front door, inviting him inside.

"How can I help you this morning?" she asked. "The schedule says you're in for 'normal service'. Is there anything else you'd like us to look at? If not, we'll get started with a quick courtesy check to ensure the vehicle is in 'top shape' and go on from there."

"That's it, Allie," Kurt said. "Oh, and, is Robert here?"

"Sorry," Allie shook her head, "Robert is out this morning. He should be back before noon. Is there anything I can help you with?"

Kurt thought about it for a second.

"Robert and I have been talking about KPIs," he said. "I have some questions about Drivers and Outcomes. Is that something you would be comfortable discussing?"

"I know a little about KPIs," Allie said. "Especially how Drivers and Outcomes fit in. Once I get all these cars taken care of, we can talk about this if you'd like to."

"Absolutely," Kurt said.

Allie turned her attention to the line of other customers while Kurt gazed through the shop window, admiring the intricate choreography of repair work taking place there. He was fascinated by the calm, purposeful nature of everything going on.

After the morning's rush, Allie walked over to Kurt.

"Okay," she said. "Is this a good time for you?"

"I'll make it a good time." Kurt replied with a smile.

"What would you like to know?"

"I think you know I'm in construction," Kurt said, "and while I understand how the Dirty Dozen works for you guys, and how the KPIs apply here, I'm still having trouble relating them to my business."

"Well then," she said. "I'm definitely the one you need to be talking to. I actually worked for a construction company before I landed here."

Allie grabbed a piece of paper. She scribbled out a series of lines and diagrams as quickly as she could.

"Okay, let's get started," she said. "Deciding which KPIs are Outcome KPIs or Driver KPIs is tied to how they are being used. There can be only one Outcome KPI for each formula, and any and all KPIs on the other side of that equation will be Drivers controlling that outcome.

"If you think about it, NOP, Net Operating Profit, is theoretically the only consistent Outcome KPI. GPD equals Gross Profit Dollars, right? And, in my opinion, gross profit is one of the most critical of all KPIs. If GPD isn't high enough, nothing else is going to work. That's where watching your margins comes in.

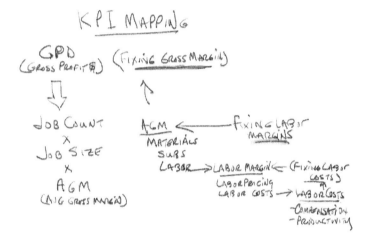

"In construction, GPD is really a function of three factors: Job Count, Job Size, and Average Gross Margin.

Job Count is how many jobs you did or are doing; Job Size is the scope of the job or what we call Average Invoice—the total of all your invoices for a fixed period of time divided by the number of cars worked on.

"Job Count is an Outcome KPI. In other words it's what it is—unless you make an effort to change it, to do more or less projects. Whereas Job Size can be both a Driver or an Outcome KPI.

"Average Gross Margin is calculated by taking your average margin on materials, the average margin you experience on work done by your sub-contractors—how much you mark that work up —and your average margin on your own labor.

"If your Gross Profit Dollars are inadequate, you've got to start looking around to see what needs to be 'fixed' first. In most cases, it's going to be your Average Gross Margin. That's generally the best place to start."

Allie drew a vertical line with an arrow pointing up from AGM toward GPD and another horizontal line with an arrow pointing back toward the GPD number.

"Fix your Average Gross Margin," Allie continued, "and the GPD number will follow. That's when it goes from being an Outcome to a Driver. But how do you do that, right? Which is the easiest to fix? Which gives the greatest improvement the fastest?"

Kurt examined the diagram, then pointed.

"Labor should be the fastest and easiest to attack," he said.

"Right," Allie agreed. "Of the three items I've listed under AGM —Materials, Subs, and Labor—Labor is the easiest to fix and the one you have the most control over. I've drawn another horizontal line from Labor to Labor Margin. See it?

"Labor Margin is an Outcome KPI. But it can also be a Driver. It's an Outcome KPI because it's a direct result of your Cost of Labor and whatever it is you're selling that labor for. But it's also a Driver KPI when one of those two factors change. If Cost of Labor goes up, what happens to your Labor Margin?"

Allie looked at Kurt, waiting for an answer.

"Well, uh, the Labor Margin would go down," Kurt mumbled.

"Are you sure?" Allie asked. "You don't sound sure to me."

Kurt nodded. He was sure.

"Good," Allie smiled. "If the Labor Cost goes down for some reason, then the Labor Margin would go up, right?

"The same holds true for your pricing. Raise what you charge for labor and the margin automatically goes up. I guess I should mention that if you raise the price of your labor, not only will your Labor Margin go up, but your AGM and GPD should go up with it.

"Raising your price on labor is the easiest thing to do. But it's also the hardest, because most of us are terrified it will drive business away."

Kurt nodded, recognizing that fear all too well.

"Fear is the big motivator here," Allie said, "the greatest single factor inhibiting success. So before we say, 'the hell with it' and raise whatever it is we're going to charge for labor, let's look at costs.

"Labor Cost seems like an obvious place to start, but that isn't often the case. Sure, it's determined by what we pay our craftsmen and laborers—but there are other factors to be considered."

"Like what?" Kurt asked. Allie pointed to the paper.

"Like the cost of worker's compensation insurance, for one. And, the productivity of those laborers and craftsmen for another.

"If your people complete the job in less time than you've budgeted or estimated, you should probably make more on that job —because increased productivity increases the bottom line either directly or indirectly. If nothing else, you might be able to start another job sooner than otherwise scheduled.

"If you shop around and find a 'better' comp policy—one that provides the same protection for a few dollars less, maybe through an association or another affiliation—your labor costs are going to go down. They're going to be 'driven' down.

"When you change a KPI, and it impacts another KPI, it's a Driver. When a KPI is changed by something you've done, it's an Outcome.

"Change one thing and everything associated with it changes. All we have to do as managers or owners is make sure that change moves things in the right direction."

Allie smiled, handing the diagram to Kurt.

"Get it?"

"Got it," Kurt smiled.

Flow

Ever since Allie had gone over mapping KPIs with him to better understand what was being measured and the impact change would bring, in either direction, Kurt was focused on developing his own set of KPI Maps for Kerrigan Construction.

It was difficult tedious work, but he threw himself into it with the same intensity he brought to tai chi at the park and workouts at the studio. And his attention to KPIs was beginning to pay off.

With his new understanding came opportunities to change this KPI or tweak that one. He found himself at the computer for hours at a time breaking the numbers down until he was certain—certain that he understood how each one operated and how it worked in conjunction with every other connected KPI.

And, just like his experience at the park or at the studio, he found the hours flew by without his conscious awareness. Chou Li called it 'unity' when he found himself caught up in the flow of his practice, those moments when time and space seemed to stand still.

"It is the unity of all things," he said. "The singular oneness of the Universe. It is you, and the yin and yang of the movements coming together. It is joining with nature in time, space, and motion. When you find this place, magic happens. Your power and energy are magnified, multiplied. And you cannot be diminished."

Robert described it in similar way. He said that when Kurt performed beyond the boundaries of where he thought his training and abilities should be, he was in a 'state of flow'—a place without conscious thought or effort.

When that happened, Kurt no longer told his body what to do; he didn't have to. The repetition of the exercises and his growing understanding of the power of letting go, unleashed a state of awareness that took over—allowing his mind and body to soar.

There were times when Kurt experienced this flow state while sparring. Times that he prevailed, but couldn't tell you what he did, or how and why he did it. It happened at the park when he gave himself over to the rhythm of the Long Yang, when an hour passed by in what seemed like seconds.

Kurt thought of it as an expression of *mushin*: no mind.

Oddly enough, the times he stopped trying to control everything were the times when he had the most control and made the most progress.

Now he was experiencing unity and flow at work, sitting at his desk. That single fact was making Kurt's life more bearable than it had been in years. It was also having a positive impact on his company's bottom line. It seemed that the small adjustments he was making were having a disproportionate impact.

It was the discussion he'd had with Allie months earlier about force and impact coming to life, and it didn't take a lot of force to get the impact he was looking for. It just took focused application delivered at precisely the right spot.

Kurt didn't fully understand it, but he wasn't sure he had to. The more he practiced, the more he meditated, the more he stopped contending against the Universe, the more often and completely he found himself in a state of being he couldn't fully comprehend, but nevertheless enjoyed. The one thing he was sure of was that it couldn't be forced; he could not command himself there.

He was certain mindfulness and meditation were both flow states, unity states. They were states you could enter under the right circumstances with the proper preparation, but they were not likely to appear on demand.

In fact, Kurt's experience suggested quite the opposite. The more you chased it, the less likely you were to experience it. It was like the circular discussions about enlightenment he would sometimes have with Chou Li after a practice.

"By searching for *qi shì*, or enlightenment," Chou Li said, "you deny yourself the possibility of its discovery. You ensure it will never be found."

Kurt had almost the identical discussion with Robert.

"The gates to *satori*, awakening, are hidden and can only be found and opened by the 'beginner's mind'. Coming to each new project with an innocent, empty slate. There's a similar concept, *kenshō*—which means to see one's true nature.

"When you empty the mind," Robert continued, "it opens like a flower and that opening allows enlightenment to find you."

Kurt was beginning to understand that, and the results had been nothing less than transformational.

Unnecessary Exposure

It was one of those workouts everyone at the studio seemed to enjoy. Casual, but not too casual. Easy, but not too easy. Just enough intensity to keep everyone interested and involved. A kind of 'work on what needs work' session.

Kurt chose to work on his combat skills: his kicks in particular. He was practicing within a small group of students when he saw Allie off to the side, leaning back with her arms crossed. Her body language suggested she wasn't excited about what she was seeing.

There were few people in the school Kurt respected more than Allie. She was absolutely beautiful to watch. Her form was perfect, and she was a formidable fighter. More than that, she was incredibly generous when it came to sharing her skill and knowledge.

Kurt decided that she had to be watching someone else, as his form was especially crisp that evening. Or so he thought.

After doing a flurry of extended side-kicks aimed at the skulls of various opponents, Kurt moved to a few crescent-kicks and then to combinations of front-kicks to the head, followed by side-kicks to the body. Allie walked to the perimeter of the group.

Kurt was convinced he had demonstrated an impressive show of flexibility, physical ability, balance, and power. He was confident that no one, not even a senior instructors, could dispute that.

"That was impressive, Mr. Kerrigan," Allie said. "Kicks like that are important to know and master. Specifically, the dynamics.

"You need to learn how to do those kicks properly. You need to understand their application—when, where, and how to use any one or all of them effectively—in order to progress here. But are they really as effective as you seem to believe they are?"

With a few words Allie transformed Kurt's confidence into insecurity. Allie may have been speaking directly to Kurt, but all the other students had stopped practicing. They were listening as well.

"Let me tell you a little story," Allie continued, "about something that happened just after I started practicing here."

Allie motioned for the entire group to take a place on the floor.

"Once upon a time, in another era, it was common for a martial arts master—either when traveling, or from the same community—to visit other studios. It was a chance to share knowledge, to learn another style. Sometimes the meeting was collegial; sometimes adversarial. An opportunity to challenge another school or master to show everyone whose art was more effective, more powerful.

"Even today, this still occurs. There've been a number of times someone from another school or style has visited here. And that's what happened that night. Someone came, but they came to fight.

"This alleged master came to challenge Robert and our mixed style. He came to show us that his pure style of karate was better."

Allie had captured the undivided attention of everyone in the group. She lowered her voice to engage them even more deeply.

"This master came with two of his senior instructors in tow. At first, the three of them were pretty much okay. They followed the workout and moved through the drills.

"But things got a little strange when they started making cracks about how their style was better, more 'pure'. They stopped doing our drills, insisting their techniques and combinations were superior in every respect.

"They weren't behaving as guests should, not respectful of where they were. Finally the leader of the 'pure' style called Robert out."

Every one of the students leaned in closer—like kids around a campfire, seduced by their counselor's storytelling.

"He challenged Robert to a match: full contact, no rules. It was to be his style against ours, his karate against Robert's. He'd brought his two instructors to witness what he thought was going to be a serious ass-kicking.

"At first, Robert was reluctant and said a match wasn't necessary. He said if they wanted to believe their martial art was superior that was fine with him. He had nothing to prove.

"But the 'pure' master just sneered. He found that response weak, bordering on cowardly. His attacks became more personal and derisive until Robert really felt he had no choice.

"Now this master's 'pure' style used plenty of sexy-looking high and extended foot work. Kicks very much like the ones you were demonstrating."

She looked straight at Kurt. He looked down, uncomfortable being associated with a story that was centered on a rude stranger calling out his *sensei*.

"In all honesty," Allie continued, "it was impressive to watch this guy warm up. He did flying kicks, spinning back-kicks, kicks that looked more like vertical splits than combat kicks. It seemed like he had an entire trunk filled with theatrical moves: high crescents and beautiful extended front and side kicks.

"I'd just started my training here, so it was intimidating, too."

Allie paused. She scanned the faces of the group circling her. Finally one of the students begged her to continue.

"I started worrying," she said. "I didn't know any better. I felt that Robert would be no match for this guy with all his fancy dancing around. His 'pure' style looked like it was straight out of a movie: big and bold and dangerous.

"You have to realize that I'd never seen Robert matched against anyone like this in the few months I'd been here. Never seen him matched against anyone at all for that matter.

"What I didn't know was that Robert had distinguished himself as a National Champion in a number of different disciplines, some of which were full-contact.

"Everyone could tell Robert wasn't happy. He didn't like this kind of stuff happening at the school then and still doesn't like it to this day. It was easy for me to confuse frustration with apprehension.

He didn't like being backed into a corner. But the look on his face had nothing to do with the fear of sparring with someone from a completely different background and style.

"The match started and this guy—this self-proclaimed martial arts master—came at Robert hard and fast! As far as any of us could tell, neither one of them had on any protective gear on except for maybe a cup. And here's this guy coming at Robert like this was a life-and-death street fight, a blood match.

"The other guy started throwing full-force punches and a bunch of wicked flying kicks. But Robert remained calm. Incredibly calm.

He was dodging just about everything this other guy threw at him with seemingly little or no effort. Most of the kicks and punches never connected. When they did, they were blocked and barely made contact.

"Robert was watching this guy, measuring him the whole time, barely throwing anything. From the outside, it was scary, because it looked like he didn't have a chance.

"Then the guy tried to deliver a really powerful knife-edge side kick right at Robert's head. It was poetry in slow motion.

"The kick looked like it could have taken Robert's head off—if it connected. But it didn't.

"That's when Robert stepped inside the kick facing the inside of his opponent's thigh. He had his left arm in front of him, with the fingers forming a 'ridge hand' extended six inches from the center of his chest, and his right fist close to his hip, parallel to the ground.

"Robert dropped his center of gravity, moved his right forearm in front of his chest and slid to his right landing his elbow—full force—just below his opponent's sternum. Wham!

"Then he threw a combination of three quick but vicious straight punches, each with deadly force. First, a right to the inside of his opponent's thigh. Second, a punch to the left side of this guy's knee and third, to the precise location of the first punch. Then Robert followed that with a second elbow to the ribcage."

Everyone gasped, including Kurt.

"It happened so fast you could barely see it." Allie exclaimed. "The guy's kick had started off with the toes of his left foot barely on the ground and his right leg fully extended and exposed. It was an open invitation to anyone with the ability to see the vulnerability and the skill to exploit it. That someone was Robert.

"Mr. Pure Karate went down like a rock.

"All it took was three punches and two elbows. And his adversary was on the ground. Robert's strikes were targeted to ensure this guy wasn't going to get up or even think about continuing. He couldn't. His right leg was useless. In fact, his two senior instructors had to carry him off the floor and out of here.

"There's a lesson here. A lesson for all of you. But one especially for you, Kurt," Allie said firmly.

"There's a difference between arrogance and confidence. One that suggests arrogance is almost always fatal.

"That lesson is about unnecessary exposure, a willingness to open yourself to risk that isn't required. High kicks that expose your groin, your thighs, or your core, or that make it easy for someone to take your center away, to knock you off balance, all bring with them a fair amount of risk.

"They may look cool, but they amplify whatever weaknesses you might have or are trying to hide. Our style rarely makes use of any kicks targeted above the waist. In fact, most of our kicks are targeted below the waist, at your opponent's legs—calves, knees, hamstrings, and thighs—unless there's an opportunity to strike higher, and it isn't a trap.

"Think of it for a moment. When you're delivering a kick, any kick, you're placing yourself in a vulnerable position. You've only got one of your two legs rooted in the ground, if that. Unless you get very lucky, you're always a hair's breadth away from finding yourself wildly out of balance and on the ground.

"The question has to be: Is it going to be worth it?

"I'll bet that 'pure'-style master was asking himself that same question on the way back to his dojo—unless they decided to stop at a local Urgent Care Center or Emergency Room first."

‡

After class was over, and everyone had bowed off the floor, Allie came up to Kurt.

"You know there are important corollaries between the story I told the group tonight and being in business. There are plenty of times you may find it easy to place the company at risk because you're trying to impress someone or make a pointless point."

"The question must be: Is the risk going to be worth the reward?"

"The answer demands that you know exactly why you're doing whatever it is you're about to do. Is it worth it? Who are you trying to impress with your 'cool moves'?"

Kurt's mind was racing.

Am I guilty of the kind of behavior Allie is warning against? Have I put the company at risk because of my own ego?

Kurt listened more carefully as Allie continued.

"Ask yourself: Are risky business maneuvers the most effective way to accomplish my goals and objectives? Or are you taking a risk because it makes the company look good? Because it makes you feel good?

"Don't get me wrong, Kurt. Every tool at our disposal—every kick, punch, strike or take-down—is there for a reason. Each has its own unique value. But each can be executed improperly, or under the wrong circumstance.

"Anything that puts you or yours in jeopardy, at extreme risk, may not be the appropriate tool for the task at hand."

Kurt was shaking his head.

This is starting to sound a little too familiar, he thought.

"With a high kick, you've got to ask yourself," Allie continued, "Would I be using this particular tool if no one was watching? Did I pull it out of the tool box because it was the right tool for the job? Or did I do it to impress myself or someone else?

"On the street, the answer—the right and honest answer—might save your life someday. In business, it can just as surely save you thousands of dollars and more anxiety than you can imagine.

"High kicks can be the perfect example of unnecessary exposure. So are countless other risks you are likely to confront in business. Learn to recognize them for what they are and then deal with them appropriately."

Kurt silently absorbed every word. When it was obvious she was done, he bowed respectfully realizing the gift he'd been given.

"One more thing," Allie said as she started to walk away. Kurt stopped and looked up. Allie's smile lit up the room.

"Your form on those kicks was killer. You've come a long way. Strong work."

Uncomfortable Dream

Kurt grunted, then awoke with a start. Laurie was shaking his right shoulder as hard as she could.

"Are you okay, honey?" she asked. "You were all over the bed, thrashing around and talking in your sleep. What's wrong?"

Kurt sat up and pulled his knees to his chest. He paused a moment—cradling the back of his head with both hands, fingers interlaced—then he rested his elbows on his knees.

His head was pounding and his heart was racing. The pillow case and sheets were damp from perspiration. Kurt knew it had to be a dream, but it didn't seem like a dream while he was in it.

Laurie slipped out of the covers and twisted around to face her husband. She reached out to touch his knee.

"What's wrong? You're scaring me."

Kurt took Laurie in his arms and held her close. Then let her go as he tried to explain what he had just experienced.

"It must have been a dream," he said. "But it felt so real.

"It was dark. Black, really. I could see someone walking toward me from very far away. Far enough so I couldn't tell who it was. Then I saw it was Chou Li. But it wasn't."

Laurie was holding Kurt's hand.

"What do you mean, 'it was Chou Li, but it wasn't'?"

Laurie could see that Kurt was shaking his head as he spoke.

"It was Chou Li, but he was younger, much younger. He was dressed differently, too. I mean, he wasn't wearing workout clothes like in the park. He was wearing a traditional white tai chi uniform.

He looked incredible. Like he must have looked thirty years ago. And he was glowing, glowing in the darkness."

"Glowing?" Laurie asked, tilting her to the side.

Kurt nodded.

"There was an aura radiating from all around him. It was beautiful, Laurie. My God, it was so beautiful!

"He looked at me and smiled. Then he said, 'Thank you, Kurt. Your friendship has been an unexpected gift that has given me much joy over these last years of my life.'

"Then he reached out to me and said, 'Don't worry about me. I am good… And so are you.' Then he was gone. He disappeared, you were shaking me, and I was awake."

Laurie reached out to hug her husband. She embraced him, then got back under the covers.

"Don't worry, honey," she said. "It was just a bad dream. Let it go. It's the middle of the night and we both need to get some rest ."

She's always right when it comes to stuff like this, Kurt thought.

It was late and he really did need to get back to sleep. But there was still something about the dream that left him feeling uneasy, something he couldn't quite put his finger on.

Maybe it was the way Chou Li had a that glow around him. It could have been the uniform, the way it hung on his master. Maybe it was how much younger he looked.

Whatever it was, it was the first time Chou Li had ever come to Kurt in a dream. That, in and of itself, was unnerving.

He was one of those people who believed dreams weren't anything more than a function of indigestion, a bad meal or the wrong food. And, yet, now Kurt found himself desperately trying to make sense out of what he'd just experienced.

What was Chou Li trying to tell me? What does it mean?

He turned his pillow over, so he could lay his head on the dry side, and got back under the covers. There would be plenty of time to figure out what the dream meant in the morning.

That is, if he still remembered it.

Is the Owner In?

Kurt had trouble falling back to sleep. He tried everything he could, including meditative breathing. But nothing worked. That is, until he remembered he had one or two guided meditation MP3s stored on his smart phone.

He reached across to the night table, opened the top drawer, grabbed his ear buds, and placed one in each ear. He found the recording he was looking for—the one he thought had the best chance of knocking him out—and pushed 'play'.

He was sure he remembered hearing the first few minutes, but that was about it. He was gone until his alarm sounded the next morning. However, even with the guided meditation, it still wasn't a very restful sleep.

Nevertheless, he was at his desk at Kerrigan before anyone else arrived that morning, working his way through some documents, when he heard a familiar voice up front.

It was familiar, but out of place. It was a voice that belonged in the park, and not at work. It belonged to one of the seniors in his tai chi group. Yet, here it was floating across the office.

Kurt got up, stepped out from behind his desk and moved to the door to his office, where the conversation up front was a bit easier to hear and understand.

"Yes," the voice said, "I know I don't have an appointment to see Mr. Kerrigan. But this is important, important and personal.

That doesn't sound like Peter, Kurt thought. He started to make his way up front to investigate.

"Could you please tell him that Morris Goldberg, from the Senior Center and his tai chi group, is here to see him?"

Kurt was halfway to the front desk when he called out.

"Morris! It's me! What's up? Is everything okay?"

The old man looked up. He was one of Kurt's favorite seniors—diminutive in size, but mighty in stature. Morris was a slightly hard of hearing, elderly Jewish man with a booming voice, a wicked sense of humor, and a very thick New York accent.

However, this morning, Morris' perpetual smile was nowhere to be found. His eyes looked tired, bloodshot and swollen.

"What's going on?" Kurt asked. "We're not supposed to see each other until later on today." He reached out to touch Morris on the shoulder. "Need a good contractor?"

Morris didn't laugh. The little old man's body language said it all. His shoulders were stooped, his head bowed. He seemed somehow even smaller than he had the day before.

"*Takeh*," Morris said, "this afternoon is why I'm here. I'm here because I knew you would want to know."

"Know what?" Kurt asked.

"There isn't going to be a 'this afternoon,' Kurt. It's Chou Li… When he wasn't at the table for breakfast this morning, I went to see if everything was okay. That's what people do when you live in a place like ours. They check up on each other.

"I banged on the door, but he didn't answer. So I went and got the manager. He opened the door and we went inside together. Chou Li was in bed.

"*Alav ha-shalom*! May he rest in peace. He must have slipped away in his sleep."

Kurt's body contracted. The pain was physical, overwhelming. He felt as if he'd been kicked in the stomach.

"I thought you, more than anyone," Morris said, "would want to know. I didn't want you to show up at the park today… Show up to find no one there. And then wonder what was going on."

"Thank you, Morris," Kurt said softly.

He was trying to process his feelings when he realized he hadn't given himself any time to go over the dream that awakened him in the middle of the night. Kurt only knew that he needed to be near someone, anyone who had been close to Chou Li.

"Have you got a minute?" Kurt asked.

"Have I got a minute? Yeah. Maybe a minute," Morris said. "After all, I'm old. Where else do I have to be? But, if I'm going to stay, maybe you have a little water? A little water would be good, if that wouldn't be too much trouble?"

Kurt guided the old man down the hall to his office.

"Would you like a cup of coffee or a little tea instead?" Kurt asked. "Or will it be just water?"

"Water is good, thank you." Morris replied. When he looked up he could see the tears forming in the corners of Kurt's eyes.

Kurt pulled out two chilled bottles of water from the small refrigerator in the corner of his office. Morris sat down by the desk. As Kurt returned with the water, he chose a chair on the client-side of the desk to be closer to Morris.

"You know, he really cared about you," Morris said. "He talked about you all the time. He told me about the times you both spent after class, just chatting. How much he enjoyed being with you.

"*Nebach*. You know, when you get old, nobody wants to spend any time with you. Nobody wants to listen. You're an inconvenience and no one wants to be bothered."

Kurt took a swig of cool water. Suddenly, he remembered the gleaming white tai chi uniform. He leaned toward Morris.

"You know, I dreamt about Chou Li last night—"

"He came to you in a dream?" Morris interrupted. His tired old eyes popped open in excitement.

"What kind of a dream? What did you see? What did he say? This is important, Kurt! More important than you could know!"

Kurt sat back in the chair. Something in the old man's demeanor caught him off guard. Kurt composed himself, then closed his eyes trying to recreate the wispy memory.

"It was dark, pitch black. Chou Li came to me. He was walking toward me from far away—"

"How did he look?" Morris jumped in. "What was he wearing? Did he say anything? Did he talk to you?"

"Take it easy, Morris! What's this all about, anyway?"

"It's about the soul. It's about the *neshamah*. We believe—"

"We, who?" Kurt interrupted.

Morris sighed in frustration. He was obviously frustrated.

"We who? We old Jews! We old orthodox Jews. That's who! We believe that when the soul, the *neshamah*, leaves the body to return to its home, it can stop to say good-bye to the person still in this world it loved most. You know what that means, Kurt? It means that Chou Li's soul came to see you. That's what this is all about."

"I don't know," Kurt shook his head. "This makes no sense to me. I'm not Jewish. I certainly don't think Chou Li was Jewish."

"You don't have to be Jewish to be a *mensch*," Morris laughed. "You don't have to be Jewish to have a soul, to be a human being. Now, tell me… What did he say to you?"

Kurt sighed, then shared more about his dream with Chou Li. Morris was leaning forward, barely on the edge of his chair.

"He said 'Thank you, Kurt. Our friendship has been a gift that has given me much joy.' He reached out and said, 'Don't worry about me. I am good. I am good and so are you.' Then he was gone."

Morris was smiling as he shook his head back and forth.

"Do you know what that means? It means he loved you. He cared about you like family. He cared enough to stop on his way to heaven just to let you know he was okay, and that you would be okay, too. Do you realize what a blessing that is?"

Kurt didn't answer; he was lost deep in thought. Along with the profound sadness he was feeling at the loss of his mentor came a renewed sense of commitment to his memory and the principles that were the foundation of his teachings. He looked at Morris.

"Listen," Kurt said, "I think we all need to take some time off before going back to the park. We need time to mourn Chou Li's passing. But I think it's really important that we continue with the group. Do you think a week would be enough?"

Morris thought for a moment. He nodded slowly.

"Yes, a week is enough. A week after the funeral. That should give everyone at the Center time to mourn."

"Then it's decided," Kurt said. "Let's tell the others that we'll get together in the same place at the regular time seven days after the funeral. Tell them to be there so we can celebrate Chou Li's legacy, his memory. So we can celebrate his life. And…"

Kurt hesitated, unsure if he should finish his thought. He considered what he was thinking carefully, then continued.

"And tell them, if no one else is there to lead the group going forward, I'll do it."

"You will?"

"I will," Kurt said confidently. "I asked Chou Li once how to thank him for everything he shared with me. He said I could do that by being generous with my time and knowledge, by living a life of service, by honoring others and then honoring myself.

"He said if I did all that, I would honor him. And that's exactly what I intend to do."

Morris wiped the corner of his eye with his sleeve.

"You know something," he said. "We have a word for a person like that in Yiddish, a person like you."

"You do? What is it?" Kurt asked.

"We call him a *mensch*."

‡

Over the next few days Kurt could think of nothing else but the time he spent at the park with Chou Li; times he would never have again. He cherished the old man's insight and understanding, his approach to learning and to life.

Chou Li had become the eye of Kurt's storm, the calm center of his turbulent universe. Kurt was trying hard get past the initial shock of Morris' visit and Chou Li's passing when he was called by an attorney representing Chou Li's estate.

The call was about the old man's personal library, an extensive collection of books on every possible subject from leadership and management to Western philosophy, Chinese martial arts and the Tao. It was a library that Kurt had no idea even existed.

The attorney made it clear that the bulk of the collection was large enough to fill a small storage unit. And it was Chou Li's final wish that the whole thing would now belong to Kurt, including all the volumes written in the original Chinese.

Kurt shared the news of Chou Li's incredible gift with Robert that evening after class. That was when he mentioned he would be taking over the tai chi class in the park. As Kurt uttered the words out loud, he realized it was a spur-of-the-moment decision he was already unsure of. A torrent of doubt grew louder in his head.

How can I take his class? How can I presume to take my sifu's place? I'm not the man or the martial artist he was.

Green Belt Master

Seven days passed. It was a beautiful sunny day in late March, cool and crisp, with the majority of Chou Li's group already waiting on the grass when Kurt arrived.

He was late and he knew it. He was late and it made him crazy. Anyone who knew him knew he'd rather not go somewhere, than be late. And, yet, here he was in the parking lot—late, but still there.

Agitated and unsettled were the two words that kept scrolling across the inside of Kurt's eyelids. This was wrong and there was no one else to blame, no one to point a finger at but himself.

What have I done? he thought. *What was I even thinking? Why do I keep doing things like this? Saying 'yes' without considering what the hell it was I just agreed to.*

I have no business being in front of them. I'm not qualified to lead anything. Shit! I almost wrecked my business. I damn near tanked my marriage! They need more than me, more than I can possibly give.

Kurt glanced at his watch and shook his head. Ten minutes is ten minutes, and he was a full ten minutes late.

Nevertheless, he made the conscious decision not to let anyone down—least of all himself. He had made a commitment to Morris, to all the seniors in the group. It was then Kurt realized that the commitment he had made was to Chou Li and to his memory.

He removed his sunglasses and pulled himself together—resisting the urge to shove the Vette in reverse and run for his life.

Everyone was relieved to see that Kurt was there as he walked across the grass. That is, everyone but Kurt. The hot sun beat down on his head. His 'lizard brain' was in hyper-drive, panicking.

What the hell am I supposed to do now? How do I start?

Chou Li made it look so easy—the movements, the explanations, everything. And, why not? He was a goddamned Tao master, with a lifetime of practice and knowledge! I'm barely a student..."

The anxiety Kurt felt was real and growing.

He closed his eyes and took a deep breath. He decided the best way to start the class would be for everyone to share their favorite stories about Chou Li. But each of the seniors seemed content to wait for someone else to begin.

Finally Kurt took the initiative. He talked about the planning problems he was having at work and how Chou Li had convinced him to share those problems with him during one of the many talks they had after the day's practice.

He shook his head, as he related how he dismissed the idea of Chou Li's help initially. He kept talking simply because he didn't know how to avoid the subject without insulting the old man.

Kurt was overwhelmed with emotion as he recounted the story, laughing out loud as he remembered just how foolish he felt when Chou Li informed him that he had a rich, full life that preceded him entering the Senior Center.

That he had graduated from Cal Berkeley with a degree in Business and had gone on to pick up an MBA from Stanford. That he had started and run a number of small businesses successfully.

As Kurt approached the end of the story, he choked up. He shared how instrumental Chou Li's help had proven as he worked to turn his business around. His respect and admiration for the old man was evident in every word.

That broke the ice. Others took their turn in the circle, and lots of Chou Li stories followed. Each was a testimony to the long rewarding life he lived so unselfishly. Chou Li had led the class for many years and it was obvious he had managed to touch a number of lives along the way.

When everyone finished Kurt urged them find a place in line. He opened his iPad, swiped his way to one of the many tai chi music recordings he had, and adjusted the volume. He stood at the front of the group, ready to begin.

He tried to remain centered as he called out the individual movements: Preparation, Lifting and Sinking, Parting the Wild Horse's Mane, Ward Off Left, Roll Back and Press, Push, Single Whip and Lifting Hands.

When he reached White Crane Spreads Its Wings, he realized Robert had joined the group, taking what had been Kurt's original position all the way in the back.

Kurt pulled his focus back to the form and pushed through to the end of the first section, even though the thought of his *sensei* watching him, judging him, was just short of crippling.

He marveled at how smoothly Robert was able to move through each posture, how fluid and graceful he was. Kurt admired how deep his stances were, how low to the ground and powerful his movements. Suddenly, he realized how much better Robert was at this than he was. Kurt felt like a fraud, a true imposter.

He should be the teacher, not me, he thought. *What do I know?*

He became aware of his own perspective—standing in front of the group, trying to lead—rather than hiding in the back of the class like he did on his first day and for many weeks thereafter.

As Kurt reached a movement called Carrying The Tiger To The Mountain, the terrible weight of responsibility crashed in on him.

He was crushed by the prodigious weight of his own doubts and insecurities, the responsibility of leading a group he was in no way prepared or qualified to lead, a group of seniors who deserved more that he was capable of giving them.

This isn't Carrying The Tiger... I'm not doing it right!

Kurt was hesitant and unsure, and the result was a series of choppy and stilted movements that rippled through the group.

It's wrong. Just plain wrong.

Robert being there, moving like the master Kurt longed to become, only compounded the inadequacies he felt in his soul.

Robert is perfection. I'm a fraud!

His arms trembled and his voice quavered as he continued to call out the postures. Kurt's and Robert's eyes locked. He was embarrassed to have someone he respected so much witness his failure: this travesty to everything Robert and Chou Li held dear.

Kurt's knees buckled.

That was it. He was done.

He was kneeling on the grass with his hands covering his face.

His chest heaved.

All the seniors in the group stood silently, frozen in mid-posture, trying not to look.

Kurt had never experienced anything like this before. Nothing as shattering. Nothing as humiliating.

He had pushed too hard. Gone too far.

There was nothing left.

This time *he* was the misfire; he was living it. The Corvette was fine, it had been fixed long ago. This time it was Kurt who wasn't firing on all cylinders. Kurt who was unable to flow with Robert's grace and mastery, with Chou Li's wisdom and ease.

Kurt who was broken and unrepairable.

He moved his hands from his face to his thighs and pushed himself to a standing position. He was breathing hard, shaking his head back and forth. He was still looking straight down at the grass as he addressed the group.

"I can't," Kurt said. "I thought I would be okay. I thought I could do this. But I was wrong. I don't have the strength. I don't have the skill. I don't have the experience."

He forced himself to look up at the stunned faces of the old men and women standing before him.

"You deserve better. You deserve more than I can give you. You deserve Chou Li. Not some incomplete, half-assed copy!"

Kurt's voice cracked. Tears ran down his cheeks. He was gasping for air, heaving out each word.

"I had no idea what I lost with Chou Li's passing until now. How much I depended on him. How much I leaned on him. I had so much more to learn. Chou Li had so much more to teach me."

Kurt's eyes searched the back of the group, hoping he had left. But Robert was still there, witnessing the whole thing.

"My *sensei*, Robert—my karate instructor—is here in the back. He can tell you what a travesty this is. He can tell you that me being here, in front of you, leading a group like this is just plain wrong.

"You deserve more than some 'Green Belt Master.'

"You deserve a real master. Not someone halfway to knowing what he needs to know. Not someone with just enough skill to fool someone who doesn't know any better, who can't tell the difference."

Kurt felt his chest tighten. He couldn't breathe.

"I'm sorry… So sorry."

With that, he turned and ran to the parking lot. The group was visibly shaken. They looked to each other for answers, shocked and saddened. But there were none.

Kurt slipped behind the wheel of the Corvette and took off like he was leaving the scene of a crime—tires screaming and clouds of black acrid smoke filling the air. As he made a hard left out of the parking lot and onto the street, the Corvette's rear end broke loose and Kurt nearly lost control of the vehicle.

Kurt's fingers gripped the steering wheel and worked the shift paddles. He drove like he was possessed. He needed to escape the park and what had transpired, to get away and put it behind him.

So he drove as hard and as fast as could.

He drove like he was being chased.

He drove that way until he finally lost traction completely and slid helplessly along the dirt shoulder—until the black Corvette came within inches of sliding off Drexel Canyon Road and down into the canyon.

It was then Kurt realized where he was and what he was doing.

He pulled into the first scenic viewpoint he encountered and stopped the car. His hands were shaking so badly when he released the steering wheel that he had trouble opening the door.

He walked to the guard rail and stopped. The sun reached down and laid its warm hands on Kurt's head and shoulders. The sky was egg shell blue. The Valley was as beautiful as he'd ever seen it, spread out before him like a giant post card. The kind you can find in almost every hotel gift shop.

Kurt wasn't sure how long he'd been standing there, staring across the Valley. He didn't remember how long it took for his heart rate to return to anything close to normal.

However long it was, it was long enough.

Long enough to realize that he wasn't suicidal. At least not yet.

Kurt turned, got in the car, and headed back to the office.

Unfinished Business

'Interminable' was one of Kurt's favorite words. Not because he used it all that often, but because of the way it sort of rolls off your tongue. He'd been back from the debacle at the park—'debacle' was another favorite—locked in his office for a few hours.

He had barricaded himself inside to avoid anyone asking anything about where he'd been or what he was up to. If they had asked, he would have told them the time he spent in the park was 'interminable': never-ending.

Nevertheless, Kurt managed to gut it out until it was time to head home for what he hoped would be a nice quiet dinner with Laurie and the kids.

He was still lost deep in thought when he rounded the corner to his cul-de-sac. He hit the brakes hard. The black Corvette jerked to a stop in the middle of the street.

Parked in his driveway was an ultrasonic blue Lexus RC F. The glamour plate read 'NO MIND'—leaving no doubt who the car belonged to. At least no doubt in Kurt's mind.

Suddenly Kurt's despair over what had transpired in the park, his despondency, transformed itself into something bordering on blind rage. He could feel every muscle in his body tighten; the blood pounding in his head and behind his eyes.

He could hear the words in his head as clearly as if someone was shouting in his ear.

What the hell is Robert doing here? What's he doing at my house? Goddammit! Who the hell does he think he is? Does he really think coming here is going to change anything?

Kurt parked on the street and headed up the walkway to his front door. He left everything in the Corvette—papers, backpack, computer, everything—as he fumbled for his keys.

He was still fumbling when the door opened.

Laurie was standing there with Max leaning against her left hip.

"HiiIIIii, honey!" she chirped brightly. "We have company! An unexpected guest."

Robert was sitting in the family room, his body wedged into the corner of the couch. AJ was sitting on his lap. He smiled and whispered something in her ear. She giggled, then slid off Robert's knee and ran to her father. AJ gave him a hug and then went into the playroom. Laurie tapped Max on the shoulder; grudgingly he headed down the hall to join his sister.

Laurie looked over at Kurt and smiled.

"Robert just accepted my invitation to join us for dinner, honey! Isn't that great? I was going to call you at the office to let you know, but you surprised us by coming home early."

Kurt refused to acknowledge Robert's presence by working hard not to make eye contact. He tried hard to keep his agitation hidden.

"I'll leave you two to visit while I get dinner started," she said.

Kurt recognized the tone in Laurie's voice. That, and her body language, made it crystal clear Robert would be joining them. There was nothing in heaven or on Earth that was going to change that.

Kurt walked into the room.

"Can I get you something to drink?" he offered. "A beer? Cold water? A soft drink? Maybe something more substantial?"

Robert searched Kurt's face for clues. He was looking for the pain and humiliation he'd seen earlier in the park. Trying to find the man hiding inside. Kurt looked away.

"I'll have whatever you're having," Robert said. "How's that?"

"Then I think it's going to be something more substantial," Kurt said dryly. He tilted his head toward the built-in bar in the corner. "I've got just about everything back there. What'll it be?"

"As long as you're asking," Robert replied, "I'll have a bourbon, club soda, and a lemon twist. That is, if it isn't too much trouble."

"Not a problem. No trouble at all."

Kurt walked into the kitchen. He needed a fresh lemon.

He locked eyes with Laurie for a second before she went back to working on dinner. The glance wasn't enough for Kurt to figure out what had transpired before he came through the door. And that bothered him.

He had no idea if Robert had shared what happened in the park. No way of knowing if he'd discussed the story of Kurt's breakdown with her. Nevertheless, he was somehow certain she knew.

He walked into the family room, lemon in hand, and moved behind the bar. Kurt spoke in Robert's general direction.

"I'm a bourbon drinker myself. Do you have a preference?"

"A preference?" Robert repeated. "Well, when I drink, it's usually Maker's Mark, Blanton's, or Basil Hayden. If you have 'em, that is. Maybe Angel's Envy? But I don't want you to go to any trouble just for me. I'll have whatever you're drinking."

Kurt was quiet for a moment.

"Really. It's no trouble at all," he mumbled.

Kurt fully expanded his chest with a deep cleansing breath.

"In fact, I'm kind of glad you decided to stop by," he said.

He took a second breath.

"In all honesty, I guess I'm *really* glad you're here"

Kurt pulled down two highball glasses from a shelf above the bar and filled them with ice from the bar fridge. He opened one of the cabinet doors behind him, grabbed an open bottle of Blanton's, and poured. He cut a few twists, added club soda, and then wiped a twist around the rim of each glass. Kurt took a moment to inspect both drinks, then nodded his head in approval.

Definitely the 'right' color, he thought.

He pulled out a few napkins, retrieved a couple of coasters, and placed everything on the wooden coffee table between him and where Robert was already seated.

Kurt called out to the kitchen. "Would you like a glass of wine while you're in there slaving on our behalf?"

Laurie peeked around the corner smiling.

"Well, Mr. Kerrigan," she said. "I thought you'd never ask."

"White or red?" Kurt asked, smiling back. It was the first time he had smiled since he left the park.

"Red, hon… Maybe a glass of Syrah."

Kurt went to the wine fridge and poured his wife a glass, then delivered it to the kitchen. She said 'thank you' without looking up.

Kurt's smile drained away. He still had no idea whether or not Laurie knew about the episode at the park.

Why won't she look at me? he thought.

Kurt shook the paranoia out of his head before going back to the family room. He didn't want to wander down that road again.

He sat down opposite Robert and reached for his drink. This was his favorite chair, his father's favorite chair, before it found its way to Kurt's family room.

He felt safe in that chair, as safe as he felt anywhere. As safe as he felt every time he found refuge there when he was a child.

The two men sat in silence.

Finally, Robert picked up his glass and held it out toward Kurt. Kurt responded in kind unsure of what was to happen next. The glasses made contact.

"To Chou Li's memory and to better times," Robert said.

Kurt felt an overwhelming wave of emotion well up from a place deep inside. It was unexpected and unwanted here in front of Robert. He wiped the corner of his eye with his free hand.

"To Chou Li's memory—" Kurt said.

He stopped there, letting the words hang in the air. They hung there until Robert finished the phrase.

"And to better times."

They sat quietly, slowly sipping away at their drinks until Kurt couldn't deal with the quiet—or the suspense—any longer.

"What are you doing here, Robert? Why did you come?"

Robert glanced up slowly from his drink.

"I came because a friend was in pain. That's what friends do."

Kurt scoffed out loud.

"That's it?" he asked. "You've got the studio and the shop. An army of people who depend on you. You want me to believe that you're here simply because 'you have a friend in pain'? Really?"

Robert set his drink down, and nodded his head.

"Yes," he said deliberately. "Really."

Robert clasped his hands together and leaned forward.

"If you want to talk about what happened this afternoon, I'm here. If you want to sit and just think about what happened, I'm here. If you'd like to try and throw me out… Well, I'm still here.

"You've got lots of options, Kurt. But, if that last option is the one you choose, you'd better have one of your construction crews on stand-by, because it's gonna get ugly. Ugly, and more than a little expensive."

Kurt chuckled. The implication was perfectly clear and it was anything but funny. Kurt stared down at his glass.

"Guess I should choose Option One, huh?"

"Good choice," Robert nodded, returning the smile.

"Listen, Kurt, I'm not going to tell you I know how you feel. I don't. I can't. Your relationship with Chou Li was yours, not mine. But I know your feelings were deep, and I'm willing to bet, at least some of them were left unresolved.

"That's what happens when someone dies. There are words that will never be spoken; promises that will never be kept. Death is messy that way. There's always lots of unfinished business."

Kurt listened intently. He could tell Robert's words were coming from a special place, one of care and concern. He was speaking from place of love and deep personal loss as well.

"I know that pain. I understand it. Even when I had the time to share what needed to be said, I didn't always do it. And, in the end, there were too many things left unsaid and undone."

Robert took his glass off the table and sat back for a moment. He sipped the bourbon slowly. Kurt had mixed the drink almost perfectly. It was thick and smooth with just the right amount of smokey burn as it went down.

He was focused on the far corner of the room, as if he could see someone Kurt couldn't. Someone who wasn't there, but was—a woman standing there, listening to the conversation with special interest.

Robert set his drink down. He looked Kurt in the eye, then proceeded to share the story of his wife's illness.

Robert described Margie's passing and how he found himself lost and disconnected; disengaged and alone. He told Kurt the story of his *sensei*'s visit and how they had come within seconds of destroying his home.

It was clear Robert was sitting in Kurt's family room for two reasons. The first was to clean up a debt. To pay it forward by helping his student just as he'd been helped when he was the one lost and in pain. The second reason was much simpler: Robert cared. He truly cared about Kurt.

With that realization, Kurt was both humbled and grateful. He felt honored that Robert shared the story of his love for Margie— their love, her illness, and her subsequent passing.

Kurt began to open up as he struggled to share his feelings for Chou Li and the seniors in his tai chi group, the seniors he spent his lunch hours with every day for the last couple of years.

Robert's eyes burned a hole straight through him.

"If that's how you feel you have to tell them," he said. "You have to tell everyone you care about the truth. You have to tell them you care about them. They need to know. That's the only way you can be sure you're not going to leave any unfinished business of your own behind. The only way.

"Chou Li got to tell you how much you meant to him. He did that through his Will. He told you with the gift of his books, his personal library, his lifetime of learning.

"But, Jesus, Kurt. Wouldn't it have been better if you didn't have to find out through some attorney after he was gone? Do you want to do that to the people you care about?"

Kurt tried hard to choke back the tears. He was grateful for Robert's friendship and wisdom. He was proud to have this man as his friend and teacher.

"Thank you, *sensei*. I understand," Kurt said. "But, no matter what, I will never go back to that park again. I can't."

Work in Progress

Kurt was not going back to the park. He had made that crystal clear. But, if the group was to continue, it was still going to need a leader, someone experienced enough to take the group through the forms with confidence and grace. Kurt was convinced that someone was Robert. Unfortunately, Robert did not share his conviction.

When Kurt began to suggest as much, Robert smiled and shook his head. That wasn't going to happen. Kurt need not even ask.

Robert looked across the coffee table and spoke quietly.

"I understand the emotions you were feeling this afternoon. I do. It's a 'been there/done that.' You suffered a meltdown. But you aren't the only one who has been down that road.

"The only question that matters now is: What happens next?

"Are you going to allow this to define the rest of your life? Are you going to let it haunt you? Corrupt everything you touch from now on?"

Kurt's body straightened in his chair.

"Don't you understand?" he pleaded. "I can't go back. I'm not ready. I'm not good enough. Even if they don't know that, I do!"

Robert bit his lower lip. He leaned forward to reposition himself against the couch's left armrest.

"Not yet…" he whispered.

"What?" Kurt asked. "I'm not sure I heard what you just said."

Robert looked deep into Kurt's eyes and repeated himself.

"Not yet. You're not ready… yet," he said calmly. "Doesn't mean you'll never be ready. It just means you aren't ready now.

"You feel you aren't ready to lead the group… right now.

"You feel you don't have the knowledge… right now.

"You feel you don't have the skill… right now.

"But that doesn't mean you will never have the knowledge or the skill—that you will never be ready. It just means you're at a crossroads, a decision point. Only you can decide whether this incident is permanent or temporary. Whether it's just for now or will be forever."

Kurt leaned back and took a sip of his drink. He wasn't sure he liked where this was going. He wanted to hide in the bullpen after getting hammered at the end of a bad inning, and it felt like Robert wanted to send him out to the mound before he had recovered.

Robert rubbed his hands together. His calloused fingertips resting on the pads of his palms. Some were from a lifetime of hard work in the shop, others were from the early mornings and late evenings spent in the studio.

"I still work out with other martial arts masters in every discipline I teach," he said, "because there's still so much to learn. You see I wasn't always ready either. But I made a choice—the conscious decision to get ready, to be prepared. To do the work.

"Whether you see it or not, that's where you are right now. You're a work in progress. But you're also the artist. You're the writer. You decide what goes on the canvas. You decide what goes on the page. It's up to you. No one else."

Robert's voice dropped back to a whisper.

"Listen, Kurt. Your business was in trouble. You decided to do something about it. Your life here at home was crumbling. You wouldn't accept the obvious outcome. You did something about it.

"You are the author of your own life's story. You get to write the next chapter and that means you get to decide what the rest of your life is going to look like.

"What happened in the park is a scar you will always carry with you. Please don't let it become a permanent disability."

Kurt stared at his empty glass, searching for an answer.

"But…" he stammered. "But how do I get through it? How do I overcome what happened today? Where am I going to find another teacher like Chou Li? How can I make this work without him?"

Robert's eyes were half-closed, his face serene.

"When the student is ready," he said. "The master will appear. I won't take over the class, Kurt. But I will help you with your tai chi practice and I'll continue to help you with the business.

"I think a portion of what happened today is tied up with your confidence level and that relates back to Kerrigan Construction. It's apparent there is still a lot of work to be done before you or your company is really fixed.

"I was watching you while you were in front of the group today. You did a lot better at leading those seniors than you think you did. You were patient, generous, gentle, and caring. Everything a good teacher, a great master, must be in order to succeed.

"You fell apart because you lost a dear friend and found yourself standing in his place, trying to fill his shoes. That's understandable. Hell, it would've been kind of weird if you didn't fall apart out there.

"But, after watching you this afternoon, I can't think of anyone more able or better qualified to lead that group than you. All I have to do is help you see that for yourself."

Kurt played with the fabric of the old chair in much the same way he had when he was a child, raking the velour with the fingers of his right hand. The result was four discolored and equidistant parallel lines worn into the armrest. It was amazing how many crises the two of them had weathered together—this chair and its current occupant. And, yet, here they were again.

Kurt was humbled by Robert's faith in him.

"I should have known," he said, "that you would know the long form. Each posture was perfect, so rooted and deep. And your transitions were beautiful—"

"While you were busy watching me," Robert interrupted, "I was watching you. Chou Li would be proud of the work you've done to master the form. In fact, I'm sure he was.

"A good teacher recognizes when he is presented with a great student. The right person was leading the group today. You're the only person who should lead it. Besides, it's the best way for you to get better with your own practice.

"But if you're still convinced that you can't or shouldn't do it, I'll help you find the confidence you need to overcome whatever it is inside that's stopping you."

Robert reached across the wooden coffee table. He placed his hand gently on Kurt's forearm.

"It was karma that brought you to Chou Li. Just like it was karma that brought you to me."

Kurt gazed into Robert's eyes. They were clear and deep.

"This is your destiny, Kurt. It's your ministry. This is your Why. You just haven't figured that out yet. I'll continue to help you if you promise to allow the Universe to take you where you need to go. If you do, I guarantee you'll enjoy the journey."

"Thank you, *sensei*," Kurt said. "That means a lot."

As if on cue, Laurie was at the family room door. While the men had been involved in their conversation, she had managed to get dinner on the table, and the kids washed up and ready to eat.

She looked at her husband. The change in Kurt's demeanor was was evident. He was calmer, more centered. She couldn't help but think it had to be Robert's positive influence.

"If you two gentlemen are done solving the world's problems, I think we should sit down and enjoy the incredible meal I've just thrown together while it's still hot."

Robert smiled his approval at the thought. He turned to Kurt.

"We're here talking about lifetime learning, while there was a true master at work in the next room and we didn't even notice."

"Why, Mr. Taylor," Laurie blushed, "thank you!"

She gave Kurt a mischievous wink.

"See? Finally someone appreciates me."

Kurt smiled and shook his head as he stood up. Laurie beamed at Robert.

"I hope this won't be the last time you decide to join us."

Before he could answer, Kurt responded.

"No, it won't," he said. "This is just the first of many dinners."

Robert was the wise, caring father Kurt longed for as a child.

He waited for his *sensei* to get up from the couch. When he got close enough, Kurt shook his hand, and thanked him. Then he pulled Robert into a bear hug that said everything that needed to be said between the two men, between two good friends.

The "Dirty Dozen" Rides Again...

Kurt let a couple of weeks pass before making arrangements with Robert to stay after class at least one evening a week to work on the long Yang form. However, Kurt was at the door to Robert's office to ask his most pressing business questions in less than a week.

Robert was prepared; he had brewed two cups of green tea in anticipation of Kurt's arrival. He handed one to his eager student as they both took a seat .

"Like I mentioned on the phone," Kurt said, "I wanted to get an earlier start tonight. I think I'm finally ready for the the rest of your Dirty Dozen KPIs."

"Happy to oblige," Robert said. "I think we got through—"

"All the Profit stuff," Kurt interjected.

"Right," Robert agreed. "That means Car Count is next."

He cleared his throat and closed his eyes. Then took a sip of tea.

"Car Count is a critical KPI for shops like mine. It's a measure of through-put. I get that you don't have cars to count in your line of work, but I bet there's an equivalent metric that's just as important.

"What I mean by Car Count is the number of vehicles that pass through the shop every day, or any time period you're measuring. That includes all vehicles, even those for which there is no charge."

"Every vehicle your people touch?" Kurt asked.

"Absolutely," Robert said. "And it's one of the easiest KPIs to track because of our computerized management system.

"We use sequentially-numbered repair orders that are created automatically. In fact, the management system calculates Car Count for us along with several other KPIs—the Dirty Dozen along with some others we track—because all the numbers are already in the system. Your software might do the same thing, if you 'ask' it to.

"The most crucial metric that Car Count leads us to is Average Invoice. For us, that's simply Total Sales divided by Car Count, the number of vehicles it took to generate those sales."

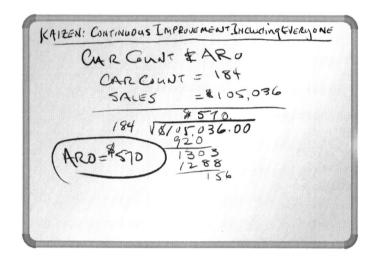

Robert walked over to the white board, writing down examples of everything. Kurt made a funny face.

"Hold on," he said. "You wrote 'ARO'. What's that again?"

"Sorry," Robert smiled. "Sometimes I write faster than I think. ARO stands for Average Repair Order. It's just another way to express Average Invoice. We use that term more often."

"Here's an example. Imagine that we worked on 184 vehicles; that's our Car Count. And then our Total Sales was $105,036. When we divide Sales by the Cars, we come up with an Average Repair Order of just about $570. That's a critical KPI for us, especially since the industry average is well below $325.

"Like I said before, you need to translate this into your trade. You could look at the total number of events in which you perform a service. Then tally up all the sales dollars generated from those.

"For you, it's probably projects, the number of houses and buildings you send crews out to every day. For somebody else, it might the number of widgets they manufacture and sell.

"Whatever it is, there's going to be one kind of critical event or another associated with your company's 'car count'. You have to know what that number is, because I'm sure there's a best practices guideline in your industry that you can compare it to."

Kurt copied down everything on the white board.

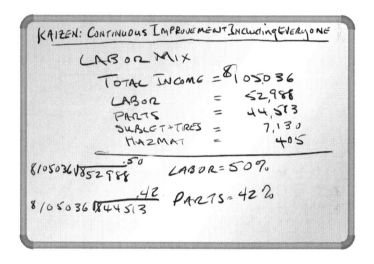

"I'm going to look at that," he said, "first thing tomorrow."

"Good," Robert nodded. "Let's move on then."

He erased the board again.

"The next metric is a thing we call Labor Mix. For us, revenue comes almost exclusively from the sale of Parts and Labor. Labor Mix is the relationship of Labor Sales and Parts Sales to Total Sales.

"In other words, what percentage of Total Sales came from Labor and what percentage was attributed to the sale of Parts."

Robert found a Profit & Loss Statement in a stack on the edge of his desk. He used a black pen to draw a circle around the Labor and Parts Income totals.

"The reason we track this," he said, "is there's a significantly higher Gross Profit realized when we sell Labor.

"For auto repair shops, we're looking for about a 60/40 split in our ratio of Labor Sales to Parts Sales. That's the industry target. Labor Mix tells us if we're hitting the mark."

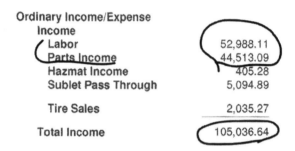

Ordinary Income/Expense	
Income	
Labor	52,988.11
Parts Income	44,513.09
Hazmat Income	405.28
Sublet Pass Through	5,094.89
Tire Sales	2,035.27
Total Income	105,036.64

Robert went back to the white board.

"The next KPI is Labor Content per Job. It starts with Labor Mix as its base, but it's different. A lot of shops overlook it, but it can play a critical role in scheduling if you understand it. I stumbled across it by accident while working on Mushin's metrics.

"I was working my way through Average Invoice calculations when I wondered what role Labor Mix could play. I mean, if the Labor Mix percentages are accurate, you should be able to apply the Parts/Labor ratios to your Average Invoice. Doing that would leave us with a breakdown of Parts and Labor."

"What could you do with those numbers?" Kurt asked.

"Good question," Robert said. "I found that if you know the Average Labor Dollars per Job, and the Effective Labor Rate, you can divide Average Labor Dollars per Job by your Effective Labor Rate and the result will be your Labor Content per Job."

"Effective Labor Rate," Kurt said. "That's from the first time we talked about KPIs. It's the thirteenth one, the Baker's Dozen."

"Exactly," Robert nodded. "For us, Effective Labor Rate is the amount we're actually receiving per hour for the labor services performed—not what we have posted on the wall.

"It's your Posted Labor Rate divided by your Service Bay Productivity."

Kurt stopped writing and looked over at Robert.

"What exactly does that mean?" he asked.

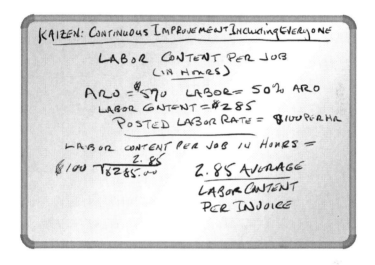

Robert laughed.

"It means that what you think you're charging per hour may not be what you're actually receiving per hour. It means if your posted labor rate is $100 per hour, but your Service Bay Productivity is only 80%, your Effective Labor Rate is going to be $80 per hour not $100.

"But, for now, we're going to calculate a 'down and dirty' Labor Content per Job using a Posted Labor Rate and not an Effective Labor Rate because it's just plain easier. I'm certain you will find out there's an Effective Labor Rate in contracting that will become as important in your journey toward success as it was in ours."

"I think of Labor Content per Job as a 'super' KPI, because it helps us to schedule work with far more accuracy than most other shops are able to do. It's our ace in the hole."

"Why do you say that?" Kurt asked.

"If we know what the Labor Content is," Robert said, "which is figured in hours, then we know the average amount of time each vehicle is going to spend in the shop. Count the license plates or appointments and you know what you have going on for the day."

"That's fantastic," Kurt agreed.

"I was pretty happy when I figured it out," Robert said proudly. He turned back to the white board and erased it again.

"That brings us to the next two: Technician Efficiency and Service Bay Productivity. These are vital numbers to watch because of the impact they can have on so many of the other KPIs we've been talking about.

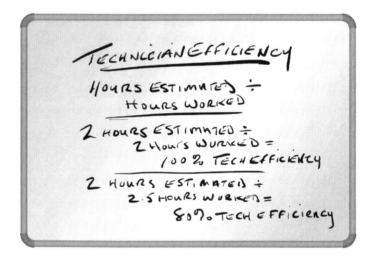

"Technician Efficiency is the relationship between the number of hours projected for each job assigned to a technician, and the amount of time it actually took that person to complete the job.

"If I have a job that should take an hour to perform, that's what I sell it for. If I assign it to a technician and it takes that technician one hour to complete, then Technician Efficiency is 100%.

"If it takes longer, Technician Efficiency drops to below 100%. If that keeps happening consistently, I need to look into why.

"Now if it takes the technician less time, maybe as the result of training, experience, or better tools, we'd say that the technician is more than 100% efficient. And, ultimately, that's what you want."

"Wait a second," Kurt said. "I totally get what you're saying. But how is this different from Service Bay Productivity?"

"I know, the two metrics are often confused," Robert agreed. "Service Bay Productivity is an indication of how productive or efficient the entire business is. It's the relationship between the number of hours the business has available for sale every day and the number of hours that are actually sold.

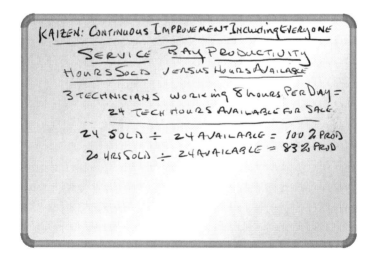

"There are only so many hours available for sale each day depending upon your company. Typically, it's a simple calculation of the time available. For us, it's the number of hours the business is open, and the number of technicians we have on staff that day. If you have three mechanics each working an eight-hour shift, you have twenty-four tech hours available for sale.

"But time is perishable. It's non-replaceable. Unlike parts that you can pull out of inventory and return if you don't sell them, if you don't sell any of the tech hours available today, they just flat won't be there to sell tomorrow or the day after.

"So if you have three techs and sell eight hours of work for each of them, then your Service Bay Productivity is 100%.

"But, realistically, that's a terribly elusive goal for most shops. In fact, most independent shops run at barely over 50%. That means, on any given day, only slightly more than half the hours available for sale are being sold. And that's a tragedy."

"*Sensei*," Kurt said, "I don't even want to think about what ours is. I'm almost afraid to look."

"Well," Robert sighed, "this is yet another step in the type of clear-headed assessment of 'where you're at' that you need to do. You have to find out. It's the only way to improve."

Kurt nodded in agreement. He and Rick were going to have plenty to do when he returned to the office. A mountain of data to dig through, a bunch of calculations to make.

"Now," Robert continued, "your Service Bay Productivity can be impacted by any one of many factors. If your people are less than 100% efficient, it doesn't make sense to sell eight hours in one day. They're just not going to get the work done.

"That might be a training or experience issue. Or there could be a marketing or sales failure. In other words, the failure of the office to bring enough vehicles in to fill the day or the inability of the Service Advisor to sell all the hours of work that are available.

"Either way, at less than 100% Service Bay Productivity, the shop is under-performing and probably will not be able to generate enough revenue to keep the boat afloat."

"This is critical," Kurt said. "I can see that."

Robert nodded, then headed to the white board once more.

"If you have any pages left in that legal pad," he said, "I've got two more metrics in the Dirty Dozen to share."

"Go for it," Kurt smiled, turning over to an empty sheet.

"Total Sales per Service Bay," Robert said, "and Total Sales per Service Technician. I think they're both kind of self-explanatory.

"Total Sales per Bay is the Total Sales divided by the number of service bays in the shop. The result of that calculation is only meaningful in comparison to an 'ideal' target. The most common number I've seen thrown around our industry is somewhere around $25,000 per bay per month.

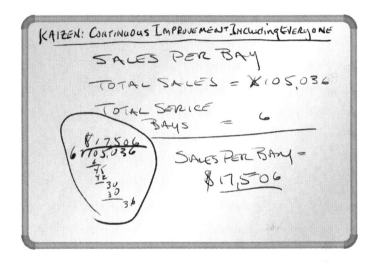

The other number, Total Sales per Technician, is calculated almost identically with the exception that the number of service bays is irrelevant. This number is all about what an individual technician can contribute working at 100% efficiency or better."

"I'm going to have a heck of a time," Kurt said, "trying to figure that out for my guys. They do so many different jobs."

"Your people work in teams, right?" Robert asked. "I'd suggest starting simple. Figure it out for each crew, I mean the people at the worksites, before you try to drill down and get too complex. That first 'rougher' number will give you a starting point. And you can always refine that calculation over time, if you need to.

"Remember that the number you come up with for Total Sales per Technician is an 'ideal' number under perfect conditions. That's rare, if not impossible. Nevertheless, it's still a good number to know, because it gives us something worthwhile to strive for.

"It also serves as a pretty good indication of what we should be doing if we were doing everything 'right.'"

Kurt looked down at his legal pad, then back up at his teacher.

"We got to twelve plus Effective Labor Rate," he said.

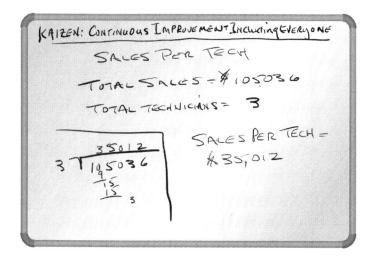

"Yes, we did," Robert agreed. "Listen, everything you do in business can be distilled into a set of numbers that reflect every aspect of your company and are intimately related to each other.

"Actually, it's not really that different from what you're learning across the alley at the studio. Each skill provides the foundation for additional skills, which create larger patterns. These combinations are assembled into forms or *katas*, and the *katas* provide the structure for just about everything else we do.

"When it comes to business, each number is dependent on another. A change in one can often cascade through all the others.

"Understand what they are and what they are trying to tell you. Then you can engage in a true dialogue with your business. These metrics can provide you everything you need to know to make intelligent decisions about what to do now—and what to do next.

"The Dirty Dozen I shared are the most critical numbers to master in auto repair. But I'm willing to bet there are a set of almost identical numbers in your business that correlate perfectly with ours. Different and yet the same."

Robert looked over at the clock and smiled.

"It's getting late," he said. "I hope that helped you, because it's almost tomorrow."

"And tomorrow is?" Kurt asked.

"Tomorrow's the best day to start implementing what you've learned today," Robert smiled.

Kurt laughed and nodded. He realized what a wonderful gift he had been given and had no words to express his gratitude.

"Tomorrow, *sensei*," he said humbly. "And thank you."

Robert nodded in return, then took a sip of his now-cold tea.

Kurt's hand was on the door, ready to leave when Robert stood and placed his left hand over his right fist and bowed.

Balance

Kurt was in the men's locker room, getting ready for class, when he saw Jason approaching out of the corner of his eye. The big man greeted Kurt using his best faux Brooklyn accent.

"Yo! Mr. Kerrigan. How you doin'?"

"Pretty good, Jason," Kurt responded. "And you?"

"Not bad at all," Jason said. "If you have a minute, Robert would like to spend some time with you after class this morning."

"Okay," Kurt said, unsure of what Robert had in store for him.

When class ended, Kurt bowed off the floor and headed toward Robert's office. He'd been there many times, but the simplicity of the room always seemed to catch him off guard. There wasn't a lot of clutter. Everything seemed to have a place and there was rarely anything that seemed out of place.

He knocked. Robert waved him in.

"How are you doing?" Robert asked. "How are things going at home and at work?"

"Pretty good," Kurt said.

"That's it?" Robert asked. "Pretty good? What exactly does that mean? What does 'pretty good' feel like?

"Things are pretty much good everywhere," Kurt said. "Training has made a huge difference in every area of my life—physically, mentally, financially, even socially."

Robert was one of the most intense human beings Kurt had ever known. He had a single-mindedness of purpose that Kurt admired and steel blue eyes that burned right through you when you were the object of their focus.

"Really?" Robert asked. "I know you're at the studio five or six days a week.

"Based upon how you apply yourself when you're here I can only imagine the number of hours you devote to your business and your people. It certainly doesn't seem to leave much time for anything else. Certainly, not a lot of room for your family.

"I appreciate your dedication to the contract we entered into but there has to be more to life than just work and martial arts training. If that's all you've got, there are elements of your life you have to be sacrificing or ignoring altogether.

"I'm just trying to make sure that isn't the case, Kurt. Because balance is critical when it comes to happiness."

Kurt was uncomfortable with where the conversation was going.

"No, Robert, really," he insisted. "Things are fine."

Robert looked across the desk at Kurt, unconvinced.

"Great," Robert said. "Then you won't mind stopping by the shop tomorrow or the next day, so we can finish this conversation."

With that, Robert smiled and went back to the paperwork he'd laid out across the surface of his desk.

‡

As it happened, Kurt had an open block of time before the Wednesday evening class he tried to attend whenever he could. So instead of hanging out at one of the nearby coffee shops that dotted the neighborhood around the studio, Kurt called to be sure Robert was available and headed to the shop.

He left the keys to the Corvette with Allie, since the car was almost due for its next oil service—a simple job they were willing to squeeze in for a loyal customer at the end of a busy day.

Robert was waiting for him at the back of a service bay under a sign that identified the area simply as Wheel Service.

"Hey," Robert said. "Thanks for making the time."

He pointed to a large red machine positioned at the rear of the bay. Kurt had already noticed it. In fact, there was no way to miss it.

"Know what this strange-looking thing is?" Robert asked.

Kurt didn't have a clue and confirmed his ignorance by shaking his head accordingly.

"This is a computerized, road stress-simulating wheel balancer. It's one of the most accurate ever created. Its sole purpose is to ensure the wheel and tire being worked on are perfectly balanced.

"I'd like you to see just how dangerous out-of-balance can be when it comes to your Corvette, so you'll know what it looks and feels like when it occurs in your personal life. That's if you don't mind, of course."

Suddenly, Jason pulled Kurt's Corvette into the service bay. Before Kurt could protest, the two men had raised his vehicle up and removed the right front wheel and tire.

"Are you sure this is part of my oil change," Kurt joked uneasily.

"In a way, I guess it is," Robert said. "Don't worry, Jason will get to that as soon as we're done here. I just want you to see this first."

Robert placed the wheel and tire on the balancer and ran the test sequence. The machine indicated the wheel and tire were very close to being in balance.

He called Kurt over and showed him the weights attached to the inside of the wheel. Then he removed them. Robert closed the wheel guard and ran the test cycle again. This time the wheel and tire vibrated violently. The difference was obvious.

Robert handed the unbalanced wheel and tire over to Jason who put it back on the Corvette, lowered the vehicle, and backed the car out.

Jason got out of the car and kept the driver's door open. Robert ushered Kurt outside to where the vehicle was idling.

"You know how your car felt before I pulled the weights off?" Robert asked. "How it felt when it was pretty much in balance?"

Kurt nodded. Robert crossed to the car's passenger side.

"Good," he said. "Then get in. It's your ride, so you drive."

Both men sat in the black Corvette. Kurt backed out of Mushin, and navigated his way to the freeway on-ramp.

The shaking started at just over 45 miles an hour. It got worse as speed increased. By 65, the vibration was so violent that Kurt was hearing rattles and noises that he'd never heard before.

So violent he was losing confidence in his ability to control the Corvette. Kurt glanced over at Robert who seemed oddly serene.

Kurt decided to exit the freeway at the next off-ramp, exhaling deeply as the vehicle slowed to a point where it no longer shook. He crawled along the surface streets back to Mushin Automotive and slowly pulled to a stop outside the Wheel Service bay.

Robert encouraged Kurt to get himself a hot tea in the front office. By the time he returned, Robert and Jason had removed and balanced all four tires and wheels on his Corvette.

Jason had backed the vehicle out of the bay. He handed the keys to Kurt and winked. "Better than new," he said.

Kurt and Robert got into the car again. Both men buckled up. Without having to be told, Kurt retraced his 'road test' route.

The Corvette hit the on-ramp and Kurt accelerated aggressively.

In a few heartbeats, the car went from 35 to 85 miles per hour— all without any noticeable vibration other than what was caused by irregularities in the road's surface.

"Feel that?" Robert asked.

"Feel what?"

"The vibration, the shaking."

"I can't feel any vibration," Kurt said. "The ride is solid as a rock. Better than when I came in."

"Correct," Robert said. "It's better than it was because the wheels and tires are balanced.

"Now take your hands off the wheel."

"What?" Kurt asked, startled.

"Take your hands off the wheel," Robert replied calmly.

Kurt complied. The black Corvette moved down the freeway as if it was on rails. Robert beamed proudly.

"This vehicle is properly aligned. As a result, the vehicle tracks exactly as it was designed to. I know it's set perfectly because we were the ones who aligned it on one of your last service visits.

"If it wasn't, it would pull to one side or the other. The tires would wear unevenly, it would shake, or it just wouldn't feel right.

"If what you do in your life, or in your business, isn't aligned with your core values—with those things that are most important to you—you'll find yourself out of alignment. The result is conflict, unnecessary pressure, frustration, and ultimately failure.

"If you aren't taking enough time for yourself or your family, if you aren't taking a moment to 'smell the roses' or appreciate where you are, if you aren't in the moment, the results will be the same. Your life will start to shake itself apart."

Kurt slowed down to pull off the freeway, then crossed the overpass, and re-entered—heading back to the shop. Robert looked over at him with a fatherly concern.

"You spend all your time at the studio or at work. That's all you ever talk about, all that seems to consume you.

"Hell, before Max and AJ enrolled at the studio, you rarely ever talked about your family. I guess, now that I've been a dinner guest, I feel a certain responsibility to advocate for Laurie and the kids.

"A very wise mentor of mine told me very early in my career that I could either live to work or work to live. You can either sacrifice every waking moment to your business and career, or you can build a business that works for you—allowing you the time to pursue those things most important to a balanced, aligned life.

"Think about that. Then try to reconcile it with where you are. I think you may find you're a bit out of balance and have more than a little work to do there as well."

Kurt pulled back into the Mushin Automotive lot. Robert got out of the car. He looked at Kurt with his steely blue eyes.

"Your Corvette's in balance and aligned properly," Robert said. "Are you? Where are Laurie and the kids in all of this?

"Please promise me you'll think about it."

Leverage

It was a valuable lesson, so Kurt remembered it well. He was on the floor with eleven other students: two rows of six, facing each other just a few feet apart.

It was another drill.

Each opposing pair would take turns as the aggressor or the defender—throwing a punch, a kick or a combination—while the other defended against it. Their goal was to take the aggressor down. It was an introduction to grappling, something Robert felt should come later in a student's martial arts training.

The process was simple, work the drill ten times, then alternate. After exactly twenty repetitions, each line would move to its right with the last person on each line moving to even up the pairing.

Thus, every participant would have the opportunity to practice with every other student in his or her cohort, regardless of their size or body mass. The drill was all about muscle memory and balance; physical balance.

It was Kurt's turn to be the aggressor, to attack in this case a much smaller opponent.

"*Hajime*," Jason said. Each side bowed formally. Jason dropped his right hand.

"Rei!" he called out.

Kurt found himself standing in front of a young lady he had never worked with before. She was less than half his size. His first concern was not hurting her—exercising enough control not to break anything when he threw a 'light contact' front punch.

Kurt was in a fighting stance—his left leg forward and his right leg back—angled slightly toward his opponent. His right fist was at his hip; the left arm and fist guarding his head and upper body.

On command, he shifted his weight, 'c-stepped' forward with his right leg and delivered a twisting right punch to the center of his tiny opponent's chest.

All he could think about was fracturing her ribcage because of her failure to move away or block his punch. Nevertheless, he knew better than to pull that punch with one of the senior instructors standing right there beside him.

What happened next, Kurt could only be sure of because of what he was told about it afterward.

He threw his forward punch aimed straight at the center of his opponent's chest. She stepped inside the punch with her right foot forward, threw up an upward block using her left forearm as a weapon, deflecting the punch up, out, and away from her body mass—driving Kurt off center to his right.

Then she reached out, grabbed his wrist, and drove the open palm of her right hand up and into Kurt's shoulder just below his collar bone. She followed that with a right-hand, knife-edge strike to Kurt's neck. Still moving, she maneuvered her right leg around and behind his right leg and continued pressing forward with her right elbow wedged into Kurt's chest.

Kurt was totally unprepared. He went spinning backward on to the hardwood floor. He was sure he felt the back of his head bounce when he went down.

He shook his head to clear the cobwebs and looked up to find Allie standing over him, smiling. He smiled back.

Well, this isn't at all what I expected, he thought.

"Leverage," Allie said, shaking her head at Kurt.

"Do you know what just happened? You underestimated both the situation and your opponent. You thought you would be able to use your size and mass to overwhelm her. It makes sense. It's intuitive. But isn't always true."

Kurt was woozy, struggling to sit up straight.

"You're bigger, taller, heavier, and stronger," Allie continued. "You have every advantage. But those advantages can work against you if you aren't careful, if you allow your opponent leverage over you. And that's exactly what she did."

Kurt picked himself up off the floor, trying to figure out how big the knot on the back of his head was going to be. The young girl who had taken him down so effectively came over to be sure he was okay. Kurt assured her he was fine. Allie wasn't convinced.

"Shower up," she said. "Then come and see me."

Kurt reluctantly made his way to the locker room.

‡

Kurt's head was still throbbing when he found Allie guiding the group through the remainder of the class. He took a seat near the mirrors at the back of the room.

Cold condensate from the ice pack he had pressed against the lump on the back of his head was running down the back of his neck. It was almost as uncomfortable as having to watch everyone else complete the exercises as he sat, useless, on the floor.

When the workout was over, Allie bowed off the floor and took a seat next to Kurt. Without hesitating, she continued their talk as if it had never ended.

"Leverage is the multiplication of force. She threw you off balance by driving your right arm out and away. She stopped your momentum with a strike to your upper body, then continued her defense by trapping your right leg and forcing you backward.

"Your body went up, back and to the right and while your leg was trapped. The only way you could have recovered would have been to get your legs back under you—under your body, restoring your center of gravity. The only way to do that would have been to anticipate what she was about to do and not over-commit. But you did over-commit and, as a result, you wound up on your butt."

"I never thought it was possible," Kurt said, "for all the reasons you suggested, not the least of which was her size. I underestimated an opponent and based on the lump on the back of my head, it isn't likely I'll ever do that again."

"It's more than that," Allie said. "More than just size. What she did was leverage her *energy*—her power, position, and strength. She used every physical tool she had at her disposal against you. So when you went down, you went down hard.

"Leveraging is not about strength, Kurt. It's not about size. It's all about position—multiplying your advantages against whoever it is you are contending against."

Kurt rubbed the back of his head as Allie continued.

"It's Archimedes' old adage about 'Give me a lever long enough and a fulcrum upon which to place it, and I shall move the world'. You need to recognize, understand, and learn to use that leverage to your advantage. This is equally true in business.

"Mushin is a small independent repair shop. We compete against eight dealerships that fill both sides of the street on two solid blocks less than a half-mile from here. If that isn't enough, there's a half-dozen franchises and retailers in the immediate area.

"There are countless shops, both large and small, in the area and yet we're always working at capacity—booked at least a week or two out. Our service bays are filled, while their bays are often empty.

"How can we do that?"

Kurt shrugged his shoulders. "How do you do it?" he asked.

"Leverage," Allie said firmly. "We leverage our strengths and minimize our weaknesses.

"We're small and agile, able to act and react more quickly than our competitors. We're intimate and involved with our clients where others are often distant and detached. We're all about relationships where they are far too often transactional.

"We've become so good at it that our competitors often react to what we are doing instead of the other way around. What are you doing, Mr. Kerrigan, to leverage your special advantages?"

‡

As Kurt drove home from the studio, he realized that he was stuck. He could hear Allie repeating herself over and over again inside his head.

'What are you doing to leverage your special advantages?'

He couldn't stop thinking about it, because he knew he didn't have a decent answer.

What are my special advantages? And how can I leverage them?

Is it our people? Our size? Is it this new commitment to our Why?

Is it everything I've learned from Robert and Chou Li?

Without knowing exactly how he got there, Kurt suddenly found himself standing in the center of his garage, staring up at the boxes of Chou Li's library he had stored there.

With as much as I learned from Zen in the Martial Arts and The Tao of Jeet Kune Do, how much more wisdom is waiting for me here?

Here was the combined wisdom of the Tao, Eastern Philosophy, Zen and the martial arts peppered with books on management and leadership. Kurt's mind raced.

Robert's friend was right when he told him, 'I am the competition!'

I am the competitive advantage. No one else has my experience. No one else has my perspective. And, together with my people, we are the leverage.

We are unique in everything we do, in the way we respond to every challenge.

Transformational Math

Kurt appreciated the opportunity that conversations with Robert provided. It was a chance to put everything he was struggling to learn in perspective. Each time his *sensei* asked a question, Kurt could almost feel himself pulling all sorts of random ideas together from where they were stored in his head.

In fact, this may have been one of the few times he was more focused on answering those questions openly and honestly than he was on how the answers would make him look or feel.

Ignoring his own self-absorption, his own ego, was liberating. It afforded him a freedom he hadn't known before he stepped onto polished wooden floor of the studio with what he later came to know as a 'beginner's mind'.

In the past, Robert had asked Kurt if he knew how to get to a 9 to 11 percent True Net Profit number on his way to even higher profit numbers. And, until very recently, Kurt's answer was always the same: 'no'.

But now he had a basic sense of where he was thanks to Peter Summerville, his de facto senior coach from the park; and Robert's sneaky 'reverse budgeting/planning backwards' tool.

Kurt struggled to use every tool available to him to work his way through the numbers, despite the discomfort and anxiety. Despite the fact he was neither a 'math genius', nor an accountant.

Still, he persevered. Having Robert there in the office helped.

He began to understand the relationships these numbers had with one another along with the impact they had on his business. If you wanted to ensure there was 9 to 11 percent left at the end of the process, you'd better have a pretty good idea of what kind of a number you needed to start with.

Kurt had been told that he should be shooting for 12 percent or better, that 9 to 11 percent, after taxes, was a 'best practices' number for most companies his size. It reflected a reasonable Return on Investment as long as the owner's compensation was calculated in as part of the company's overhead expenses.

But he'd been told there was something else to think about as well. And that had to do with the economic cycles that were an integral part of operating a contracting business. The boom/bust cycles that every contractor had to live with.

Everyone Kurt talked to agreed that contractors needed to have reserves sufficient to survive for two or three years of break-even. Every decade seemed to have six, seven, or even eight 'peak' years that alternated with two to four years of hardship.

Put money aside and make it work for you when times are good, and you won't be begging your banker for a high-interest loan when the phones stopped ringing.

This is where reverse budgeting comes into play, Kurt thought.

He remembered how lost he felt the first time he was forced work backwards through his numbers. It was no picnic, especially when the numbers were nowhere near where they needed to be. But it felt good knowing he was narrowing the gap between his current reality and his goal of 9 to 12 percent Net Operating Profit.

It kind of makes sense, he thought. *Isn't that what Covey said, 'start with the end in mind'? Start with what you want or need and work backwards from there. Okay, then, I want 10 percent.*

Kurt grabbed his notebook and dug in to the numbers.

If I want a bottom line, True Net Profit of 10 percent, what kind of Gross Profit would I need?

If we're talking about a construction business like mine, everyone says I should start with an Adjusted Revenue of 25 percent—the part that covers my 10 percent plus my tax liability.

To dedicate 25 percent of Adjusted Revenue for taxes, and ensure the 10 percent I want, I'd need to start working with a balance of 65 percent. If I divide the 10 percent I want by that 65 percent, I wind up with just over 15 percent.

One of my KPIs is a desired General Overhead of 9 percent or less. I've got to add that number to the 15 percent I need for me and the government. Now I'm working with a Gross Margin of Adjusted Revenue that's right about 24 percent.

Suddenly, Kurt tossed down his pencil on the yellow legal pad.

"My God," he said through clenched teeth. "I hate math!"

Robert looked up. He had assumed silence was the best gift to give a student who was calculating a series of math problems. But now he leaned forward with interest.

"Having trouble?" Robert asked.

"I wish someone had told me how damned important math was going to be in real life when I was in high school," Kurt mumbled.

Robert chuckled. "What can I help you with," he offered.

"Thanks," Kurt said. "But I need to get through this on my own."

Then he picked up his pencil and pad and tried again.

Another one of the numbers Kurt was looking at was Indirect Cost. The 'best practices' target he'd been given was 22 percent or less. When that percentage was first presented Kurt bristled against it, insisting it was way too high. But then he began to understand why it wasn't.

That number included not only his own salary, but Rick's as well. Add in the cost of owning and operating the equipment—the trucks, backhoe, pumps and other stuff, as well as operating expenses like office equipment and Worker's Compensation—and that 22 percent not only felt 'reasonable,' it almost seemed too low.

Couple the Indirect Cost together with the Gross Margin and you're looking at a Direct Margin of about 46 percent of Adjusted Revenues. That means that the Direct Costs would have to be about 54 percent of the total adjusted contract revenues.

Kurt kept scribbling down formulas, then checking his math.

Convert those percentages to dollars and then divide the Margin by the Cost and I'll know what I need the company to do for the recipe to remain accurate.

Kurt stopped, his head pounding. Robert was unperturbed. He sipped his tea, and focused on his student's progress.

"Last step," Kurt announced, not sure if Robert was listening.

Kurt's pencil moved quicker as he gained more self-confidence.

If my goal is a Net Operating Profit of 10 percent, and I decide I want that to translate to $90,000, what kind of Sales Revenue is it going to take to support that number?

The first thing I have to do is divide that $90,000 by 10 percent, because that'll give me the Total Gross Margin that the Net Operating Profit is going to come out of.

I wind up with a Total Gross Margin of $900,000. If my Gross Margin is going to equal $900K, and that $900K is 46 percent of the Total Revenue I'm going to need. I need to divide it by 46 percent and I'll need to push for a Sales total of $1,956,521.72. If I do that, I'll have the $1,056,521.74 I'll need to pay all of my Direct Costs, which is close to the Direct Cost Target KPI I have of 54 percent of Sales.

That'll take care of me, Rick, the staff, our taxes—which should be about $230K—and all the expenses. That leaves room, at the end, for a Net Operating Profit of $90K. For me. That's on top of the salary I've carved out of the business by paying myself first.

I could use that $90K to cover past debts, to invest in new equipment, or to keep things going when the economy tanks again. I could use it to prepare for retirement by proving to a potential buyer that purchasing my contracting business is a good investment.

Kurt set down his pencil and yellow legal pad with pride. He'd done it. He'd figured out a path forward. Somewhere in the back of his mind he heard a football stadium erupt in cheers.

"You hear that, Robert?" he asked.

Robert scanned his office, cocking an ear to one side.

"What?" he grunted.

"The sound of a better future!" Kurt said proudly.

Mastery

Kurt looked out across the grass as a group of seniors left the Center and headed his way. The familiar shade of the ancient oaks felt somehow reassuring. It had been far too long since Kurt had visited the park.

He let his arms hang at his sides, closed his eyes, and took a deep cleansing breath, letting the scent of fresh-cut grass fill his nostrils. He could almost feel Chou Li standing by his side smiling.

I can do this, Kurt assured himself. *I can do this.*

Kurt and Robert had worked hard to reach this moment. Hours of practice and constant correction. Hours spent with other tai chi masters—many with their own Chou Li stories.

One even had an old copy of *Black Belt* magazine featuring his former teacher on the cover. Kurt smiled as he thought about the secret life of his former Tao master.

He could feel the emotional echo of that afternoon, so long ago, when he collapsed in shame while trying to lead the class. The memory reverberated through his body, disrupting his energy. But, instead of fighting to suppress it, he allowed it to find its way to the surface and embraced it for what it was: an echo of something that had happened in the past.

Something that already transpired. Something over which he no longer had any control. Something he had learned from. Something he had forced himself to overcome.

He struggled with the reality of being back in the park.

Should I say something? Should I acknowledge the breakdown I suffered and forced all of them to suffer through with me? Or should I just let it all go? Should I just wing it?

It was good to be back despite the initial discomfort he felt asking Morris if he thought it would be okay to come back to the park. But, despite Kurt's initial angst, Morris assured him his return would be anticipated with a great deal of excitement, that his participation in the group had been sorely missed.

After the initial welcome of old friends and the introduction to new members of the group and their initial interest in tai chi and its benefits, Kurt asked if it was okay to begin their practice.

Morris stood at the front of the group shaking his head.

"*Nu*, Kurt?" he said. "You have to ask?"

Kurt laughed, "No, Morris! I guess I don't. Let's get started."

Morris put his hand up and looked across the field.

"Your friend," he said, "your other teacher. I don't see him. Will he be joining us today?"

"No. We both decided it would be better if I visited the 'scene of the crime' alone. It was my melt-down. Now it will be my triumph or my failure, depending on how things go."

Kurt started the music and took the group through a number of *qigong* exercises designed to help prepare for the long form. When he was done he looked at the more than twenty seniors facing him.

"Let's try this again," Kurt said smiling. "Only, this time, without an emotional collapse."

Kurt looked up at the sky through the leaves of the giant oak. He closed his eyes for a moment.

Okay, Chou Li. This is for you.

Kurt opened his eyes again. His students waited patiently.

"Okay, everyone," he said. "Feet together, hands at your sides. Take a deep cleansing breathe—in through your nose, out through your mouth. This is always better if you curl your tongue slightly at the roof of your mouth.

"Now shift your weight to your right leg and gently lift your left leg and move it to your left and place it down, shoulder width.

Gently raise your arms up in front of you with your wrists above your fingers, like this. Elbows relaxed and slightly bent."

Kurt observed as everyone followed his lead.

"Bend your knees slightly as you sink down a bit. That's it. Lookin' good, everyone.

"With your arms still out in front, shift your weight to your left leg and turn your right foot out ninety degrees. Let your torso follow with your right arm out in front of you, shoulder height, and your left arm parallel to your left leg, palm down.

"So your direction has changed and you're ninety-degrees from where you started, facing right. Facing the Senior Center. Now, bring both hands to your left side as if you were holding a beachball shoulder height with your right palm on top."

Kurt continued through the twenty-four movements of the short form and stopped. He let out a grateful sigh of relief.

"Okay! You guys were great and I didn't fall apart. Life is good."

Everyone laughed, some nervously.

"Who'd like to continue with the second and third sections?" Kurt asked. More than half the group raised their hands.

"Then let's continue."

‡

It was a good class. Long, but good.

Kurt led the seniors through the long form, from beginning to end twice. The second time, he moved through the group gently correcting their posture and position where needed, encouraging everyone. He could feel it this time. He was 'home.'

But it was different. This practice wasn't about him, it was about the group and that meant constantly watching to ensure no one hurt themselves, that everyone felt uplifted during the hour they spent together. As Kurt finished he turned to face the group.

"I sincerely hope everyone got something out of today's practice. Especially those of you who started with Chou Li. For those just beginning, I hope you enjoyed as well. I'll be back tomorrow at the same time. Tomorrow, and the day after. And the day after that.

"I welcome anyone interested in joining me. In joining *us*. Thank you. Hope to see all of you tomorrow."

A few of the seniors hung out for a couple of minutes after class, expressing their gratitude, glad someone was there to lead them.

Kurt didn't say it, but they couldn't have been as happy as he was. When it appeared that everyone had gone, he stood in front of the massive oak tree, took a deep cleansing breath, and started his own repetition of the long form.

For the first time, he felt Chou Li's presence physically. He felt it surround him and move through him. He was immersed in it.

Each posture was deep and powerful and yet, somehow, totally relaxed. Each transition was fluid and graceful. It was his most perfect interpretation of the form and he knew it. His spirit soared.

When he was done, he saluted, and moved to collect his iPad from the beach chair he'd brought with him. He looked around, confident that he had done what he'd come to do.

As he turned to head back to the parking lot he heard Morris call out from behind the tree. The old man was smiling.

"You know something, *boychik*?" he said. "That was beautiful what you just did. Beautiful."

Kurt shook his head in amusement.

"How long have you been hiding back there, Morris? How long have you been checkin' up on me?"

Morris chuckled, then scanned the contours of the clouds. He gazed at Kurt with softness in his eyes.

"Chou Li would be proud, Kurt. Proud that you found the *koyech*, the strength to come back. Thank you."

Morris bowed his head gently.

"I'll see you tomorrow, God willing," he said.

Then the old man turned and walked away.

How to Fall, How to Fail

Kurt was lost in thought, carefully considering everything that had occurred during the past two-and-a-half years.

Two-and-a-half years since the Corvette mysteriously developed a misfire and he found his way to Mushin Automotive. Two-and-a-half years since his life changed in ways he could never have imagined the day before his Malfunction Indicator Lamp screamed a warning at him with its ominous amber glare.

He was an entirely different person than he had been before: at home, at work, and in life. Or maybe he just had found his way back to the person he always was. He was aware, fully engaged, and that awareness seemed to be at the heart of all the changes he experienced since that first afternoon thirty short months ago.

He was at the studio three to nine hours a week, learning everything he could. And he honored Chou Li's memory by starting every morning with a ritual of light stretching followed by one of the Yang style forms and by leading the tai chi practice. That and at least fifteen to twenty minutes of meditation.

Moreover, he was enhancing Chou Li's library with volumes of his own—focused on just about every aspect of Eastern philosophy and the martial arts. He was as dedicated and as disciplined to the arts as any human being could possibly be.

Even when involved in 'normal' conversation, his awareness of these ancient traditions would find its way into the discussion.

So when Rick asked him what the single most important lesson he'd learned during this new period of his life was, Kurt responded without hesitation.

"How to fall, and how to fail. That and how to be be just plain happier and more content."

"That's it?" Rick asked.

"Maybe you don't remember, but that's a lot," Kurt said. "When I started at the studio, the first thing I learned was that the polished wood floor they have there is *hard*.

"There's no mat, nothing to absorb the force of a fall. Regardless of who you are or how long you've been training, that surface is merciless and unforgiving."

"So, one of the first things you need to learn is how to fall without hurting yourself. Because, especially in the beginning, you are going to wind up laid out on that floor. In fact, you're going to wind up laid out on that floor a lot."

"Isn't that a pretty good allegory for life, boss?" Rick asked.

"You bet it is," Kurt replied. "Life is going to see that you wind up on your ass. So it makes sense to learn how to mitigate the impact of falling or being knocked down—if only so you can find a way to get back up again.

"When someone first arrives at the school, a lot of time is dedicated to the science of dissipating the energy of their body mass striking the ground. New students are taught how to fall, how to roll, and how to break a fall by striking the ground with the palm of their hand. They're taught how to deflect the fall's energy and to change the vector of that force to minimize impact.

"Sooner or later, you're going to face a critical situation with no guarantee it will work out the way you want it to. In fact, we both know that from what happened here.

"The question is what you do *after* find yourself there. The issue is, how do you mitigate that fall so it's easier to get up? So you want to get up. So you *can* get up.

"All the important lessons you learn in life are the results of your failures, aren't they? That's how we learn. That's how we grow.

"Training has taught me how to fall without hurting myself. And falling without hurting myself has taught me to fail in ways that are more positive than negative."

Rick bowed slightly, honoring the path Kurt had been walking.

"You know something, boss? You may not realize it, but your learning how to fall and fail has provided everyone here with a great example of how to recover—how to recover, then succeed."

Pain Cancels Technique

Kurt was excited. He felt like it was Christmas morning and he was nine years old again. It wasn't, but that's how it seemed.

It wasn't because in the years Kurt had been working out at the studio his business had made the journey from chaos to order—from confusion to process, policies, procedures, and a disciplined determination to succeed. From living in the 'red' to operating in the 'black'. And not because he found his personal life riding alongside, on a parallel track. Although it was.

He was like a kid about to receive a new toy because Robert had invited him to participate in the largest, most respected martial arts event in the state—the Fall edition of the Four Seasons Traditional Martial Arts Tournament.

Whether it was a true right of passage or not, that's how Kurt internalized the invitation. His hard work and dedication had been recognized. He'd been accepted as an integral part of studio to the point he was even involved in training some of the newer students.

More than that, an invitation to the Tournament implied his sparring had improved to the point that he had earned a place on the floor with martial artists from other schools and disciplines.

Kurt was pumped. However, he was reluctant to share the reason for this newfound excitement with the rest of his universe. His own insecurities demanded that he wait to see how he would do. As a result, he was careful about who he told about the event.

The fact the studio had no formal belt system beyond white, brown, and black—no rankings identified by a rainbow of colors—didn't make things any easier. It actually made it a lot more difficult.

Other studios could group their students according by rank. The first three levels—white, yellow, and orange—competed against beginners. The next group was comprised of intermediate level athletes: purple, green, and blue. And, finally, the advanced *karatekas* wore the brown and black belts.

Kurt's studio did not rank their students that way. Instead there were only three belts: beginning, intermediate, and advanced. And, despite his dedication and commitment—despite his more than two years of concentrated training—Kurt was still wearing the white belt he'd been given when he started his training. Still considered 'an experienced beginner' at the studio.

Consequently, the senior instructors registered Kurt accordingly for his first match, hoping he might be able to continue in the tournament. 'Hoping' because this, as in most martial arts events, was a single-elimination competition. Lose your match and you became an instant spectator.

Kurt was ready. Ever since he'd been invited to participate in the tournament he'd been training even harder than usual. He felt a new inner resolve, and approached the opportunity to represent the studio with deep dedication.

The day of the Tournament arrived. Now it was time to see if, all that hard work was going to pay off in the only place that mattered: the three, three-minute rounds fought on an eight-meter square.

So far the competition had been tough, but the studio was doing well. Two competitors from Mushin had already won their matches, while only one had been eliminated.

Kurt could feel his chest tighten as he sat alone outside the safety ribbon that bordered the competition mat. His breathing was anything but normal while he tried to stretch and keep from locking up, to keep from counting the others sitting across from him in order to determine who he would have to face first.

Who is it going to be? he wondered. *Whose eyes will I be staring into as we bow and touch gloves?*

There was an order to the selections, and Kurt most likely would be the next one from the red corner to be called to the center of the mat. He scanned the blue corner. It appeared he would be facing off against a smaller, younger fighter. But he had no idea who it was actually going to be.

At first, Kurt tried to ignore the large *karateka* sitting in the center of the group of blue fighters. That was until someone approached the guy and whispered in his ear. The fighter got up, glared towards the red corner, and physically moved the person who should have been called for Kurt's match.

Kurt tried to ignore the bizarre event in the blue corner. He focused instead on the three judges seated along one side of the square. They were there, along with a referee and two back judges on the mat, to ensure each match was judged fairly.

Jason came up behind Kurt, tapped him on the back and started pressing down on his shoulders to help him stretch out his lower back when, suddenly, Kurt's name was called.

He stood up immediately. Jason turned him around, placed his open left hand over his right fist and bowed.

"Y'all have trained hard," Jason said. "You know what to do. Trust your body and it'll know what to do instinctively. Remember: *mushin*. No mind."

"Hai!" Jason shouted with a glint in his eye.

Kurt slid his head gear on, adjusted the strap, and tugged on protective cage covering his face. He walked to the three-meter circle at the center of the mat. The referee tucked a red ribbon behind his belt, and a blue one on his opponent's.

Then the ref went over the instructions. There was to be light, controlled contact with no strikes to the groin or kicks to the knees. The judges were looking for form and control. They wanted to see a well-executed demonstration of basic, but effective, martial arts principles and skills.

Kurt was big. And, under most circumstances, his size was an advantage. But, now, as he stared at his opponent, he was unsure of himself. The fighter with the blue ribbon seemed exponentially larger—bigger, meaner, more confident.

Kurt was glad he wasn't wearing his heart monitor; his heart was racing. In fact, it seemed his body realized the primal nature of the contest long before his brain picked up on the danger. Kurt shifted his weight from leg to leg—biting down hard on his mouth guard. The referee held his arm aloft.

"*Hajime!*" he shouted, dropping his arm.

Kurt circled to his left, sizing up his opponent. He faked a front kick, then moved in with two left jabs and a straight right punch. They were all blocked. He recovered and started circling left again, then… Wham! He felt his head snap back from the force of a roundhouse kick that sent him to mat.

Kurt's mouth was dry and his head was pounding. He could taste something salty and metallic in his mouth.

Wonder if that's blood? he thought.

He got to his feet slowly—moving to his corner of the mat as directed. The referee pointed to the blue corner.

"One point! Blue!" he told the judges.

Kurt's legs felt like rubber.

This is surreal. What the hell am I doing here? What the hell was I thinking? I don't need to prove anything to anyone, dammit!

Through the mental fog clouding his perception, he managed to see Allie standing off the mat in his corner. She reached out and grabbed the protective cage on the front of Kurt's head gear, pulled it close, and started shouting.

"He hurt you! You were thinking too much about what you were going to do to him to see what he was about to do to you! You weren't paying attention. You weren't present. 'Too much mind.'

"He's good. Probably fighting down just to take home a trophy. But that doesn't mean you can't beat him. All you have to do is remember one thing, it's simple but it works…"

Kurt tried desperately to comprehend what Allie was saying. She sensed his difficulty and shook his helmet back and forth.

"Pain Cancels Technique, Kurt! Pain Cancels Technique!"

"You can beat this guy. You've got the tools you need to win. All you need is the desire. You need to fight your fight, not his. You need to teach him that pain cancels technique!"

Kurt nodded to her. He smacked a glove against each side of his helmet and shook his head. He bit down hard on his mouthpiece.

I'm not goin' out like this, he thought.

He bowed to Allie, as he was called to the center of the mat to touch gloves for Round 2.

"This round is mine," Kurt growled.

He took a cleansing breath and relaxed into a fighting stance. He felt his opponent moving into his circle, the radius of which was defined by the length of his leg and a front or side kick. Kurt blocked a flurry of punches all thrown with a level of malice usually reserved for a life and death struggle on the street.

Kurt blocked a right hook aimed at his head and countered with a right jab of his own. Contact was light, but it gave Kurt the confidence he needed to know he belonged in the competition. They continued to trade punches when Kurt sensed his opponent coming at him again.

The danger he was facing was real and his body responded. As his opponent raced toward him Kurt timed a front snap-kick perfectly, landing it directly to his adversary's solar plexus. He could hear the air leave his opponent's lungs. Kurt twisted his body and followed the snap-kick with a side-kick that almost sent his attacker off the platform.

"One point! Red! Match tied!" the referee called out.

His opponent hobbled back to his own corner, holding his midsection as he spoke to his coach.

Pain cancels technique, Kurt thought. *I can do this.*

Kurt saw Allie in the corner; he saw her mouth moving but couldn't hear a word. He was in the moment, in the zone.

He could see into the future. He knew how his opponent was going to come at him. He could feel it. Kurt could see the attack unfold in real time before he was called to the mat for Round 3. He was focused and determined to end the match right then.

Allie grabbed the protective cage on his helmet for a second time. She was visibly agitated. Her face was blood red and there was no mistaking the fire in her eyes.

"You remember that story I told you about the jackass who came to the studio when I first started at Mushin? The one who had two of his instructors in tow when he showed up—the two guys who carried him out of the studio?

"Kurt! Look at me…" Allie pleaded, obviously agitated.

Kurt blinked the sweat from his eyes. He leaned forward.

"That's him. The son-of-a-bitch you're fighting. He was one of the two guys with the guy who came to fight Robert. And his 'coach' in the corner… That's the guy Robert was forced to fight."

The pieces started to come together in Kurt's mind, but—before he could respond to Allie—the referee called him to the center of the square. This was the final round, the tie-breaker.

"*Hajime!*" the ref called out.

Kurt moved around the mat, dancing away from his opponent's fake advances. He couldn't get Allie's urgent message out of his mind. The attacks he was facing were furious and unrelenting. He blocked a front punch and then a right-left-right combination that went high-low-high. The punches were followed by a series of kicks that seemed to come from everywhere.

Kurt's heart pounded. He was having difficulty breathing. His anger and fear and pride worked together trying to end the match, calculating a quick way to send his opponent to the mat.

Kurt threw two left jabs that failed to connect. Then he blocked a roundhouse kick that was clearly meant to take him out.

The two fighters exchanged a series of punches at the center of the square. Kurt was clearly on the defensive. Suddenly, he winced. The pain was exquisite, sharp as a razor's cut. His opponent had masked a vicious punch to Kurt's left kidney that left him reeling, gasping for breath. None of the judges or the ref had seen it.

Kurt could hear Allie's words in his head.

'Pain Cancels Technique!'

But it wasn't supposed to be *his* technique that got cancelled. Kurt was losing it. Then, all of a sudden, he felt an eerie calm wrap him in its cold embrace. Time stood still. The venue went silent.

I deliver the pain, and its YOUR technique that gets cancelled!

Kurt recovered from the kidney punch just in time to block a violent roundhouse kick. His opponent followed that immediately with a wicked spinning back kick. That was the opportunity Kurt's subconscious had been waiting for.

The fighter with the blue ribbon failed to find his center as he tried to recover from the kick. His landing was anything but solid. He had over-committed and found himself off balance—far from where he thought he would land. As a result, he wasn't positioned to adequately defend himself.

Nevertheless, he tried to follow up with a spinning back fist using the momentum of the kick to multiply the power. But it never connected. Kurt moved out of reach and the momentum of the punch left his opponent wide open, awkward, and vulnerable.

Kurt shifted out of the way as the back fist flew past his head. He could feel the air move around his opponent's gloved fist. He reached out and grabbed his opponent's wrist with his left hand and threw a right forearm strike into his opponent's tricep just above the elbow.

The strike was controlled and executed perfectly, demonstrating how damaging it could have been had it been applied full force.

Then Kurt opened his fist, turned it into a knife-edge, and slid it down his opponent's arm connecting it to the left side of his neck below the man's ear while still hanging onto that wrist.

He pulled his opponent's arm back and down, then threw his arm left. He released his hold on his opponent's wrist and grabbed the back of his neck before it was out of range, pulling him into a high, Muay Thai knee strike that landed just below the center of his ribcage. He followed that with an upper cut, snapping his attacker's head back with abrupt finality.

The guy with the blue ribbon went down.

Point. Set. Match.

Kurt stood above him, glaring down as the man winced in pain. Slowly, Kurt took off his helmet and removed his mouthpiece. He smiled and spoke quietly.

"That's for Robert."

Kurt walked back to his corner.

Pain Cancels Technique.

That match, and three others went to Kurt. So did a trophy and the silver medal after losing to a more experienced, slightly better martial artist who was as precise as he was fit, and as strategic as he was devastating.

‡

The core of Mushin's team was in the van on the way home from the Tournament. The studio had done well. They earned a highly disproportionate number of trophies and medals for forms and for fighting; all of them tucked safely away in the rear of the van.

Allie was sitting next to Kurt—her head back, arms crossed.

"Well, cowboy, did you learn anything today?" she asked in her best fake West Texas accent.

"Oh, yeah," Kurt responded with a wicked grin.

"And what might that have been?"

"I learned that Pain Cancels Technique."

"Anything else?" Allie asked.

"I learned that using your head to block a kick is not the most intelligent way to win a match."

Everyone laughed. Jason looked back over his shoulder at Kurt.

"How could y'all apply that lesson to life and to your business, Kurt?" he asked.

Kurt thought about it for a minute. It was a great question.

"You know," he said, "no matter how much you prepare, no matter how carefully you plan or how hard you work to ensure you're ready for just about anything that life throws at you, sooner or later you're going to get hit. Hit by something. And, when you do, it's likely you're going to get hurt.

"That pain can paralyze you if you let it. It will try to destroy everything you've worked so hard to establish. In fact, that pain will try to cancel every aspect of your technique.

"The only way you're going to beat it is to embrace the pain, to accept it, let it go, dance with it, and the fear it brings with it. You have to allow all your preparation and training to take over.

"*Mushin*. No mind. Without conscious thought. If you do, you win. If you can't, you're defeated."

Allie stretched her legs out, smiled, leaned back and clapped Kurt on the shoulder.

"You've learned your lessons well, grasshopper," she said.

Jason looked back, smiling in agreement.

Life is a Contact Sport

Ice reduced the swelling on the side of Kurt's head, but it didn't help the multi-colored welt that framed his right eye. He wasn't sure if he'd ever seen that shade of green before.

The ice didn't do much for the bruises on both forearms either—the direct result of countless blocks—or for the two fingers Jason was forced to tape together to limit their range of motion in order to help Kurt deal with the pain of their dislocation.

Even after a hot shower and liberally applying a combination of *dit da jow* and Bio-Freeze to what Kurt thought must be most of his body, he still went to bed hurting in places he didn't know he had.

As he crawled into bed Laurie started to say something, but Kurt held up his right arm with his palm facing her. He pointed at the trophy he had lovingly placed in the corner of their bedroom.

"I'd like to give you a hug and say I'm proud of you," Laurie wrinkled her nose. "But you stink!"

"I'll take the 'proud of you' part," Kurt replied, "but no hug. At least, not tonight."

Laurie shook her head as she watched her husband fall asleep almost the second his head hit the pillow.

Awakening the next morning was worse.

Everything hurt to the point Kurt considered staying home. But he didn't. Instead he sucked it up; got dressed; ate a healthy, light breakfast; and headed to the office.

Getting in and out of the car itself was a project. He couldn't believe how many muscles were involved in simply reaching for the door handle and pulling it open. Each one cried out in a discreet agony of its own.

Kurt had been making it a point to be the first one at Kerrigan every morning. But today he felt lucky to be there at all, proud to be upright and walking. He was uncomfortable, in a lot of pain, and that meant it wasn't going to be a good day.

He was halfway to his office when Rochelle intercepted him. She was visibly shaken when she realized the extent of Kurt's injuries.

"Oh my God, boss!" she said. "What happened? You look like you were in a hatchet fight and everyone had a hatchet but you."

Kurt tried not to smile at her joke.

"You know that martial arts tournament I've been talking about for the past few months?" he asked. "Well. This is what second place in my division looks like."

Rochelle shook her head, staring at Kurt's discolored eye.

"There are only two things I can think of," she said. "The first is: If this is second place, what does third place look like? And second: I hope it was worth it, because you look like hell."

Kurt thought about all the time, effort, and energy that he'd put into his martial arts training over the past few years. He thought about what he'd learned and how it helped drive the transformation of his company. He smiled broadly.

"You know something, Rocky? It was worth it," he said proudly. "Everything I've done. Everything I've learned. All the effort and sacrifice. It was all worth it."

Kurt sat down on the corner of one of the desks along the path to his office. He looked relaxed, satisfied with himself and what he'd accomplished over the weekend.

Rochelle's head tilted to one side, curious.

"But you're not done yet, are you?" she asked, "There are more lessons. I mean, there have to be. Right? Any idea what's next?"

"I don't know, Rocky," Kurt said smiling.

"If there are lessons waiting to be learned, I'm willing to bet they have something to do with the fact that life is a contact sport. And that business, when you understand it, is a reflection of that, only more intense. More visceral and certainly more immediate.

"I guess the question at this point isn't what *I've* learned. The real question is what have you and everyone else here learned?"

Rochelle was caught off guard. She tried her best to recover.

"I guess, when you think about it," she said, "it's all a battle. You can't get anywhere in life without getting knocked down, can you? And there are lessons to be learned in that, right?

"Like respect is important. And empathy. You've taught all of us that patience works for you more often than it works against you. I know that was an important lesson for me."

Kurt smiled like a proud father; she got it. Rochelle continued.

"You taught me that thinking doesn't always make it so. That it takes action. And, action takes work.

"You've demonstrated that it is its own reward. And, that work is a lot like prayer, in that it can elevate you."

"Thank you, Rochelle. But, you left something out." Kurt winced as he repositioned himself on the edge of the desk. "You failed to mention that Pain cancels Technique. But only if you let it. A lesson that was reinforced at the Tournament."

Kurt smiled, "And that's a lesson you'd rather teach a competitor than have them teach it to you."

Rochelle laughed.

"There is something else I learned over the last few years and that is everyone has something to deal with—and most of the time it's their own personal demons. And to achieve success you have overcome your worst fears."

Rochelle picked up the conversation from there.

"We learned something else, boss, by following your example. To do great work, you have to start by starting. And sometimes that means failing: falling on your butt wondering why you're working so hard to do something that's obviously impossible. But it can't be impossible if someone's already done it. And if they have, quit whining and get back to work.

"In other words, with a modicum of effort you will probably succeed by default, because most people aren't willing to do the work."

Kurt smiled, "There is one more thing, Rochelle. Change—change of any kind—starts right here." Kurt pointed to his right temple. "It starts here in the mind.

"And that perception is reality. That if you change the way you see things—you change everything."

Rochelle smiled in agreement as Kurt slowly raised himself off the desk. He grunted a bit at the effort, stretched a little, then started to hobble back to his office. But, not before Rochelle asked if it would be okay if she gave him a hug.

Continuous Learning

Kurt felt a deep sense of satisfaction as he pulled two highball glasses down from above the bar. He filled them with ice and reached for a brand new bottle of Basil Hayden's. It was going to be a nice evening.

Laurie had already scored the lemon, so peeling the twists off wouldn't be a problem. He showed his appreciation by bringing her a lightly chilled glass of Chablis as she was putting the finishing touches on dinner.

Despite trying hard not to disturb Robert and Kurt, AJ and Max still managed to create an intermittent, albeit not unpleasant, distraction with their antics. Through all of it, AJ left no doubt that she liked Robert much more than she liked the stern authoritarian Mr. Taylor who watched over their classes at the studio.

Having Robert over for dinner had become one of Kurt's favorite new family rituals. One that everyone in the Kerrigan household looked forward to with great anticipation. More than that, it was an opportunity for Kurt and Robert to explore their growing relationship outside the studio.

Kurt held the highballs up to the light, admiring his handiwork.

Angel's Envy. Club soda. Lemon twist. Nectar of the Gods!

There is no more perfect shade of amber!

He grabbed a couple of coasters and carefully set his precious cargo down on the table separating the two men.

Robert held his glass up to the light then took a long, slow sip.

"Are you sure you were meant to be a contractor? Because, I'm willing to bet you would have made one world-class bartender."

Kurt chuckled, "No. With someone as obsessive/compulsive as I am, I can almost guarantee that would have turned tragic."

Robert laughed and then seemed to drift away. Kurt had gotten used to these gaps in conversation, knowing that Robert was deeply lost in what would come next.

"You know you may be the only student we've ever had who never questioned why there are only three belts at the studio. Why there is no rainbow bridge taking you through all the belts with all the artificial levels in between."

Kurt sat quietly, knowing not to interrupt. He knew Robert's point would become evident soon enough.

"Don't misunderstand, he continued. "I'm actually glad you never asked. You never asked how long it would take to achieve mastery over our system either. You must have been curious, especially in the beginning when you were unsure and feeling awkward all the time."

It was just over three years since Kurt started his martial arts journey. Three years of really intense training at the studio, and still more practice at home.

Robert was done. Kurt took the opportunity to respond.

"I don't know, Robert. I think the fact there weren't all those artificial plateaus helped me to concentrate on my training without the pressure of all the testing and preparation that students at other schools endure.

"I never thought much about the belts either, I guess.

"After I got started, I was more interested in mastering the art than in proving to myself, or someone else, that I'd reached a certain level. That's when I realized I was addicted. It was all about the learning, Continuous Learning—never getting to the point I felt like I didn't need to train any more, that I'd learned enough.

"You helped me understand that, right upfront, when you told me a black belt was the beginning, and not the end, of our training.

And, truth be told, you're the perfect example of continuous learning, both at the shop and at the studio."

Robert looked down at his glass uncomfortable with the praise.

"Besides," Kurt continued, "where is the benefit in standing still? You're certainly not learning anything when you're just coasting on what you already know."

"Good to know you feel that way," Robert said, smiling. "Good to know you're not likely to quit after you receive your black belt."

Robert called out out the door to the kitchen.

"Laurie, can you break away from that incredible dinner you're slaving over and come in here for a moment?"

Laurie poked her head in the family room.

"Is everything okay? Or have the you boys gotten into trouble already? I swear, leaving the two of you alone is more dangerous than turning Max and AJ loose at the mall."

She caught the twinkle in Robert's eyes and knew something special was in wind. She went grabbed a dish towel, and was drying her hands as she walked back into the family room.

Robert caught Max trying hard to make it look like he wasn't interested in what the adults were up to.

"Max. Would you do me a favor and bring me my jacket? I hung it up in the hall closet when I got here. Then ask AJ if she'd like to join everyone in the family room."

Max went into the playroom, took AJ by the hand, then went to the hall closet. He returned with the jacket cradled across both hands. He held it in front of him and bowed to Robert.

"Here, *sensei*."

Robert returned the formality.

"Thank you, Max."

Robert took the jacket and reached inside its right sleeve. He removed a twelve-inch-long rectangular box, meticulously wrapped in rice paper. His eyes twinkled as he handed the box to Kurt.

"I figured there was only one way to see if you would continue with us after you received your black belt. When I was pretty certain I knew what the answer would be I came up with a plan."

AJ's excitement filled the room, "What's in the box, Daddy? What's in the box?"

"I don't know, honey. You'll have to ask Robert."

AJ looked over at Robert while Kurt carefully peeled the paper back. He opened the box and found a brand new black belt embroidered with 'Kurt Kerrigan', and his new rank written in *kanji* along with the name of the studio, also in *kanji*.

Laurie's eyes got wide as she took a step backward. Both kids pounced on their father. Kurt tried to control himself, but he was overwhelmed. Robert sensed his mood and spoke gently.

"Of course, there will be a formal presentation at the studio and you will have the opportunity to invite your colleagues from work and the seniors from the park. But I wanted a private moment to let you know how much I've enjoyed your being at the studio with us, you and the kids.

And, of course, I wanted to personally let you know much I hope this will not be the end of your training."

Kurt bowed his head in appreciation. Laurie was standing alongside the chair when she signaled Kurt to get up. She gave him hug and then kissed him gently on the lips.

"I'm so proud of you, honey," she said. "So proud of everything you've accomplished."

The kids showed their excitement and pride as well, first by saluting their father and then with a volley of hugs and kisses.

"Do you know how the belt system originated?" Robert asked. "There were no rankings of any kind when the arts were first developed. Instead a student would be given a white belt when his training odyssey began and that's the only belt he would ever ever formally receive. It would be worn and rarely washed."

"Just the belt, of course, he said smiling. "Not the *gi*."

"Ultimately, the belt would become soiled to the point that it appeared brown and then worn until it turned black. And that's the origin of the belt system: a lack of adequate laundry facilities."

Kurt laughed at the joke. The children were amused as well.

"The good news is," Robert continued, "if your learning is continuous, both here and at the construction company, the mastery you achieve—the black belts you will earn—will become frayed to the point that the entire outer covering will wear away and the belt will become white again. A beginner's mind yet again.

"When that happens, you will truly become the master you were meant to be, here at home, at work. and at the studio."

Kurt stood up, clutching the black belt tightly in his hands. He smiled and bowed deeply to Robert, his *sensei*, his friend.

All this from a Check Engine Light. All this from a simple misfire.

"I'll be there in the morning, *sensei*," Kurt said. "Tomorrow, and the morning after, and the morning after that."

Happy Wife...

It was a crystal-clear morning with just a hint of mist on the surface of the lake as the sun came up. But it was chilly enough for Kurt to think twice about removing his sweats.

He put down his insulated coffee mug, moved to the center of the lawn, and followed the grass down to the beach with his eyes.

My beach, he thought.

The boat was tied up at the dock, ready for one last run around the lake before they headed home. Kurt wasn't looking forward to driving the truck around and backing the trailer into the water to pull the boat out.

But he couldn't resist smiling as he thought about rocketing across the lake with the wind in Laurie's hair, and the kids reveling in the motion of the waves—waiting for their turn at the controls.

He took a few deep cleansing breaths, centered himself, saluted the rising sun, and proceeded to work his way through the last two *katas* he'd mastered at the studio. They were second degree black belt forms, appropriately long and difficult.

He was halfway through the first form when he remembered what Robert had told him about the *katas* he was introduced to when he first started.

"When you start, all you will be able to do is work your way through the movements as they were taught you. You won't understand what you're doing or why, and that's okay.

"If you practice long enough and with enough intensity—if you think about what you're doing, the motions you are demanding your body to master—you will eventually understand.

"You'll understand the form's purpose: why the combinations are put together the way they are and in the order in which they flow.

"Do the form a thousand times with the same level of intensity, the same perfect practice, and you will see your opponents. Do the form ten thousand times, and anyone watching you will see them just as clearly as if they were there.

"When someone who is watching can see your attackers as clearly as you do, you will truly have become a master."

That's the level of intensity Kurt brought to everything at the studio, his continuing journey, the *katas* he mastered, and the classes he taught now that he had become one of the senior instructors himself.

By the end of the second *kata* he was ready for his morning tai chi practice. It wasn't long before he was lost in the form, the beautiful sunrise, the mist on the lake, and the joy of having shared the last few days with his family.

For him, the long form was a moving meditation and it was rare that he missed the opportunity to do it. It had become an integral part of his day—either on his own in the morning, at the park, or during a break in the afternoon with Rick and any of the other team members who could break away.

He was working his way through the form when he realized he had company. Laurie was behind him, practicing in concert with his movements, while Max was on his right and AJ was on his left, attempting to do the same.

He smiled, first to himself and then to his wife.

I guess it's time for the student to become the teacher, he thought.

It was a beautiful sight to behold.

When everyone had finished, Laurie and the kids headed back into the cabin for breakfast. Kurt took one of the chairs on the porch, wiped the dew off, and sat down to drink his coffee. His mind wandered back to Friday, late in the morning, close to noon.

Kurt had called Laurie from the office.

"HiiIIii!" was her musical response on the phone. Kurt could hardly contain the excitement in his voice.

"Hi, honey," he said. "How soon can you get packed up and ready to go, so we can head for the lake house this weekend? I'm done here at work and Rick's got everything under control. I know it's 'spur of the moment,' but I'd really like to get away for a couple of days. That is, if we can, of course."

There was no response. Kurt waited in anticipation.

"Who is this, *please*?" Laurie said, both measured and stern.

"Come on, Laurie! It's me, Kurt, your husband! You know, the guy you liked better when he wasn't home disrupting your life, under your feet all the time. I'm the tall one, your third child."

Kurt could hear his wife working hard to suppress her laughter.

"I'm sorry," Laurie said. "My husband would never leave work to spend time with his family. He's incapable. Too committed and way too neurotic. He would never ever do something on the 'spur of the moment.' You must have the wrong number."

She pursed her lips to hold the laughter in. Kurt rolled his eyes.

"You're killin' me here. Can we get serious for a moment? Do you think we can get away or not? If you think we can I can make it happen, I'll be out of here in less than a half-hour. If not, we can plan it for another time.

"It's just that the weather is supposed to be incredible up at the lake and, for all intent and purposes, the place will run just fine without me for the next few days. We could head up today and come back Monday night. Whaddya say?"

Laurie was giggling like a school girl. She covered the phone with her hand and called out into the family room.

"Kids! How soon can you get packed up and ready to head for the lake? There's a strange man on the phone impersonating your father. He says he can take time off from work to go to the lake house, just because he can. Do you think we ought to go with him?"

Kurt heard the excited laughter of his children bursting through the phone. He beamed with joy.

"Does that mean we're going?" he asked.

Laurie was still laughing as she answered him.

"Listen, I don't know who you are or what you've done with my husband, but I'm not missing an opportunity to escape to the mountains for a few days.

"Get here as soon as you can, honey. In the meantime, I'll do whatever I can to whip your two barbarians into submission and have everything ready by the time you arrive. I'm starting to really like these Friday morning surprises. Drive carefully, Mr. Kerrigan. And no more speeding tickets!"

Kurt smiled broadly. He liked them, too—these unscheduled Friday morning getaways. More than that, he was really starting to appreciate the freedom this new life offered.

All the planning, all the hard work and effort, had paid off in the creation of a business that turned out to be everything Kurt had dreamed of when he first made the leap and went out on his own. It was a business that worked as hard for Kurt as he worked for it.

Now he could say that Kerrigan Construction worked for him, for his family, for everyone at the company—including his clients.

Business was good. Profits were up. And the company's reviews were all 5-star. He'd accomplished all that and still managed to find time for his family, and time to explore his own interests.

Kurt finished his coffee as he looked out on the lake. He took a deep breath—in through his nose and out through his mouth—then headed inside.

It was going to be another great day.

Luck?

Kurt was sitting in his office staring at the ceiling fan. It was set on 'low' and barely turning. The shadows the blades cast on the ceiling and the corners of the room were mesmerizing. A rhythmic pattern of light and dark beckoning Kurt's subconscious to take control.

Kurt couldn't be sure how deep he'd gone. A knock on the door returned him to reality. Rick entered without waiting to be signaled in. After all, Kurt was would be leaving soon and Rick still had to prep him on a pre-proposal meeting.

Kurt had a meet-and-greet scheduled with the Parsons to establish the scope of their vision and the nature of the project, in order to see if this was going to be a 'good marriage' between contractor and client.

Rick pulled up 'his' chair, one of two on the guest side of the desk. Kurt was still focused on the fan blades, so Rick dropped the folders he had brought, allowing the sound to pull his boss back into the here and now. Kurt sat up straight.

"Gone again?" Rick smiled.

"Yeah, I guess," Kurt said sheepishly.

"Well, where were you this time? Here? Home? Or on the floor at the studio?"

"We need to stop meeting like this," Kurt said, chuckling. "You know me too well. I was here, actually."

"Should have known you were working," Rick said.

"Yeah," Kurt replied. "Thinking about how we do things today— the discipline we bring to everything we do—and the chaos and inconsistencies that infected everything we did before. How haphazard everything was. How we never did anything the same way twice. I was thinking it's a wonder we're still here: here and doing well."

"Guess we're just lucky," Rick said, shaking his head. "Lucky that your Corvette decided to misfire when and where it did."

"Think that was it?" Kurt asked. "Luck? Really? I'm not so sure.

"You know Peter? The older gentleman who stops by here every Tuesday? He says there is no such thing as luck. He says Luck is what happens when Opportunity meets Preparation. But I'm not sure about that either.

"The Corvette misfired on the freeway, right at the foot of the Blue Ridge exit. The off-ramp you have to take to get to Mushin Automotive.

"You could call that 'opportunity', I guess. But was it really? And what about 'preparation'? My only preparation for meeting Robert that day was imminent doom. Cataclysmic failure.

"Hell, Rick. They say, 'If you fail to plan, you plan to fail.' If that's true, I was well on my way to failure—and I was taking everyone here along with me."

"Jeez, boss," Rick said. "I think you're makin' it sound even worse and more random than it was."

"I don't think so," Kurt responded. "I don't think it was random at all. In fact, I'm sure it was anything but. Robert and I talk about it all the time. The Universe aligning itself just for us. Just for me.

"Think about it for a minute. Why in the world would anyone in Robert's position agree to help a complete stranger without knowing what that would mean? And why would I accept his offer?

"Sure, things here were awful and I was desperate. But, you have to admit, the whole thing is more than a little crazy. And yet..."

Rick leaned forward in his chair. He completed Kurt's thought.

"And yet, here we are. It's hard to imagine the business doing any better. We're growing, dominating our market. And we're profitable. Hell, more than just profitable.

"And from what you've told me, things couldn't be better at home. Laurie is happy. The kids are growing like weeds. It won't be long before you're car shopping with Max so you can get that new ZR1 you keep talking about, and pass this Corvette along to him."

Rick chuckled. Kurt eyed a photo of Max on his desk.

"You got two great kids," Rick continued. "They work out with you at the studio. Laurie meets you at the park for tai chi when she can. Know something, Kurt? Luck? Opportunity? I don't care what it was. But there's one thing you should consider."

"What's that?" Kurt asked with genuine curiosity.

"It took both you and the Universe to make it all come together," Rick said. "The Universe may have worked its ass off to align itself for your benefit—for the benefit of everyone here at the company— but if you didn't smile back, if you didn't accept the opportunity you were presented with, the business would have gone under, your marriage would have gone to hell with it, and I'd be driving some other boss nuts."

Kurt laughed. Rick stood up and shrugged.

"So 'fuggedaboudit,'" he said in his best Italian accent. "Now. Let's focus on your meeting with the Parsons."

Rick opened the folders he'd brought and spread the contents across the desk. Kurt got up, walked to where Rick was standing and gave him a hug.

"Time to rock 'n roll!" Kurt said enthusiastically.

"Okay. Here are the notes we took when the Parsons first called, along with their answers to the questions we've established on our First Contact Check List where they talk about what they'd like.

"Here's a list of all the other jobs we've done in their area, large and small, all within a five-mile radius. And I put in a list of 'comps' from a local realtor that pretty much nails down how much other properties in the neighborhood are selling for. We have a pretty good idea of what their place is worth now, so we can project what it might be worth after our work is completed.

"And here's the Blackstone project folder. They live right around the corner and are the family that referred the Parsons.

"We've already sent a letter to the Blackstones thanking them for the referral, along with a gift certificate for any future projects they might want to do.

"I put a copy of our company binder in with everything else as a 'leave behind.' It's got pictures of past projects, endorsements, testimonials, stories from web, articles from the local paper, and stuff about all the charities we support.

"Oh! And a gift certificate for dinner at Nick's Italian in appreciation of the opportunity to sit down with them.

"One last thing, do you still have a box of 'hospital booties' in the truck to cover your feet when you enter their house? If not, I can throw a box in before you leave. I think that's about it."

Suddenly, Kurt smiled a huge grin.

"Do you remember what a client meeting used to be like?" he asked. "My God! We'd show up and talk about anything! It was just a matter of measuring whatever needed to be measured and then just blurting out an estimate. Now it's all part of a detailed process.

"I mean, really. How many other builders or remodelers have someone call every day to follow up on what was done the day before and to ensure there are no problems? How many are willing to commit themselves to discussing what's scheduled next, and when to expect that work to begin?

"We went from nothing to Meticulous Attention to every Detail and the results speak volumes about the difference all of that has made."

Rick sat back in his chair. His head was tilted to the side, his arms crossed in front of him.

"Well, boss? What were you saying about Luck, Opportunity, and Preparation a minute ago? Wasn't it something about Luck occurring whenever Opportunity and Preparation collide?

"Well, isn't that what we're doing? Isn't it what we've done? What *you've* done?"

Full Circle

Kurt checked his GPS one last time. He made a right turn onto Applegate, drove past three nice houses, found the right numbers on the curb, and parked. 19985 Applegate: this was the place.

The address was correct, but there was no sign of life anywhere. No car in the driveway. No evidence of anyone around.

He walked to the front door and pressed the small white button. He heard the bell inside the hallway, but there was no response. He pulled out his phone and checked his calendar app: date, time, and address. Everything was correct.

He pressed the doorbell again, waited a reasonable amount of time, then decided to leave. That's when he heard a truck bump the curb and screech to a halt in the driveway behind him. He turned to see both doors fly open as a man and a woman exited the truck. The man's face was flushed, beads of perspiration running down his forehead. He extended his hand to Kurt.

"Hi! I'm Jim Parsons. This is my wife, Ellen. I'm so sorry we're late. I set everything up so I could leave our business in time to be here, but I just couldn't get away. Too much going on. Too much."

Jim paused for a second to catch his breath. He was panting.

"It never fails, everything goes straight to hell every time I get ready to walk away, every time I get ready to walk out the door. It's almost as if there's a conspiracy working against my having a 'normal life'—whatever that means.

"It's always like that. No matter how hard I try, every day, it's crisis management. Nothing ever goes the way it's supposed to."

Jim looked at Kurt and smiled a sheepish grin.

"You have a business. You understand."

Kurt took a deep breath. There was something too familiar about the desperation in Jim's voice. Something he remembered, but didn't miss at all. He shook Jim's outstretched hand.

"Hi, I'm Kurt. Kurt Kerrigan."

Before he could continue, Jim unleashed a litany of complaints about how hard he was working for his business, bemoaning the fact that it was all one-sided and wasn't the other way around.

Kurt thought back to the Corvette's misfire, the Service Engine Soon warning, and his first trip to Mushin. He smiled, knowing exactly where the Jim's desperation was coming from.

"Your business isn't running the way you want it to?" he asked. "I can relate. There was a time my company was misfiring all over the place. In fact, there was a time it was barely running at all.

"I was lucky, though. I found a great 'mechanic,' and he and his crew helped me get everything back running the way it's supposed to. More than that, they taught me how I could help myself."

Jim protested, "But I'm talking about my business running like hell. Not my truck."

"I know," Kurt replied as he held up his right arm, palm up and open. "The same guys who fixed my car taught me how to fix my business. So, in a way, it was a kind of 'two-fer'. I wound up getting both fixed at the same time. Only fixing the business took longer.

"Really, when you think about it, I got three things fixed, because I got my life back as well."

Jim's jaw dropped open. He was dumb-founded.

"That sounds unbelievable. Very attractive, but unbelievable," he said. "How did you do it?"

Kurt laughed, "I earned a black belt."

At that point, both Jim and his wife, Ellen, were staring at Kurt.

They'd made an appointment to get information and maybe an estimate on remodeling the home they had just bought. Kerrigan Construction came up at the very top of everyone's list of who to call: 5-star ratings on the web, a neighbor that swore they were the best, and nothing but praise on every neighborhood chat-room.

Now, instead of talking about the house, they were talking about their business—their business and, somehow, martial arts.

"You have to tell me," Jim said curiously, "what in the world does becoming a black belt have to do with fixing your business?

"You must mean you became a 6-Sigma Black Belt? Right? Because that's the only thing that would make any sense at all."

"Well, first of all," Kurt said. "I mean a martial arts black belt, not a 6-Sigma Black Belt. Although, over the years, I think I've certainly learned enough to accomplish that as well.

"Martial arts had everything to do with my success. From when I started, right up until today. More than that, it was the smartest thing I've ever done. But please don't misunderstand. I was lucky."

Jim tilted his head to one side, "Lucky?"

"Yes, lucky. I found the perfect place to train. The perfect place to learn. A place where my master understood both martial arts and business management and how the two complement each other. How the commitment and discipline necessary in one, helps build success in the other.

"So I'm not sure if picking a different school and working toward a black belt there would deliver the same result. In fact, I'm pretty sure it wouldn't.

"But in the case of my school and my teacher," Kurt grinned, "I *know* it would. Or, at least, I know it could, because it worked for me. Or, rather, it helped me make the connections that allowed it to work for me."

Jim was shaking his head back and forth.

"Listen," he said. "I know we made this appointment to talk about the house and I don't have much time. I told you, everything falls apart when I'm not there and the clock is ticking.

"But I've got an I.T. business and I need to hear more about this magical solution you came up with to fix your car, your business, and your life."

Kurt thought back to his first meeting with Robert and their ensuing conversation. He took a deep breath, and began to share.

"Well, it's not magic. I can assure you of that. It was lots of hard work, and it meant confronting all the things I avoided, failed to do or failed to do well. All the things I wasn't doing but had to do in order to succeed."

Kurt stopped, thought about it for a moment and smiled.

"But I'll tell you what I will do. And that is make the same deal with you my master made with me.

"There won't be any money involved, at least not at my end. But there will be a cost to you, a little 'skin in the game' if you know what I mean."

Special Thanks

Writing is both a calling and a privilege. It is lonely, isolated, and most times doesn't acknowledge all the individuals who support the author's struggle to share in the telling of that story. In my case, it begins with all the publishers and editors I've been privileged to work with, and ends with the talented and committed professionals who inspired and guided me.

It includes Art Epstein and Ray Walker, who taught me there was a world beyond the automotive repair shop; and includes my parents, without whose guidance and example, I would never have written for anyone.

Most of all, I want to acknowledge my wife, Lesley, who has made my writing possible through her love and abundant patience; and also our kids, Ryan and Dana, for their unyielding support throughout my career.

I'd like to thank everyone I've written to and for over the years: the repair community, jobbers, warehouse executives, counter professionals, and members of the manufacturing community. They read and listened, even when it left them feeling more than a little uncomfortable.

There are a few more acknowledgments that belong here.

Two are for Chris "Chubby" Frederick of the Automotive Training Institute, and Ken Brookings of Aspire, for the vital role they have both played in my life. And, I would certainly be remiss if I didn't include my coach and dear friend, Paul Colison. The importance of our Thursday morning coaching calls was critical.

The final acknowledgment goes to Seth Godin and the altMBA Program. Without Seth's writing and shared wisdom, the prodding and encouragement of my coaches and cohort, the completion of this long odyssey would never have come to pass!

Thank you all.

Finally, if you are compelled to do work that matters, you must be willing to invite the comments and suggestions of people you respect to produce the best that you are capable of. To that end, I asked several individuals to read *Misfire* with a critical eye to ensure it turned out to be everything I hoped it could be.

It was a big "ask," but their involvement helped shape *Misfire*, and I would like to show my appreciation by recognizing their generous efforts here.

So, thank you Alex Alcantro, Robert Ayers, Nikki Ayers, Ken Brookings, Mark Chadroff, Chris Chesney, Corey Garnett, Jim Gourley, Jeanette Hardy, Sarah Huoh, George Jensen, Ed Kohn, Mitch McDaniel, Chris Munier, Greg Olson, Jon Popiel, Jason Simms, Arthur Singer, Andy Steinborn, Steve Weiss, and Paul Zappardino.

Special thanks go to my editor, Fredrick Haugen, who helped me craft *Misfire*, and to our son, Ryan. Without his involvement and support, this entire project wouldn't have been possible. The final work is better as a result of his participation.

About the Author

People say that those who can, do; and those who can't, teach. Mitch Schneider has proven that you can do both: teach and do. And exceed at both extremely well.

Mitch is an accomplished businessman, writer, educator, and speaker focused on the issues confronting small business owners in today's rapidly changing world.

As a 52-year veteran of the automotive service industry, Mitch has experienced the challenges of small business ownership as both an active participant and as a trained observer. During that time, he's been a certified master automotive technician, an independent repair shop owner, and a trade journalist .

Mitch has written a successful eight-volume series on leadership and management. *Misfire*, however, is his first novel. The book overflows with relatable characters facing real-world challenges. It is a direct result of hist vast knowledge and experience.

As a martial artist with years of experience in several different disciplines, Mitch has shared the hard lessons learned in the studio with his readers. As a stem cell/bone marrow transplant and cancer survivor, Mitch provides a unique view of the determination and dedication required to succeed both in life and in business.

You can follow Mitch's video blog and writings, and learn more about the concepts presented in *Misfire*, including free business resources, at his website: misfirebook.com

Made in the USA
San Bernardino,
CA